The Financial Times Guide to Wealth Management

The Financial Times Guide to Wealth Management

How to plan, invest and protect your financial assets

Jason Butler

Harlow, England • London • New York • Boston • San Francisco • Toronto • Sydney • Auckland • Singapore • Hong Kong
Tokyo • Seoul • Taipei • New Delhi • Cape Town • São Paulo • Mexico City • Madrid • Amsterdam • Munich • Paris • Milan

PEARSON EDUCATION LIMITED

Edinburgh Gate
Harlow CM20 2JE
Tel: +44 (0)1279 623623
Fax: +44 (0)1279 431059

Website: www.pearsoned.co.uk

First published in Great Britain in 2012

© Pearson Education 2012

The right of Jason Butler to be identified as author of this work has been asserted
by him in accordance with the Copyright, Designs and Patents Act 1988.

Pearson Education is not responsible for the content of third-party internet sites.

ISBN: 978-0-273-74299-9

British Library Cataloguing-in-Publication Data
A catalogue record for this book is available from the British Library

Library of Congress Cataloging-in-Publication Data
Butler, Jason.
  The Financial Times guide to wealth management : how to plan, invest, and protect your
financial assets / Jason Butler.
     p. cm
  Includes index.
  ISBN 978-0-273-74299-9 (pbk.)
1. Finance, Personal. 2. Investments. I. Title.
  HG179.B8768 2012
  332.024--dc23
                         2011038680

10 9 8 7 6 5 4 3 2 1
15 14 13 12 11

Typeset in 9.5pt Stone Serif by 30
Printed and bound in Great Britain by Ashford Colour Press, Gosport, Hampshire

Contents

Acknowledgements

Writing a factual book when you are also working full time and have a young family is a challenge! Unlike a fiction book, where the author can pretty much make things up as he or she goes along, a factual book like this one requires a lot of prior research and many drafts before anything coherent or useful – let alone accurate – is produced.

I am very grateful to my colleagues at Bloomsbury Financial Planning for providing the support that permitted me to devote large chunks of my time over the past year to researching and writing this book. They are a great bunch of people who share a common desire to do the very best for our clients and I am very proud to work with them. I would particularly like to thank Robert Lockie, who reviewed several of the chapters and also created many of the charts and tables under a very tight deadline. Thanks also go to my long-serving assistant Elaine McErlean for all that she does to keep me organised and supported as well as being a great sounding board, not to mention her input on creating many of the book's graphics.

Thanks go to Sam Adams, Alison Broadberry, Justin Bryant, David Lane, Tim Hale, Alan Pink and Jo Summers, who generously took time out from their own busy schedules to review various chapters and offer valuable feedback. I am lucky to know such superb, knowledgeable professionals.

I would like to thank the following organisations for providing research, data or other resources: Albion Strategic Consulting; AXA Wealth; Canada Life International; CEG Worldwide Inc.; Dimensional Fund Advisors Inc.; Fidelity International; Fiscal Engineers Limited; Finametrica Pty; Financial DNA; FTSE, Lipper Fitzrovia Limited; Speechly Bircham LLP; Vanguard Group; Voyant Software Inc.; and Zurich Insurance plc.

I would like to thank my editor Chris Cudmore at Pearson Education for believing in me and providing support and guidance on the initial drafts. I agree with you Chris that less is definitely more!

I would also like to acknowledge the families with whom I have had the privilege to work over the past 20 years and who have taught me more about managing wealth than any textbook or exam ever did. Thank you also to those clients (you know who you are) who generously gave their time to explain what they would want to see this book cover. I hope I've managed to deliver.

Finally I would like to thank my wife Jane and daughters Daisy and Megan for putting up with me being absorbed in the book project for a year. I promise I'll not do another one for a while!

Any errors and omissions in this book are mine but any value that is created from its contents is yours.

Jason Butler

The material in this book is based on the author's understanding and interpretation of current UK legislation and practise (as at September 2011), both of which are subject to change. No material in this book should be constructed as financial advice as defined by the Financial Services and Markets Act 2000, and you are strongly recommended to take independent and personalised advice from a suitably qualified and authorised financial advisor.

Publisher's acknowledgements

We are grateful to the following for permission to reproduce copyright material:

Figure 1.1 excerpted from Bill Bachrach's *Values-Based Financial Planning*, Aim High Publishing; provided courtesy of Bill Bachrach, Bachrach & Associates, Inc., www.BillBachrach.com/ © 1996–2011 Bill Bachrach. All rights reserved; Figure 1.2 reproduced by kind permission of George Kinder and The Kinder Institute of Life Planning, www.kinderinstitute.com; Figure 1.3 courtesy of Maria Nemeth, Ph.D., MCC, Licensed Clinical Psychologist and Master Certified Coach, Founder and Executive Director of the Academy for Coaching Excellence; Figures 4.7, 4.8, 4.9 and 4.10 courtesy of CEG Worldwide; Figure 4.4 courtesy of Schneider, L./FTSE Group; Figure 5.1 courtesy of Dr Jean-Paul Rodrigue, Department of Global Studies and Geography, Hofstra University; Figures 8.1 and 8.2 courtesy of Vanguard; Figure 8.4 courtesy of Dimensional Fund Advisors Inc/FTSE Group; Figure 8.5 courtesy of Dimensional Fund Advisors Inc/FTSE Group/Morningstar; Figures 14.3 and 14.4 and Tables 14.2, 14.3 and 15.1 courtesy of Axa Wealth; Figure 15.2 courtesy of London and Colonial; Figure 18.1 courtesy of Speechly Bircham; Table 18.1 and Figures 18.5, 18.6 and 18.7 courtesy of Canada Life International.

We would like to thank Dimensional Fund Advisors Inc for permission to include their data.

In some instances we have been unable to trace the owners of copyright material, and we would appreciate any information that would enable us to do so.

Introduction

We are all living longer, inflation isn't going away and we have an ever-increasing expectation of the quality of our desired lifestyle. With increasing taxes and volatile investment markets, historically low interest rates and the prevalence of divorce and second marriages, managing personal wealth is a serious responsibility that can be challenging and time-consuming.

There are so many vested interests in the financial services sector, misinformation available from the internet, unsubstantiated claims made by product providers and a very 'noisy' media that even the most well-informed person would be forgiven for being totally confused! There are, however, no short cuts, easy answers or perfect solutions because the fiscal and demographic landscape is constantly changing. Whether you manage your own wealth or are engaging professionals to help you or do it for you, this book should make you to feel more confident, be better informed and gain a clearer understanding of the key planning issues that you need to consider.

Managing wealth does not require you to have exceptional intelligence. Instead what's needed is a sound intellectual framework for making financial decisions and sticking with them through the inevitable changes that will arise. Making sure that you are clear about what you are seeking to achieve in your life – your 'what' and 'why – will then help you to work out the 'how' in terms of specific solutions so that you can make good decisions and avoid bad ones.

Wealth management is a very big subject so no one book can cover every issue or go into sufficient detail without making the book so large that it becomes less accessible or interesting to the majority of readers. My approach has been to think of the subject matter like an iceberg: I assume that all readers will want to know the broad concepts and ideas – the above the waterline part of the iceberg; some will want to know a bit more detail – just below the waterline part of the iceberg; but only relatively few people will want to know all the detail of a particular issue – the bottom of the iceberg. I have, therefore, tried to avoid the bottom of the iceberg, so to speak, and keep things as easy to understand as possible. This inevitably means that in some areas I couldn't cover every aspect or go into great detail and further reading might be advisable or necessary.

This book is set out in three main parts.

Part 1 covers strategic planning issues, including the importance of developing and maintaining a proper overall wealth plan that is in tune with your mission, vision, values and goals. In addition, I have explained the value of taking proper advice and when and how to choose suitable professionals to work with, as well as the negative impact that the media can have on your financial well-being!

Part 2 provides a condensed and 'elegantly simple' investment framework that is likely to be the core of your wealth plan. While there are lots of investment-related books that go into lots of detail and explain all the various approaches you can adopt, I've tried to explain the subject matter on the basis of what matters and, more importantly, what works. My view is that the simpler you can make your investment approach then the more likely it is to be effective.

Part 3 provides an overview of a range of tactical planning issues including use of insurance, general tax planning, pensions, later life planning and wealth succession, as these are inevitable components of most wealth plans. Some of these subjects are complicated and wide-ranging, so I've tried to cover what I think will be the most important issues to the majority of readers. I could easily have written three times as much material, so bear that in mind when reading those chapters.

Don't feel that you have to read the whole book from beginning to end; you aren't studying for an exam and there will be no test when you've finished! If you want to you can read random chapters that take your fancy or read one whole part. If you read this book in small chunks, you will probably get more out of it than thinking you need to absorb every word. The language is as jargon-free and clear as I could make it, but where I judged that further explanation might be helpful, particularly for readers who like more detail, I have included these in the footnotes.

I do not know all the answers and I don't think anyone does. Nor do I seek to suggest that there is only one way of managing personal wealth. The contents of this book are the product of my 20 or so years of practical experience of working with and advising affluent and wealthy families on managing their wealth in a comprehensive way, as well as the thousands of hours spent studying, training and updating my technical knowledge. I would hope, therefore, that this book becomes your trusty companion along life's financial highway and gives you the inspiration, understanding and the confidence to make good decisions about managing your wealth or to hold to account professionals you engage to manage it for you.

If you spend less time and effort worrying about your money and more on living your life to the full then it will have been worth the effort.

Strategic planning

1

Know where you are going and why

It's a fact that you can't live in the past, because the present is already happening. We all have dreams and aspirations for the future, but some of us can envisage a bigger future than others. Even if you have achieved a ripe old age, you'll probably have aspirations for your grandchildren or other young people or other important causes.

Many people go about planning and managing their wealth in a haphazard and random manner. They have a vague idea of what they want, gain some information and go from one financial solution to the other, without any real plan or context. Over the years I've answered many readers' questions for the *Financial Times* and other weekend newspapers and a common question is 'How should I invest my capital?' This is the same as asking 'How long is a piece of string?' The answer is 'It depends.'

Viktor Frankl, in his classic book *Man's Search for Meaning*, wrote about his observations of human motivation when he was held in a Nazi concentration camp. His central observation was that 'A man can always find the "how" if he knows the "why".' Before you can go about making good financial decisions you need to know your 'why'.

The key to a successful wealth plan is setting personal life goals and objectives in the context of your money values. In addition, agreeing and articulating overarching financial planning principles will assist with future decision making.

Money values

Abraham Maslow was a psychologist who developed the theory of 'the hierarchy of needs', which provides a basic framework for all human motivation and associated actions. At the bottom of the ladder are basic needs like food, shelter, sex, etc. Once these basic needs have been met the individual will seek to fulfil higher-level needs that serve to meet their wider personal desires like friendship, love, material possessions and status. Once these intermediate needs have been met, an individual will seek much higher-level needs, which at their highest level are known as 'self-actualisation'. These needs generally relate to wider society and the desire of the individual to find their real meaning or place in the world.

The self-actualisation stage is where real meaning and contentment can be found. For many people this concept of self-actualisation can appear a bit woolly or vague, even frightening. We can adapt Maslow's ideas to help us make decisions that are in tune with our 'money values'. Money values are overarching beliefs that you have about money and these follow a progressive hierarchy. The 'values conversation', as it is known, starts with asking the question: 'What's important about money to you?' (see Figure 1.1.) This approach was pioneered by Bill Bachrach in his excellent book *Values-based Financial Planning*[1] and this forms the basis of the training that his company provides to progressive financial planners.

Usually the first response to the question 'What's important about money to you?' will be general and basic answers like 'financial security', which is a perfectly reasonable response. However, if you keep following this line of questioning with 'And what's important about financial security to you?', it will allow you to discover more deep-seated values. It is this process of self-actualisation that really helps us to find real meaning and purpose for the future wealth plan. Some people find this process a bit uncomfortable as it requires a level of reflection and contemplation about money that we rarely give to it. However, this reflection can be highly liberating and might allow you to develop a better sense of priorities and objectives.

---

[1] Bachrach, Bill (© 2000–2011) *Values-based Financial Planning: The Art of Creating an Inspiring Financial Strategy*, Aim High Publishing.

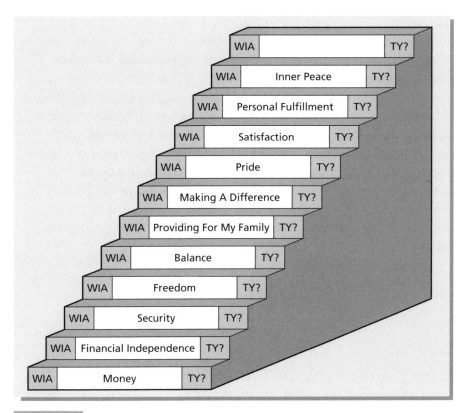

Figure 1.1   The values staircase: what's important about money to you?

Source: The Values Conversation® and The Values Staircase® was excerpted from Bill Bachrach's *Values-based Financial Planning* book. It is provided courtesy of Bill Bachrach, Bachrach & Associates, Inc., www.BillBachrach.com.
©1996–2011 Bill Bachrach. All rights reserved.

Life planning can provide deeper meaning to goals and dreams

Over the years I've met many financially successful people who have stopped dreaming. They have 'switched off' from identifying real meaning, purpose and authenticity in their life. It is not uncommon for a business owner to work hard for years, sell their business for a significant sum and then lose all purpose in their life. This is because their central focus, their business, is taken away. They then drift along slowly losing motivation and purpose. Other times they jump straight from the sale of their business to 'investing' some of their hard-won capital into a new business venture, only to see the business, and their hard-earned capital, slowly dwindle to nothing.

When I was looking for ways to help my clients to envisage a better future and to articulate their life goals and objectives, as well as to improve my own happiness and life meaning, I discovered life planning. In essence life planning is about living life on purpose, whatever that means to you. George Kinder is considered by many to be the father of life planning and his ground-breaking book, *The Seven Stages of Money Maturity*,[2] sets out a radically different way of approaching managing wealth. I attended a training workshop during one of George's regular trips to the UK a few years ago, which I found very enlightening as it made me question a number of my principles and ideas about my life and the role that money played in it. A consequence is that eventually I realised how much was 'enough' and what is really important to me.

The three difficult questions

A key element of the Kinder approach is to ask yourself three difficult questions.

- ■ **Question one**. I want you to imagine that you are financially secure – you have enough money to take care of your needs, now and in the future. The question is, how would you live your life? What would you do with the money? Would you change anything? Let yourself go. Don't hold back your dreams. *Describe a life that is complete, richly yours.*

- ■ **Question two**. This time, you visit your doctor who tells you that you have five to ten years to live. The good part is that you won't ever feel sick. The bad news is that you will have no notice of the moment of your death. What will you do in the time you have remaining to live? *Will you change your life and how will you do it?*

- ■ **Question three**. This time, your doctor shocks you with the news that you have only one day left to live. Notice what feelings arise as you confront your very real mortality. Ask yourself: 'What dreams will be left unfulfilled? What do I wish I had finished or had been? What do I wish I had done? What did I miss?'

---

[2] Kinder, G. (2000) *The Seven Stages of Money Maturity: Understanding the spirit and value of money in your life*, Dell Publishing Company.

The purpose of these questions is to help uncover your deepest and most important values. Equally important is uncovering what is standing in the way of leading the life that is truly the one you want to live. In this context another home or expensive car might not be the answer.

What's really important?

Kinder sets out a framework for helping us to identify what is really important in life. The values grid, as it is known, determines between 'heart's core' – what really matters; 'ought to' – things that you feel obliged to do; and 'fun to' – irreverent things that aren't really important but nevertheless are possible goals. (See Figure 1.2.)

Life can seem complicated, things get in the way and we sometimes do things we would rather not do and don't do the things that we'd rather do. Maria Nemeth is a clinical psychologist and a Master Certified Coach. Maria asks her clients 'Would it be OK if life got easier?' Maria has developed a useful tool called 'the life's intentions inventory' and this is reproduced in Figure 1.3. Why not take some time now to go through the inventory and score the relative importance of each of the intentions. You might find it quite enlightening and it might make you rethink what's important to you and why.

Financial planning policies

Once you have uncovered your purpose, motivations and money values, you can then use these to help you to formulate financial planning policies. Financial planning policies are tools for making good decisions in the face of financial uncertainty. They transcend the current situation by expressing, in general terms, what you plan to do and how you are willing to do it in terms not limited to the current circumstances. Such policies are broad enough to encompass any novel event that might arise, but specific enough so that we are never in doubt as to what actions are required. We'll see the value of having planning policies in Chapter 10 when we discuss withdrawal rates from an investment portfolio.

In the adjacent table, you will find a number of possible uses to which you could put your current or future wealth. For each one, please place an 'X' in *one* of the four boxes to the right based on the following definitions.

Heart's core: a deeply held core value of yours, as to how the wealth should be used. This is a value that you 'stand for'.

Ought to: something you feel obligated to do, based on a commitment you may have made or a belief held by your family, someone outside your family or society in general.

Fun to: the "icing on the cake'. Doing this would add zest or spice to your life, is not an obligation you feel and is not truly a deeply held core value, but it sure would be fun!

Possible uses of your wealth	Heart's core	Ought to	Fun to	N/A
Providing for my family's ongoing needs (Note: this involves day-to-day living expenses, mortgage and car payments, holidays, funding children's education, etc.)				
Supporting parents, siblings and other family members in need				
Providing an inheritance for my children				
Adjusting selected elements of current lifestyle (a second home, a boat, an aeroplane, travelling, an 'expensive hobby', etc.)				
Supporting a major change in my work and career				
Actualising a very different direction for my life				
Charitable giving/philanthropy				
Other(s) please specify				

Figure 1.2   The values grid

Source: Adapted from the Kinder Institute of Life Planning, which trains Financial Life Planners all over the globe using the EVOKE Client Interview process. Reproduced by kind permission of George Kinder and the Kinder Institute of Life Planning. www.kinderinstitute.com

Life's intentions represent underlying purposes that give meaning to our goals and dreams.

Please rate the intentions that are currently important to you. Use 1 for Relatively Unimportant and 5 for Very Important. This is only a snapshot in time, reflecting where you are today. How you rate your intentions could change at a later date.

My intentions are to be:

Financially successful	
Physically fit and healthy	
A successfull painter or sculptor	
A successful musician or composer	
A successful author, playwright or poet	
A contributor to my community	
A visionary leader	
Spiritually developing	
A loving family member	
A trusted friend	
A well-respected professional	
An effective manager	
An effective teacher	
Well educated	
An effective coach	
A successful business owner	
An effective mediator	
Well travelled	
An effective mentor	
A successful entrepreneur	
An adventurer	
Politically active	
A successful communicator	

Figure 1.3 The life's intentions inventory

Source: Reproduced by kind permission of Maria Nemeth, Founder and Executive Director of the Academy for Coaching Excellence

Examples of financial planning policies.

- I will give 10% of my gross annual income to charity.
- I will only do work that I love.
- I will maintain sufficient life insurance to cover my children's education costs.
- We will provide family members with financial literacy support but will not give them money.
- I will not invest in any investment or tax planning that I do not understand.
- I will only invest in 'positively screened' ethical investments.
- I will delegate everything in relation to my finances that I either do not enjoy doing or can be done by someone else at lower cost, taking into account the value of my time to be able to do other things.
- I will always maintain a minimum of one year's living costs in cash and if my portfolio falls more than 20% in a 12-month period then I will reduce the amount of regular withdrawal I take to 50% for up to 2 years.

Financial policies are the anchor points of your strategy to help decision making in difficult times or where there are competing objectives. Think of the policies as the keel of your financial boat, keeping you from capsizing in rough financial seas.

Clear goals

There is something incredibly enabling about defining and writing down clear life goals. Notice that I refer to life goals, not financial goals. My view is people don't have financial goals, they have life goals that have financial implications.

In 1961 President Kennedy set the incredible goal of sending a man to the moon and safely returning him before the end of the 1960s. He didn't tell the NASA people to see what they could do in space over the next few years and come back to him with a few achievements; Kennedy was specific about what he wanted and had a clear timeline. In my experience people who have clear and realistic life goals tend to make better financial decisions.

Life goals that will be common to everyone are maintaining financial independence and staying fit and well. This means being able to fund your desired lifestyle until you die, regardless of your desire or ability to work, and that your money lasts a lifetime, including a time when paid work is optional as you have enough financial resources available to fund your desired lifestyle. If you work for money you do so because you want to, not because you have to. The term 'financial independence' is much more meaningful to people today than the concept of 'retirement' and is something worthwhile to aim for. This is because, unlike retirement, which for some people means a time of doing nothing but playing golf or gardening, financial independence means you have the choice of doing whatever you wish.

The four key factors that will affect this objective are: how long you live; how much you spend; the return you achieve on your capital; and the rate at which the cost of living rises. We'll cover these issues in more depth in Chapter 3 and determine what are reasonable assumptions to use when formulating your overall plan.

Clearly your lifestyle, genetics and sense of purpose will play a large part in determining your standard of health, but if or when your health deteriorates, you'll want to make sure that you can afford any additional costs for health- and long-term care and continue to enjoy a good quality of life. With people living longer and continual advances in medical treatment the importance of planning for declining health will affect more and more people. Life expectancy in the UK has been rising for many years and some commentators have described 90 as the new 70. But life expectancy isn't the only issue that you need to factor into your plans, quality of that life is also important because it can have significant cost implications.

Other goals

There may be any number of other goals that are important to you. The following are real-life examples that I have come across in my work with clients. Some have more of a financial implication than others, but it is important to get the goals written down so that you can get excited about pulling together your wealth plan:

- funding part or all of the education costs of a child, grandchild or other family member or friend
- leaving a specific legacy to an individual or charity
- funding the cost of your child or children's wedding
- taking up a hobby, such as sailing, shooting, scuba-diving or flying, which has a cost implication
- taking up further study or further education at a university or college
- mentoring young businesses and possibly providing development funds
- indulging an interest in culture such as opera, ballet, musicals or performance art at home and abroad
- learning a foreign language and staying in the home country for some time
- buying a second home in the UK or abroad
- moving abroad to live permanently
- helping your children or other family members to buy their first home
- setting up a small 'lifestyle' business such as a country pub, restaurant or shop
- travelling around the world to indulge an interest in historical buildings and/or interesting places
- learning a new skill such as dancing, martial arts or rock climbing
- buying a boat, classic car or plane
- collecting art or other items
- buying an expensive musical instrument
- visiting relatives more often, particularly those living overseas
- writing a book (take it from me, it takes a lot of time!)

While setting clear life goals is essential to developing a wealth plan that works, not all goals are of equal importance. I have found it helpful in my own planning and when working with clients to categorise goals in order of importance. Goals are therefore either 'required', 'desired' or 'aspirational'.

Required goals

The 'required' goals are the most important and must be met come what may – they are non-negotiable – and will usually revolve around maintaining financial independence throughout your lifetime and remaining fit and well or obtaining treatment and care to enable you to have a high quality of life. You should state the minimum annual lifestyle cost that you'd be prepared to accept – your basic financial independence target – in the event that things like taxes, investment returns or inflation turn out worse than you expect. There may be other goals like funding school fees, which are equally important and must be met but for which you could substitute a cheaper option as a base scenario.

Desired goals

'Desired' goals are important but not at the expense of the required goals. You might, for example, wish to fund a slightly more expensive lifestyle than that assumed under the required goals. Examples of other typical desired goals might include making regular gifts each year to individuals, a trust or charity; preserving assets for your children; investing in a new business; or funding a holiday home. In essence, desired goals are important and broadly reflect the middle values in the values staircase referred to earlier. They usually, but not always, reflect a desire to help the wider family.

Aspirational goals

'Aspirational' goals are essentially those goals that you wish to achieve if everything else has been catered for and perhaps investment returns have been consistently above those assumed or you've spent less than anticipated. Such goals often reflect the desire to help wider society. Such 'aspirational' goals might be giving money, time or both to good causes in your lifetime or after death. The point is that if the investment strategy has produced returns below the original assumption, it is the aspirational goals which take the back seat, not your core lifestyle expenditure.

Philanthropy is a possible example of an aspirational goal, although it may be the quantum of philanthropy rather than the act. For example you might have a 'required' goal to support a charity or cause with time or modest financial gifts, whereas you might have an 'aspiration' to give much more substantial amounts of money if you are able to do so.

Example

The unhappy surgeon

Many years ago, on one of my visits to the annual conference of the Financial Planning Association in the United States, I heard the following story that illustrates how we can think differently about work and 'retirement', sometimes with life-changing consequences.

A well-respected and ostensibly successful surgeon, let's call him Mr Jones, visited a financial planner. During the initial goal-setting discussion the planner gently asked Mr Jones what his key concerns were. Mr Jones revealed that he really didn't enjoy his job any more; his relationships with his wife and 13-year-old daughter were under strain; he had high blood pressure and suffered bouts of depression, for which he was on medication. In addition, Mr Jones, despite earning a high salary and having built significant wealth, didn't feel wealthy or successful.

Mr Jones' plan was to work hard for the next five years, earn as much as he could so that he could afford to 'retire' to Florida and have enough time for both his wife and daughter and his other hobbies like fishing and cycling, neither of which he currently had time to pursue. The planner took all this in and suggested that Mr Jones come back in a few weeks, once the planner had been able to run the numbers and see whether this would work.

Mr Jones duly returned a few weeks later. The planner showed a picture of Mr Jones' overall wealth and confirmed that the numbers did seem to support the strategy that Mr Jones was currently pursuing. However, the planner pointed out that with the current approach Mr Jones would continue to be unhappy over the next five years and possibly find that he might not survive long enough to enjoy his life when he stopped work.

The planner then showed another picture of Mr Jones' wealth that was also sustainable. In this alternative scenario Mr Jones would actually work about half his current hours, with immediate effect, but instead of stopping work in five years he would work at the new reduced rate for the next ten years and an even more reduced amount for the following five years. The planner explained that the benefits of this approach were that Mr Jones could do surgery, which he really enjoyed, he would have enough time to spend with his wife and daughter and pursue his hobbies *now* and he would be able to schedule exercise and rest. Mr Jones had not considered this alternative approach and cautiously agreed to give it a try.

At the progress meeting with the planner about a year later, Mr Jones explained that he was really enjoying his work again, and the paradox of making himself less available meant that his value went up and he was almost earning the same income working 2.5 days a week as when he was busting a gut working 6 days a week. His blood pressure was now under control and he had lost about a stone in weight. His relationship with his wife had improved considerably and while no amount of planning could change the fact that his daughter was a typical teenager, with all the usual associated challenges, he felt much more able to understand her and flew off the handle much less.

The message here is that thinking differently about the big picture plan could, quite literally, save a life!

Time horizon

Different goals will require different approaches based on whether they are short-, medium- or long-term goals. Funding a wedding or house in a couple of years will mean that the need is to avoid the potential for capital loss; inflation is less of a concern. Funding your long-term lifestyle, however, means that inflation will be more of a threat and therefore you could accept some risk to capital in return for a potential of generating real returns over the long term.

Current/desired lifestyle expenditure

The clearer you can be about what your current and future lifestyle costs are, the better your overall plan and associated financial decisions will be. This is because funding your lifestyle will have an influence on your investment strategy, tax planning and wealth succession planning. In my experience the vast majority of people rarely have a clear idea of the cost of their current or desired lifestyle and they consistently underestimate how much they are spending. Sometimes this is because they feel guilty about how much they are spending. In other cases the attributes of their personality that helped them create their wealth may not be those required to manage it well. Entertainers are a classic example of individuals who have high earning capabilities, but often have poor financial judgement. Elvis Presley was well known for being very generous and gave Cadillacs to strangers. Who knows how much Elton John has spent on flowers over the decades!

Over the years I've had clients tell me 'This was an exceptional year for spending.' Every year seems an exceptional year! Do remember to account for things like holidays and home improvements/maintenance. The importance of having a clear idea of expenditure, both now and in the future, will vary from person to person depending on the financial resources they have available. My advice is to be realistic about what you will spend throughout your lifetime as it is better to overestimate than to underestimate. There is no need to spend lots of time doing detailed budgets, just as long as you are totally confident that you have a true idea of how much you really are spending (or would like to spend).

Don't mention the 'R' word

If you are thinking about retirement as a goal, I suggest you ask yourself the following questions to see if that really is the goal for which you are aiming.

■ What does retirement mean to you?

■ How will you live your life differently when you are retired?

■ Have you a role model of someone who is retired and, if so, what is it about their lifestyle that you admire?

■ Do you have concerns about retirement and, if so, what are they?

■ How would you feel about working less but for longer?

'For many, a conventional retirement may not be welcome. More than ever before, we are enjoying good health to an older age and many of us are not only capable of working well beyond retirement age, we also often have the desire to do so. Today's older generation can often be found using their retirement years to start a new career, set up a business or to consult in their specialist field. As a result, the notion that an individual should cease working at a pre-defined age is more of an illusion than a reality.'[3]

People who have never created any meaningful wealth are often amazed when they learn that many wealthy people are still motivated to continue working, often until they die! The thought process goes something like 'They have all the money they could possibly need, why are they still working?' This displays a lack of understanding of both the role of work and the meaning of wealth for successful people. It also goes to the heart of one's life goals.

Frederick Herzberg was a US psychologist who carried out a study[4] on human motivation in the workplace. His main conclusion was that the most powerful motivator in our lives isn't money; it's the opportunity to learn, grow in responsibilities, contribute to others and be recognised for achievements. True happiness and fulfilment is unlikely, therefore, to be determined by your level of wealth or financial success, although life goals will, obviously, have a financial implication.

---

[3] *Barclays Wealth Insights* (2010) 'How the wealthy are redefining their retirement', Vol. 12, p. 4.

[4] Herzberg, Frederick, Mausner, Bernard and Bloch Snyderman, Barbara (1959) *The Motivation to Work*, Wiley.

When I initially start working with a new client and I explore the motivations that drive them, it often becomes clear that work is actually a creative and defining part of their life. While building wealth may well have been an early motivation, more often than not the actual process of leading people, innovating, building a business and making a difference are more important, particularly as the financial success becomes more tangible.

'...they don't stop being an entrepreneur when they sell the company. Typically, an entrepreneur's business is what defined them.'[5]

If being involved in business is something that makes you happy or enables you to pursue other meaningful life goals, then why not include that in your wealth plan, rather than aiming for a 'retirement' that may take away a lot of your purpose and meaning? It's OK to still be working in your seventies or even eighties if it is in proportion to your other priorities and it makes you happy. As long as your life goals, which have a financial implication, are not dependent on you continuing to work, then why not work until you drop? Sometimes we need to look at wealth planning in a different way.

In Chapter 3 I'll explain how you can use this knowledge with other key planning assumptions to help develop a robust framework for making key financial decisions, but first we've got to examine the role of financial personality.

---

[5] *Barclays Wealth Insights* White paper (2007) 'UK landscape of wealth', March, p. 8.

2

Knowing your 'financial personality'

'Information is not knowledge. Knowledge is not wisdom.'

Frank Zappa

With the internet, information is widely available at the click of a button and you could be forgiven for thinking that making good financial decisions should be easy. It is possible to go online and compare financial products, buy investment funds or insurance and apply for a mortgage or a loan. What is rarely considered is both the context in which those decisions are made and the psychology of the person making them.

Knowing your 'financial personality' is the key to living the life you really want and to developing and sticking with a financial plan that will help to ensure that money enables you to be true to that ideal. Your financial personality is your unique combination of natural 'hardwired' and learned behaviours. Your behavioural characteristics will have a big impact on how you see the world, process information and how you react to messages from your family, friends and colleagues. If you are employing a professional financial adviser it can mean the difference between a successful long-term relationship or not.

Your financial personality is made up of a number of interrelated elements. These include:

- your life goals, aspirations and motivations
- your natural 'hardwired' behaviour, which is instinctive

- your learned behaviour – education, upbringing, environment, career and life experiences
- how you like to receive information and communicate
- your need for information and facts
- your desire for control
- your propensity to take risks and live with the consequences
- whether you are a do-it-yourselfer, a collaborator or a delegator.

Behaviour

Natural behaviour is instinctive, very stable and highly predictable over time and is the ingrained response that shapes how you respond to external factors and scenarios. At its most basic and extreme level, these responses are triggered by the amygdala in the back of your brain, which could be described as your 'fight or flight' decision box. Natural behaviour usually surfaces when a person is under pressure – whether positive or negative. This natural behaviour is often masked by learned behaviour and as such it can become 'buried' and less obvious over time

Learned behaviours, on the other hand, are those that are shaped by your life experiences, education, environment and previous financial successes and failures, and these create your attitudes, beliefs and values. Overall your personality is dynamic, but it is driven by 'hardwired' natural behaviour and then shaped by these learned behaviours. Knowing your natural behaviour factors and how these surface in a stress or striving scenario is key to sticking with a unique life plan and avoiding 'noise' and other bad decisions that can blow you off course from leading a full life.

Communication style

Are you a 'big picture' person or someone who likes lots of detailed information? A 'big picture' person will not want to wade through a long detailed report, whereas a 'detail' person will be anxious if they don't have in-depth information to enable them to make key decisions.

Someone who is fast-paced and likes lots of variety and minimal information will not appreciate a long, slow and detailed lecture that labours over facts. A reserved, reflective and slower-paced person, on the other hand, will love this approach. Your core communication style also extends to the form that you like to express yourself in and how you prefer to have others communicate with you. To find out your own preferred communication style you can visit **www.financialdna.com** and take the free Communication DNA Profile.

Financial risk profile

We all have a unique risk profile that is determined by our core and learned personality traits. Knowing your risk profile is probably one of the most important aspects of making committed life and financial decisions. In Chapter 1, I explained that the starting point with your financial plan is to identify and quantify clear life goals and objectives. Once you know what you are trying to achieve you need to determine if your goals are achievable by investing only in no-risk assets like cash and equivalents. If the plan requires a higher return than that available from risk-free assets and you can't find more resources or spend less, then you will need to invest some of your wealth into risky assets. By 'risky' I mean that there is a degree of uncertainty about what the actual return will be and the value of the investment will vary – both up and down – sometimes extremely so. However, the payoff for that uncertainty is the probability that the overall return, particularly over the longer term, will be higher than that provided by the no-risk investment. Generally, the higher the amount of risk, then the higher the expected return.

Your ability to withstand, financially, the effect of future returns being less favourable than were predicted or expected is called **risk capacity**. It thus represents a constraint on the maximum upside that you can expect from investing, given your goals and resources. In effect 'risk capacity' represents our need to take risks and to be able to live with the consequences of an adverse outcome.

A different, but very important, measure of risk is **risk tolerance**. This represents your emotional ability to cope with investment uncertainty or loss and is based on a combination of both your 'core' personality (inherent) and also those learned (evolved) from life experience, education and environment. As a general rule we are happier forgoing potential investment returns than we are of losing money. The need to avoid the pain of loss is a powerful emotion.

Risk perception can and does change depending on current experiences and events. You will usually have a higher investment risk perception when the stock market or property values are rising strongly and the world seems full of optimism and you feel wealthy. It can also vary depending on the type of investment or whether you are under pressure or stress.

When investment and property markets and the economy were booming, and before the global credit crunch hit, it was highly likely that your inherent risk tolerance traits were hidden. As we know, when the tide comes in all boats rise! But what happened when the stock market dived or some other big negative event happened (the Iraqi invasion of Kuwait, 9/11, etc.) and your portfolio showed a large loss? The decision-making patterns for many of us can change radically when the good times turn to bad. This happens because when we are under pressure, our natural instincts instantly take over and for most of us we have little control over this: it just happens. This is why we often see a high degree of emotional decision making. This is not rational in the area of investing and it can cost investors dearly.

Tony Robbins, the US success guru, made a very good point when he said that we often overestimate what we can achieve in a year but underestimate what we can achieve in a lifetime. The same can be said of managing wealth in general and managing investments in particular. We get upset, annoyed or concerned if we don't make a decent return in three or four years because we had unreasonable expectations of what could be delivered over such a short term. However, we are pleasantly surprised when we realise that, for all its ups and downs, our pension fund has quietly delivered a return of 3% per annum over inflation over the past 10 years at a time when our cash at the bank is yielding a negative real return after tax.

Emotions and money

The world is made up of lots of different types of people all with their own idiosyncrasies and traits, experiences and preferences. The thing common to all human beings, however, is that, to a greater or lesser extent, most decisions, including those involving money, are made at an **emotional** level (see Figure 2.1). The evidence is that emotions can get in the way of making good financial decisions. Because emotions play such a large part in our financial decision making, having a great education or a high intellect is no guarantee of financial success or happiness. Sure, all other things being equal it is preferable to be well-educated and to have a good intellect, but it isn't enough for financial happiness and success. That's why history is full of examples of people with high intellect, natural ability or inherited wealth, who died lonely, unhappy and penniless.

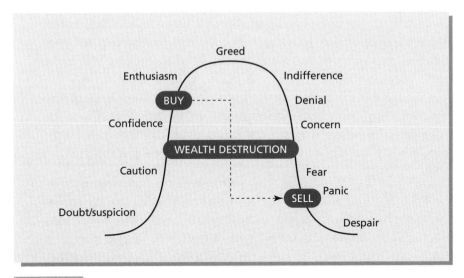

Figure 2.1   Emotions and investing

Emotional intelligence

Recent research into the human mind has found that the secret to success in any long-term endeavour, whether it is in business, relationships or investing, is an attribute called **emotional intelligence** (otherwise known as 'EQ'). EQ is a type of intelligence that's significantly different from the standard IQ-based definition of 'clever' we're all used to. The topic of 'EQ' has received significant coverage in the business world in the past few years, fuelled in particular by Daniel Goleman's books[1] aimed at helping business people to use the skill to further their careers and effectiveness.

With Goleman's model for EQ, the emotionally intelligent investor would, for instance, calmly make investment decisions based on a higher consciousness of who they are and with a positive personal relationship to money (the first facet, 'self-awareness'). This is instead of making decisions based on an emotional impulse that sabotages their financial position. They also handle stress, disappointment and uncertainty more rationally and don't allow those feelings or circumstances to control or initiate their decisions (the second facet, 'self-management').

Going further, the emotionally intelligent investor would also understand the emotions of others such as their partner, spouse or family members, recognising them and responding with empathy (the third facet, 'social awareness'). Finally, a person with high investment EQ would have the ability to maintain quality relationships with others around them when making investment decisions, knowing how to motivate them effectively and appropriately and manage their money energy using subtlety, delicacy and tact (the fourth facet, 'managing others').

The role of EQ in investment has been little publicised, even though its application can be invaluable for investors. Whether this is because the investment process is seen as an objective, numbers-based, non-emotional process or the investment industry has simply not been made sufficiently aware of the existence of EQ is unclear. My experience is that a high level of EQ *combined* with sound financial knowledge, strategy and advice can make the difference between great investors and losers.

So why is understanding investment EQ so powerful? It is the ability to give a person enough confidence, focus and rationality to remain

---

[1] Goleman, D. (2005) *Emotional Intelligence: Why it can matter more than IQ*, Bantam Books.

committed to their strategies even when the market value of their portfolio is declining, not living up to expectations or being superseded by other events.

Charles Ellis is one of the leading thinkers in investment management, the author of 6 books and 70 articles on investment and finance and has taught the graduate school investment courses at both Yale and Harvard. He is a member of the Board of Directors of the Harvard Business School and a Trustee of Yale University where he also serves on the investment committee. Here's what he had to say about emotions and investing and the key to a successful investment experience:

> 'Principles that every investor should be thinking about... [that] investing is all about you, not about the market, about you and how you would feel most comfortable through thick and thin because there will be thick and there will be thin. There will be good times, there will be bad times and that's part of life's experience. And, you must be comfortable and candid about whom you really are and what your investment capabilities are and what your emotional capabilities are so that you can set a pathway you can really stay with. Staying with it is the most important single principle.

> '.... don't be afraid of being candid about what your emotions are. Go ahead and accept who you are as a human being and if you can't handle turbulence don't invest in turbulent securities. If you are more able to handle turbulence take that chance because you can take it in stride and invest that way. But, if you will aim at the right kind of investment mission and then stay with that mission you can have a winning experience and everybody in your family, everybody in your neighborhood, everybody in the world can have a simultaneously winning experience if they each do what's really right for them.'[2]

You are more likely to make rational decisions if you have a high level of self-awareness, financial education and experience, a secure relationship with money and a high level of 'emotional intelligence'. Even then the instinctive aspects of your core personality will still have an impact on your financial decisions. With turbulent financial markets it is far more likely that your inherent risk tolerance will emerge and strongly influence your financial decisions.

---

[2] Transcript of video interview with respected investment expert and author Charles Ellis on investment fundamentals: **www.vanguard.co.uk/uk/portal/Library/interviews--video-ellis.jsp**

At the end of the day you need to accept that there are some things you can control and some things you can't and to have the wisdom to know the difference. In that context, knowing your life purpose and financial personality are likely to give you the best chance of making good financial decisions. Avoiding getting blown off course by the 'noise' from the media is difficult but, once you realise that their interests are not aligned with your own, you'll start to focus on what really matters – staying disciplined in the face of adversity and extreme events.

The nine high-net-worth personalities

In the 1990s research[3] was carried out in the USA among high-net-worth individuals to help ascertain their key motivations and concerns. As a result of the research the researchers created a psychological framework that places wealthy individuals into one of nine high-net-worth types, each with different psychological characteristics. Everyone has characteristics of more than one high-net-worth personality, but virtually every individual has a dominant personality that broadly follows one of the nine in this framework.

Key attributes of the nine high-net-worth personalities[4]

Family stewards
- Dominant focus is to take care of their families.
- Conservative in personal and professional life.
- Not very knowledgeable about investing.

Independents
- Seek the personal freedom money makes possible.
- Feel investing is a necessary means to an end.
- Not interested in the process of investing or wealth management.

Phobics
- Are confused and frustrated by the responsibility of wealth.
- Dislike managing finances and avoid technical discussion of it.
- Choose advisers based on level of personal trust they feel.

---

[3] Prince, R.A. and Van Bortel, B. (2005) *The Millionaire's Advisor: High-touch, high-profit relationship strategies of advisors to the wealthy*, Institutional Investor News.

[4] Ibid.

The anonymous

- Confidentiality is their prominent concern.
- Prize privacy in their financial affairs.
- Likely to concentrate assets with an adviser who protects them.

Moguls

- Control is a primary concern.
- Investing is another way of extending personal power.
- Decisive in decisions; rarely look back.

VIPs

- Investing results in ability to purchase status possessions.
- Prestige is important.
- Like to affiliate with institutions and advisers with leading reputations.

Accumulators

- Focused on making their portfolios bigger.
- Investments are performance-orientated.
- Tend to live below their means and spend frugally.

Gamblers

- Enjoy investing for the excitement of it.
- Tend to be very knowledgeable and involved.
- Exhibit a high risk tolerance.

Innovators

- Focused on leading-edge products and services.
- Sophisticated investors who like complex products.
- Tend to be technically savvy and highly educated.

Knowing your high-net-worth personality will be particularly important if you are looking to work with a professional adviser, because it is essential to a good working relationship for your adviser to understand you, your interest in and association with money. We'll discuss choosing and working with advisers in Chapter 4. If you want to find out your high-net-worth personality you can take the quiz at the end of this chapter.

Financial personalities

Another way of understanding your financial personality is to determine whether you are a 'do-it-yourselfer', a 'collaborator' or a 'delegator' as this will help you to determine the type of advice and service that you need and from which you would derive good value for money. The level and complexity of your wealth, as well as your available time, inclination and financial knowledge, will influence whether you need to seek help and assistance and, if so, what type.

Do-it-yourselfer

As the name suggests, this group has a very strong need for control and will seek lots of information; members have an above-average intellect. They will enjoy spending time on financial matters and be very well organised. They rarely benefit from collaborating or delegating to others as they do not value their time more than the cost of the collaboration/delegation.

If you are in this group then the only time you are likely to want or value professional advice is to help with a specific situation or one-off, more complicated, situation. Examples include complex property transactions; selling a business; setting up a family trust; structuring a sophisticated tax wrapper for a large portfolio; or selecting and arranging a tax-driven investment solution that is only available from authorised financial advisers.

Collaborator

This group is similar to DIYers but members lack the confidence to make financial decisions on their own and will usually seek advice and assistance from professional advisers, salespeople and organisations like the Citizens' Advice Bureau and the Pensions Advisory Service. They will also usually seek access to information from magazines, newspapers, websites, books (like this one) and friends and other contacts.

If you are in this group then you probably value and benefit from some form of ongoing advice and service but it will be important that this is not more extensive and expensive than you want or need. It is common for a collaborator to engage a 'full service' advisory service, which is aimed more at those clients who are looking to delegate rather than collaborate. If you are willing and able to take more responsibility for your wealth and carry out some of the day-to-day aspects yourself, then you will probably save yourself money and become more confident about your financial decisions if you choose products and services that are less extensive and as a result less expensive than a full service offering.

Delegator

This group is keen to 'outsource' most day-to-day aspects of managing their wealth, although they will want to have close involvement in formulating strategy. Looking at the big picture is usually enough for delegators, as they have better uses for their time. Delegators are usually the most financially successful people precisely because they have learnt when and to whom to delegate for best effect. Delegators rarely do something themselves that they could delegate to someone else.

If you are in this group then a full service advisory firm will probably be the best choice, as you will be able to derive the maximum value for the fees and/or commissions you will pay. When the value of your time is very high, you have little inclination to learn about financial matters in detail and/or your needs are complex, the price of a good, fee-only wealth management service will often pay for itself many times over.

And finally...

A significant majority of affluent and wealthy individuals and their families will be better off working with a decent, fee-only financial adviser, as long as they select a firm appropriate to their needs and the fees charged can be demonstrated to be value for money. This is particularly the case if you have an investment portfolio that includes exposure to risky assets, because emotions, as we've seen, can cause wealth-destroying behaviour.

A small minority would be better off doing their own planning because they have the time and inclination to acquire the knowledge and level of understanding as well as the discipline to stay the course. In that case there is unlikely to be much perceived value obtained from paying for professional advice, even if the outcome achieved by the individual is worse than with a professional adviser. In Chapter 4 we'll look at the value of advice, the types of advisers who are able to help you and how to choose one who is right for you.

Quiz

High-net-worth personalities

To determine your high-net-worth personality, take this self-diagnostic quiz. Simply prioritise from most important to least important the statements in each group. Be sure to write down the first thought that pops into your mind. Don't stop to think about it.

1 Please rank each of the following between 1 and 4, with 4 being the most important to you and 1 the least.

Funding further education for my children and grandchildren (A)

Achieving my asset accumulation goal (G)

Having enough money to have the holiday home I want (F)

Getting enough money to retire early (C)

2 Please rank each of the following between 1 and 4, with 4 being the most important to you and 1 the least.

Having a fun time investing (H)

Learning about the most sophisticated investing methods (I)

Having enough money to have the power I want (E)

Being able to maintain my privacy (D)

3 Please rank each of the following between 1 and 4, with 4 being the most important to you and 1 the least.

Finding someone I trust to do my investments so I don't have to be involved (B)

Ensuring the security of my family through my investments (A)

Minimising the risk of identity theft through proper disposal of financial information (D)

Having sufficient assets invested to be independent (C)

4 Please rank each of the following between 1 and 4, with 4 being the most important to you and 1 the least.

Being able to protect the confidentiality of my investments (D)

Having the assets to buy the things I want (F)

Being able to focus on the exciting aspects of investing (H)

Having the luxury of not educating myself on technical financial minutiae (B)

5 Please rank each of the following between 1 and 4, with 4 being the most important to you and 1 the least.

Having sufficient assets to feel powerful (E)

Using the most modern investment approaches (I)

Using my investments to take care of my family (A)

Concentrating on increasing the amount of my assets (G)

6 Please rank each of the following between 1 and 4, with 4 being the most important to you and 1 the least.

Having the asset base to live wherever I want to (C)

Having enough assets so that others respect me (F)

Hiring a top money manager to oversee my account and forgetting all about it (B)

Maintaining complete privacy over my investment affairs (G)

7 Please rank each of the following between 1 and 4, with 4 being the most important to you and 1 the least.

Finding new ways to keep investing is a thrilling part of my life (H)

Applying the most technical investment approaches (I)

Having the investment base to get people to do what I want (E)

Using investment products to transfer assets to family members (A)

8 Please rank each of the following between 1 and 4, with 4 being the most important to you and 1 the least.

Being able to avoid getting involved in the details of investing (B)

Focusing on increasing my assets (G)

Having the assets to enjoy the finer things in life (F)

Ensuring my privacy with the investment managers I choose (D)

9 Please rank each of the following between 1 and 4, with 4 being the most important to you and 1 the least.

Having advanced planning and products in my investment portfolio (I)

Being able to use my investments to influence the way things are done (E)

Having the confidence that I can live independently (C)

Staying very involved on a day-to-day basis (H)

High-net-worth personality quiz: scoring

	Totals
A	
B	
C	
D	
E	
F	
G	
H	
I	

To find out your HNW personality visit www.wealthpartner.co.uk

3

The wealth framework – the importance of a plan

'Good fortune is what happens when opportunity meets with planning.'

Thomas Edison

I've already explained the importance of setting clear goals, developing financial planning policies and understanding your financial personality. To develop a successful wealth plan, you need to put these goals into a wider context and review your overall financial position both as it is today and how it might be under various scenarios throughout the rest of your lifetime.

A good wealth plan should include the following elements:

- the wealth summary – detailing your, goals, current personal information and financial resources
- the financial plan – including analysis of your lifetime cashflow position, estate tax liabilities and insurance needs
- the investment policy statement (IPS) – detailing the investment strategy for your long-term liquid capital.

The wealth summary

Knowing what you have and where documents can be located is a simple but important element of getting and staying well organised. How you choose to do this is up to you and it could just be a handwritten summary of your assets, liabilities, financial documents, insurance policies and trusts or it could be a more formal spreadsheet.

The important thing is to list out what you've got and what you've done as this will help you to make more informed decisions. In addition, if you are incapacitated or die, it will avoid a nightmare for your family of getting to the bottom of your financial world.

Another common problem is not documenting or recording when gifts have been made. The type of gift, for example, whether to an individual or a trust, whether it is exempt from inheritance tax or not and when it was made, are all essential facts that need to be shared with your professional advisers, because this can have a dramatic impact on the eventual inheritance tax bill.

Notwithstanding the hard facts, the wealth summary is a good place to record your financial planning policy statements, goals and planning assumptions, so that you can readily refer to the goals for which you are planning. To get you started you can download a preformatted spreadsheet from **www.wealthpartner.co.uk** if you'd like to create a written summary similar to one that a professional financial planner would prepare.

The financial plan
Financial planning assumptions

When you formulate your planning projections you will need to use some assumptions. The following are the key ones that you (or your professional adviser) should include in your plan.

Life expectancy

Clearly your own health will determine how long you expect to live, but with medical advances it may be longer than you think. The evidence suggests that most people underestimate their life expectancy by quite a big margin. As illustrated in Figure 3.1, a 65-year-old male has a 1 in 3 chance of living until age 90. On average, a man and woman aged 65 can expect to live another 21 and 23.4 years respectively and this is projected to increase to 25 and 27.2 years by 2050, as illustrated by the chart in Figure 3.2.

I recommend using age 99 as the default lifespan for planning purposes as this is currently well in excess of the average life expectancy. However, recent research from the University of Denmark[1] suggests that a child born in Western Europe in 2007 has a 1 in 3 chance of living beyond 100, so you might wish to extend this to an even greater age.

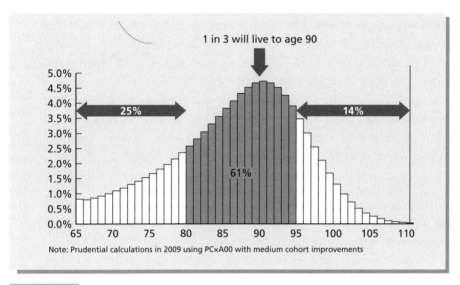

Figure 3.1 Distribution of age of death for male aged 65

Source: Prudential

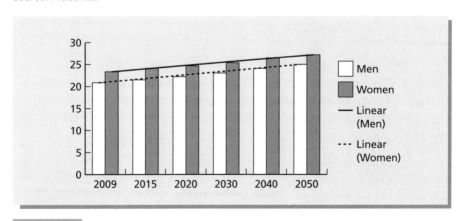

Figure 3.2 Projected life expectancy at age 65

Source: PPI (2010) 'Retirement income and assets: outlook for the future'

[1] Christensen, K., Doblhammer, G., Rau, R. and Vaupel, J. W. (2009) 'Ageing populations: the challenges ahead', *The Lancet*, 374 (9696): 1196–1208.

Lifestyle expenditure

Ensure that the lifestyle expenditure assumption in your projection is reasonable and reflects what you do, or expect to, spend, not what you think you should be spending! If you think that you are spending £60,000 per annum, why not build in an additional 'desired' goal of spending an additional £20,000 per annum and see what effect that has on your overall position. It is better to overestimate your spending than underestimate it. The importance of being accurate about your current or desired expenditure will depend very much on the ratio of your regular spending shortfall (i.e. that not met by pension or other non-investment income) to your capital base. If the ratio is under 1:30 (i.e. you need your wealth to generate 3% pa or less), then you probably don't need to be too worried about every last penny.

The reality is that we do spend less in later life as we become less active (various estimates put this as much as 40% less) but this might be countered by needing long-term care. I suggest that for planning purposes you keep the projected expenditure amount constant in real terms throughout life, rather than aim for spurious precision by assuming a fall in living costs and allowing for specific long-term care costs. If your financial resources look a bit thin then you can drill into more specific expenditure projections.

Expenditure escalation

The Office for National Statistics publishes various measures of inflation that vary widely as a result of the different items included in the indices. The two that are of interest to individuals managing their wealth are the Retail Prices Index (RPI or RPIX; the latter excludes mortgage interest payments) and the Consumer Prices Index (CPI). The CPI measures inflation on internationally agreed standards throughout Europe and is now the basis on which allowances and most State benefits are escalated each year. The main difference between RPI and CPI is that RPI includes council tax and some other housing costs not included in CPI; it excludes certain financial services costs; and is based on a smaller sample of the population. RPI also includes mortgage interest costs whereas CPI and RPIX don't.

The CPI rate has tended to be lower than RPI/RPIX. The RPI/RPIX rate excludes items of expenditure incurred by the very poorest and very wealthiest members of society, on the basis that they are unrepresentative of wider society. For this reason, it is highly likely that your own 'personal inflation rate' will be higher than any of the official rates, particularly if you employ domestic help, pay childcare and/or school fees, own a second home or pay for comprehensive private health insurance/care. I suggest that you visit the ONS website **www.ons.gov.uk** to use its inflation rate calculator to work out your own inflation rate. Failing that I suggest you escalate your expenditure by RPIX + 2%.

Convert pension funds to a simple level annuity

If you have substantial money purchase pension benefits, then it is unlikely that you will buy an annuity with all of them at the same time. For tax and investment reasons, it is more likely that you will take benefits from the pensions in stages and possibly some or all as income withdrawn from the fund or possibly an investment-linked, rather than gilt-linked, annuity, as this is likely to provide maximum investment flexibility and the option to minimise tax.

However, from a financial planning perspective, I recommend that you assume the lowest-risk, highest-tax position first, as this is the most prudent approach. Therefore, assume that any pension funds are used fully to purchase a guaranteed annuity at one point (between ages 60 and 80), inflation protected (you can always use a level annuity if the plan doesn't work) and the maximum dependants' income protection (this is usually 100% of your own pension, so it does not reduce on your own death). If your plan works with this cautious assumption then you know that you have a fair amount of 'wriggle room' if things turn out differently. You can then consider how and when you take benefits to minimise risk and tax.

Use reasonable investment return assumptions

For many years the actuarial profession consistently underestimated the present-day value of the future liabilities of many final salary pension schemes. This arose because the discount rate (i.e. the rate of expected future investment returns) used to calculate the present-day value of the scheme's liabilities (the pensions due in the future) usually assumed a higher-risk investment strategy than many of the schemes were actually pursuing. So if you have half your capital in cash and half in bonds (fixed income), your expected return for long-term financial planning purposes needs to be lower than if you held, say, half in bonds and half in equities.

There has been much written about actual and expected returns from different asset classes but, as we'll look at in Part 2, risk and return are related, and higher risks have a higher expected return. However, returns are rarely delivered in a straight line and there can be a range of outcomes (which is what makes them risky), as well as sometimes prolonged periods when actual returns are well below the long-term average. For this reason the forward-looking expected return in any wealth projection or analysis ideally needs to be well below any historic returns.

In Table 3.1 I've listed what I believe to be reasonable return assumptions for the main asset classes in real terms (i.e. after discounting inflation) but before costs, which you'll need to also take off the before inflation return to arrive at the true projected return. Those costs will be influenced by the investment approach that you adopt, which we discuss in Chapter 8, and whether you employ a financial planner or investment manager.

Tax rates

If you (or your adviser) are using professional planning software, it will most probably calculate taxes reasonably accurately. However, it is not necessary to be spuriously precise about taxes as this is a moving target and tax rates will invariably rise and fall over your lifetime. It is perfectly reasonable to assume a simplified tax rate on investments of, say, 25% as reflective of the true rate of tax likely to be paid on income and gains, after allowing for allowances and other reliefs. Another key factor that will affect the amount of tax you pay will be where and how you locate your wealth, and we'll discuss this issue in Chapters 9, 10, 11 and 12.

Table 3.1 Asset class long-term return assumptions

	Nominal return (%)
Inflation	2.50
Fixed interest (short-dated)	5.00
Fixed interest (index-linked)	5.30
UK market	8.50
UK value	10.50
UK small companies	9.50
International market	8.50
International value	10.50
International small companies	9.50
Emerging markets market	11.00
Emerging markets value	13.00
Emerging markets small companies	12.00
Commodities	5.50
Property	6.50

Source: Bloomsbury

All businesses have three key elements to their accounting: a cashflow statement, a profit and loss statement and a balance sheet. Individuals are no different, although it is rare for them to apply the same structured approach to their personal wealth planning.

The importance of lifetime cashflow

The lifetime cashflow statement is, arguably, the most important measure for individuals. Although the projection is almost certainly going to be wrong over a lifetime, as it is impossible to accurately predict all the factors that will impact on your wealth, it will give you a very useful idea of whether or not you have sufficient resources to meet your lifestyle and other goals under a number of different, but plausible, scenarios.

All good professional financial planners create a lifetime cashflow projection as a starting point to help ascertain the client's most likely financial position throughout their lifetime. Some online tools do the same thing, although they often adopt a simplified approach. Whether you use a planner with sophisticated financial planning software, a simple online planning tool or your own spreadsheet, the most important thing is to create a reasonable baseline financial scenario, from which you can draw some broad conclusions.

In Figure 3.3 I've set out two different scenarios for the same individual: the base case scenario and the worst case scenario. The latter will form the basis of our planning, investment and tax planning decisions.

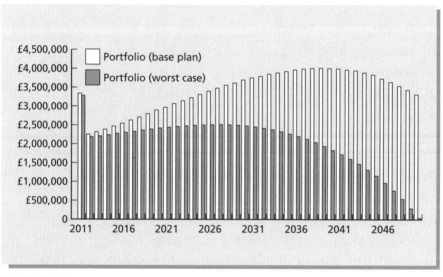

Figure 3.3   Example of financial viability analysis

Your wealth will almost certainly comprise short- and long-term liquid assets as well as used and unused illiquid assets. Liquid assets include cash deposits, most National Savings & Investments (NS&I) products, and quoted equities and bonds, both directly held and via daily priced investment funds. Used illiquid assets include your home, cars, boat or holiday home. Unused illiquid assets would include investment properties, business holdings, land/woodland, many structured investment products or alternative investments, such as hedge funds, that have long 'lock-in' periods. As a general rule, the higher the proportion of liquid assets you have, then the greater will be your financial options and security.

Low-risk liquid investments like cash or most NS&I products are easy to value as they comprise the capital and any accumulated interest. Such funds will also be accessible, depending on the terms of the account. They are also the best place to keep capital on which you expect to call within the next few years or just want to keep to hand for unforeseen emergencies. The only issue to watch is the financial security of the financial institution if you place more than £85,000 (£170,000 if you hold a joint account) in a UK-based account. Financial protection offshore is often less than that in the UK and, in any case, is only as good as the ability of the authorities in the jurisdiction to step up to the plate if an institution fails.

The importance of liquidity

Some illiquid investments, such as property, provide the opportunity to employ leverage (borrowing) to enhance returns, but this can also increase the associated risks. It is usually the case that most illiquid investments are valued less frequently than liquid ones and even then this is usually merely a matter of one person's opinion rather than the price at which the asset actually changes hands. Securities listed on quoted investment exchanges, on the other hand, are valued in real time and reflect the best collective assessment that buyers and sellers place on the present value of the current and future dividends and profits growth of companies (in the case of equities) and interest yield relative to the inflation and general interest rate outlook (in the case of fixed interest bonds). Obviously the same applies to funds that invest in these securities, although they are often valued and priced daily rather than by the minute.

Figure 3.4 illustrates the impact of daily versus annual valuation points for UK equities using the same index. The daily version looks more volatile than the annual version but this is purely a function of the different price points.

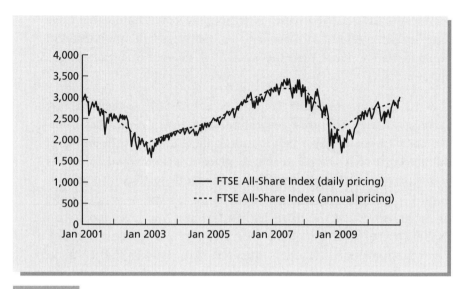

Figure 3.4   Valuation frequencies for FTSE All-Share Index between 2001 and 2010

Source: Bloomsbury, FTSE

While it is true that some unused illiquid investments can produce very high returns in a short space of time, this usually comes with additional and sometimes unanticipated risks (always remember that risk and return are related). In addition, some illiquid invest-ments such as property or unquoted trading businesses require more oversight and input from the investor and may have ongoing main-tenance costs, which must be paid from any income arising from the investment or from your other (liquid) capital or income. Don't forget that your main home may well represent a large part of your wealth and as such may mean that you already have a high exposure to property. Just because you can see and touch something doesn't make it a sure bet!

Investment property can form an asset base from which to build your wealth plan, but it is not a one-way street and to maximise your returns you either have to be prepared to spend time managing the asset or outsource this task to someone else (which has a further cost implication). Either way my advice is that you shouldn't kid yourself that property is the answer to your investment problems, nor that it provides either superior long-term returns at lower risk than a liquid, highly diversified investment portfolio. Property is affected by the reality of the economic conditions prevailing. If people and businesses cannot afford the rent you want to charge or the purchase price then these will simply adjust to reflect the reality of supply and demand.

The perceived lower risk of property compared to equities is just that – a perception. Where property is represented by an index fund that is valued and traded daily on an investment exchange, it exhibits similar (but not exactly the same) fluctuations in price and sentiment as quoted equities. Listed global commercial property (known as securitised) has a correlation of about 0.50 against UK equities and 0.60% against global equities.[2]

Investment in an unquoted business (which can include the business of developing and/or renting property), whether your own or someone else's, usually offers the highest reward but also comes with a different, and sometimes much higher, set of risks. If you have owned your own business and have now sold it for cash, then you need to think very carefully about if reinvesting your money, or at least the vast bulk of it, into another unquoted business is really in line with your future lifestyle and other life goals. If freeing up time is important to you and/or reducing the risk of losing money matters, then perhaps it would be better to invest your non-cash reserve capital into a fully diversified, liquid investment portfolio. However, there are always exceptions to the rule and the case study of Nigel and Mary (see below) is an example.

Some people who have been successful in business are interested in mentoring young and growing businesses. Sometimes this also involves investing some cash in the business, referred to as 'angel investing', and it can be extremely rewarding, both personally and financially. Allocating a small proportion of your capital to angel investing might make sense if you have the interest and necessary time to help nurture new and growing businesses. However, it is rarely good advice to put all your hard-earned capital into such a concentrated risk, particularly if preserving what you have is your key concern and you would not be able to recover from any loss. My

---

[2] Philips, C. B. (2007) 'Commercial equity real estate: A framework for analysis', Vanguard Investment Counseling & Research.

advice is to view such investments as 'fun', like indulging a hobby, and to disregard them from your overall financial resources unless they become cash again.

Case Study

The caravan couple – when business investment is best

I remember a couple who I met some years ago, let's call them Nigel and Mary (not their real names), who had sold a very successful caravan park business for several million pounds after 20 years' hard work. During the wealth planning process it became apparent that neither of them wanted to stop being involved in a business (they were in their early sixties). They also felt that reinvesting the bulk of their liquid wealth into another caravan park business might be the best solution for their wealth plan, provided that they could delegate the day-to-day management of the business to staff. The couple looked at a number of suitable businesses and, drawing on their considerable experience of owning and running such a business, they decided that those on offer were not good investments.

After a few months a more suitable business came on the market and after hard negotiating the couple bought it. The business would comfortably generate an income of £100,000 per annum for each of them, which more than funded their lifestyle after tax. In addition, Nigel and Mary could employ their daughter on a part-time basis for £40,000 per annum, which, as well as only being taxed at no more than 20%, allowed her to indulge her passion for regular travelling. The business was asset-backed in the form of the land on which it was sited and it would also qualify for exemption from inheritance tax after two years and capital gains tax at 10%, should they ever decided to sell it in later life.

This still left them with about £500,000 of surplus cash, which we decided should be spread between instant and notice deposit accounts and NS&I products so as to provide them with an adequate cash reserve while they settled into the new business. Nigel and Mary are very happy with their 'investment' and so is their daughter.

If you have attained financial independence or are almost there and have life plans that do not including spending your precious time overseeing business investments, properties or picking the next 'hot' investment and are looking for 'elegant simplicity', the best investment solution is likely to be to invest your long-term capital into a well-diversified, fully liquid investment portfolio allocated in line with your required return and risk profile.

'We ignore the real diamonds of simplicity, seeking instead the illusory rhinestones of complexity.'[3]

---

[3] Bogle, J. (2009) *Enough!* Wiley, p. 23. John Bogle is founder and former CEO of the Vanguard Mutual Fund Group.

The investment policy statement

An integral element of your wealth plan will be the design and implementation of your personalised investment policy statement (IPS) for your long-term, liquid investment portfolio. This document should detail the following information:

■ your financial goals for the investment portfolio

■ the rate of return required, as identified in the lifetime cashflow analysis

■ the monetary amount that you intend to withdraw from (or add to) the portfolio each year

■ the asset allocation strategy and specific allocation to different asset classes

■ the investment philosophy

■ the rebalancing policy, including when and how this will be done

■ a statement of the action that you will take in response to adverse life or investment events by reference to your financial planning policy statements

■ your tax management approach or policy such as it relates to the portfolio.

The IPS should act as the key reference point for your investment strategy and provide you with the discipline to stick to the plan, particularly when things don't turn out as you expect. If you decide to delegate some or all of the management of your wealth to a professional investment manager, then the IPS can also be used as the basis of the manager's brief for managing the portfolio. An example IPS can be found at **www.wealthpartner.co.uk**

Writing down your financial position and key goals, carrying out a simple viability analysis of your resources and articulating and documenting your investment approach will force you to think about the way that you manage your wealth. It will also serve as a useful reference point from which you will be able to measure your progress.

4

The value of advice

'You make more money selling advice than following it. It's one of the things we count on in the magazine business – along with the short memory of our readers.'

Steve Forbes, Publisher, Forbes magazine[1]

You probably derive much of your financial knowledge from what you read, hear or see in newspapers, magazines, websites, television and books. The internet gives us fast access to vast amounts of material, whether that is video on demand, discussion forums, social networks or knowledge archives. However, just because there is a lot of information available out there does not mean that it is necessarily accurate, objective or relevant to your situation.

The media is not your friend

The sheer amount of information, vested interests and speed of news, coupled with the huge amount of competition, means that journalists are fighting a losing battle when trying to be helpful, objective and independent in what they communicate to their readers on personal finance issues. Sometimes stories are inspired by real news events and other times by 'expert' comment from companies with some form of vested interest. The problem is that in the face of such

---

[1] Excerpt from a presentation at The Anderson School, University of California, Los Angeles, 15 April 2003.

a continual barrage of often conflicting and sensationalist news and information, the average person finds it hard not to be seduced into taking actions that they may turn out to regret. Even if you've decided on your overall planning and investment approach, it is hard not to be knocked off track by the relentless media messages that bombard us daily.

'The investor's chief problem, and even his worst enemy, is likely to be himself.'

Benjamin Graham, legendary US investor

We often overreact to news and ignore the reality of long-term, steady norms. This is normal and totally expected. We place far too much weight on what happened yesterday than we do on what has happened over the past 50 years. The media focuses our attention on the daily movements in the capital value of the stock market. In a sense this fixation on capital values is the investment sizzle, when in fact the investment steak is compound returns. The magic of compounding works away in the background, with dividend/interest and capital gains generated by the portfolio reinvested to create more income and more capital gains. Compounding has been described as the eighth wonder of the world and it is rarely understood what a powerful impact it has on investment returns (see Figure 4.1).

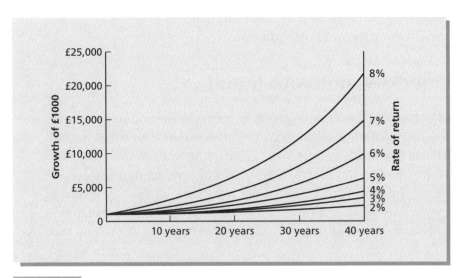

Figure 4.1   The power of compounding

The financial services marketing machine

There is a massive marketing machine deployed by the financial services industry, sometimes subtly and sometimes less so, that is seeking your attention for financial products and services. Jack Bogle, the founder of index fund group Vanguard, estimated that in 2000 the amount spent on financial media advertising was at least $1billion,[2] so today it is likely to be much more than that.

Financial services companies make claims, promises and statements that often don't bear up to scrutiny. The chief problem is that financial companies are seeking to sell their products regardless of whether they are suitable, competitive or value for money. In some cases these products offer a solution to problems that investors never knew they had! I'll talk about the cost of investment funds in Chapters 8 and 9, but remember that the amount spent on marketing is often in direct inverse relationship to the value being provided. In other words, the more spent on marketing then the higher is likely to be the real cost of the product. Oddly enough, the most profitable products for the provider may not be the best value for money for the investor.

Fund managers have a lot of form when it comes to launching new funds on the back of strong optimism about an asset class, usually following a period of strong performance. For example, at the height of the technology boom in 2000 fund managers were falling over themselves to launch technology funds on the back of tremendous past performance. I remember very well in early 2000 a taxi driver telling me that he was making more money on his investments in technology funds than he was from driving his cab! When taxi drivers start offering investment advice then you really do need to start worrying!

Aberdeen Global Technology was one of the largest technology funds around at the time and it attracted a lot of new money from private investors keen to join the party. Unfortunately the next ten years were not very kind to those investors (see Figure 4.2).

---

[2] Bogle, J. (2007) *The Little Book of Common Sense Investing*, Wiley.

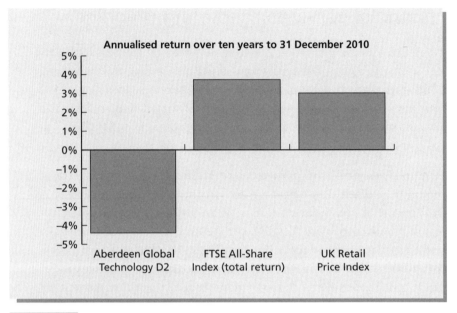

Figure 4.2 Aberdeen Global Technology

Source: Morningstar, Office of National Statistics

When it comes to promoting their funds, fund managers are usually highly selective about what they show. They typically show those funds that have outperformed the particular measure they select while saying nothing about their underperforming funds. Often they quote a very short-term (three years is common) track record of one of their 'star' managers or their five-year, top-quartile-performing flagship fund. The media also gets sucked into quoting this highly selective past performance data as part of a story or feature on investing trends, which are often based on press releases originated by smart people in public relations firms. I know from experience that many journalists want to write about 'noise' rather than the boring reality that investing and financial decision making should be dull to be successful. 'Buy and hold' doesn't have the same ring about it!

Average investors and markets

Research[3] tells us that investors rarely obtain anything like the returns the funds in which they are invested achieve. This is because the average investor flits from fund to fund based on the prevailing messages that they pick up from the media and the financial services industry – 'this time it's different'. There is a powerful and very natural human tendency to want to do something in the face of adversity or if others are apparently doing better (investmentwise) than you. As you can see from Figure 4.3 the average investor doesn't get much of the returns that are there for the taking, if only they could stay the course.

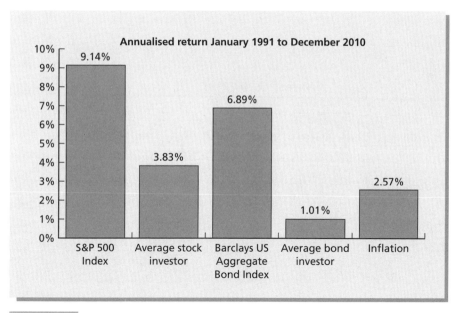

| Figure 4.3 | Investor returns compared to fund returns |

Source: DALBAR (2011) Quantitative Analysis of Investor Behavior (QAIB)

Over the 20-year period to the end of 2009 it seems that the average US equity investor achieved a return of *5% pa less* than the main US stock market index and the average US bond investor achieved a return of *6% pa less* than the main US bond index. The average equity

---

[3] DALBAR (2010) Quantitative Analysis of Investor Behavior (QAIB).

investor barely beat inflation and bond investors actually lost money in relation to inflation. This is nothing to do with fund manager competence or costs but everything to do with poor discipline on the part of investors.

'Investors should remember that excitement and expenses are their enemies.'

Warren Buffett, Chairman, Berkshire Hathaway Corporation.

Other research[4] shows that a similar underperformance can be found with UK investors, with the average investor underperforming their fund by about 2% pa over the 11-year period covered by the study. If this weren't bad enough, the average investor actually underperformed the UK FTSE All-Share Index by nearly 4% pa. (See Figure 4.4.)

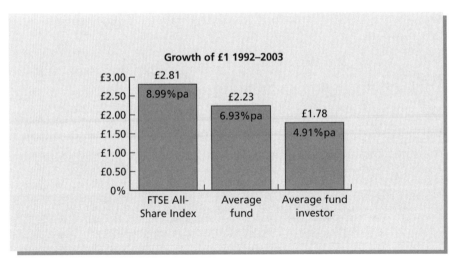

Figure 4.4   Returns achieved by average UK-based investors

Source: Schneider, L. (2007) 'Are UK fund investors achieving fund rates of return? An examination of the difference between UK fund returns and UK fund investors' returns', July. Courtesy of Schneider, L./FTSE Group.

---

4   Schneider, L. (2007) 'Are UK fund investors achieving fund rates of return? An examination of the difference between UK fund returns and UK fund investors' returns', July. Masters paper available at **www.wealthpartner.co.uk**

Responding to changing economic conditions

In a recent lecture on what investors could learn from the stock market crash of 2008–2009, Charles Ellis put it like this:

> *'People often like to say, well, there's a great powerful experience in this terrible financial crisis, are there lessons to be learned? The answer of course is "yes" but be careful you don't learn too much because it's a very unusual experience that we went through and most people will never go through anything like that again. So, you don't want to be so well prepared to go through it again that you lose the chance to have positive experiences for the more normal part of life.*
>
> *But, you really should pay attention to what was it about the experience of the crisis that really was shaking your confidence and might have caused you, or people like you, to do something that would have been horrible in the long run. Give you a good example: anybody who got so frightened last February or March [2009] that they cleared out their stock investments and put their money into either bonds or cash is someone who took a temporary loss and made a permanent loss. That's a lesson we all want to learn: don't allow current experience, no matter how acute, to be disruptive of your long-term planning. The easiest example for all of us who've had teenage children is be very careful that the worst moment of experience with a teenage child does not dominate your behaviour towards that child. Be steady, be calm and in the long run your child will grow up to be a wonderful adult, just like you.'[5]*

Media noise is just that, noise. Don't confuse the needs of media to sell copy and advertising with what is in your best interests. You wouldn't measure the distance between your home and place of work with a small ruler so avoid reacting to short-term, random news. The best antidote to being blown off course might be to work with a fee-only adviser to develop and stick with a structured financial plan that enables you to make decisions in context with your values and key life goals.

---

[5] Transcript of video interview with respected investment expert and author Charles Ellis on investment fundamentals **www.vanguard.co.uk/uk/portal/Library/interviews--video-ellis.jsp**

Decide what advice service you need and will value most

If you have relatively simple needs or wish to focus on one particular issue, for example reviewing your pension arrangements or setting up a trust investment portfolio, then you should only approach firms that have made it clear they offer advice on this basis. A majority of financial planning firms will do this but a significant minority will not. This type of service is sometimes referred to as 'focused' advice or 'project-based' advice.

Most affluent and wealthy families would derive good value for money by employing the services of a competent and qualified financial planner within a wealth management firm. The challenge is finding a good firm that is suited to your own particular wealth and situation. While there are lots of individuals and firms keen to help you manage your wealth, there are not many that are worth using, whatever your level of wealth. It is also extremely important that the promises the adviser makes are ones it is possible for them to deliver on as this is a key component of the trust you develop in order to have a meaningful and effective business relationship.

The role of a good financial adviser or wealth manager

Let's hear from Charles Ellis again on the role of an adviser:

> 'If they're very good, financial advisers will help each of their clients come to a clear understanding of themselves, their values, their dreams, their hopes and their responsibilities and that makes it very easy to work out the investment programme that will suit that specific individual.

> If investors want to get good value from their advisers they will first be entirely candid and try very hard to give all the factual information that an adviser might be able to use. All their factual information about everything financial. And, a great deal of factual information, even though it'll be qualitative, about

themselves, their families and what their experience has been in the past that might really influence their thinking now and what their hopes are for the future. The more information you can give to an adviser, the easier it is for an adviser to give you very helpful analysis, interpretation and judgement.'[6]

Many years ago I saw a presentation in the United States that explained the key roles a good financial adviser performs as part of a long-term professional client relationship and these are shown in Figure 4.5.

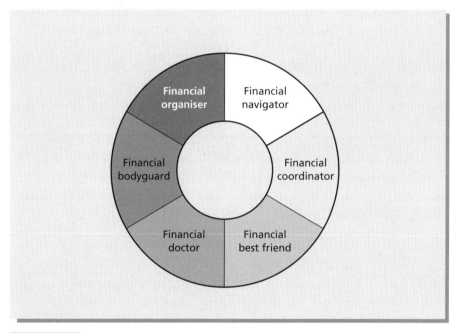

Figure 4.5   Key roles of a financial adviser

---

[6] Transcript of video interview with respected investment expert and author Charles Ellis on investment fundamentals: **www.vanguard.co.uk/uk/portal/Library/interviews--video-ellis.jsp**

The financial navigator

As we saw in Chapter 1, knowing what's important to you, where you are going and why are the keys to successful planning. A good adviser will make sure that you are clear about your goals and they are true to your values. They will also help you to resolve any mismatches between what you want to achieve and what is possible, as well as determining alternative strategies and associated tactics.

Sometimes the way forward is not clear and you might need the adviser's judgement and experience to help you to develop a sensible financial roadmap that anticipates the various life events likely to arise or you are planning to happen. Sometimes, when you have important decisions, competing priorities or an unexpected situation arises, a good adviser can help you to make a well-informed decision. They will offer guidance when you need it to ensure that you keep focused on your life goals rather than the vagaries of the investment market or changes in tax rates. Most importantly, where appropriate, a good adviser will play devil's advocate and also hold you to account for the financial decisions that you make.

The financial coordinator

A good wealth plan for most people will include a number of different elements, such as investment, tax, legal aspects and insurance. Particularly if you have more complex needs and larger amounts of wealth, you will need to use the services of a number of professionals, each with specialist knowledge and skills in different disciplines. The danger is that the overall advice is often fragmented, more expensive than it need be and quite often not as effective as it could be.

A good wealth manager will help to coordinate the advice of these professionals to ensure that the constituent parts 'fit' together to form a bespoke and comprehensive solution. Often there needs to be a series of discussions and communication between, say, a trust specialist, a lawyer and a tax adviser, to ensure that any solutions 'fit' together. The wealth manager will understand the context of the family's overall financial position and objectives and ask the necessary questions so that, when a solution or shortlist of solutions is presented to you, all the technical analysis and evaluation has been completed.

The financial best friend

As John Lennon said in one of his songs 'Life's what happens when you're busy making other plans' and a lot can happen in a lifetime. A best friend is someone with whom you feel able to share thoughts and feelings and ask their opinion without feeling silly or stupid. The best financial advisers and wealth managers are people who are also there for you in difficult times to provide moral support and can help you deal with opportunities, threats and life events. Sometimes you might want a sounding board, even if you think you know the answer to the question, to give you more confidence that you are making a good decision.

The following are typical of the range of issues that clients have shared with me over the years:

- whether to accept the remuneration package in a new job
- how to deal with aged parents' care needs
- whether to buy a new home
- how to teach children the value of money
- whether to make a gift of capital or to lend it
- whether to invest in a friend's or relative's business venture
- whether to retrain for a completely different career
- how best to determine a fair value for selling the family home to a close friend.

More often than not I didn't offer a solution as the clients came up with the answers themselves, but they found it helpful to share the issues with someone outside of the family whom they trusted. As they say, a problem shared is a problem halved!

The financial doctor

Just like the medical doctor who knows your family well and can be trusted to keep confidences, a good adviser develops a deep understanding of you and your family over many years. Sometimes relationships are not always what they seem and it can take time to uncover subtle but important information. For example, some adult children might be reckless spendthrifts with a trail of broken relationships, while others might be hard workers who value wealth and are in a stable relationship. There might be stepchildren to whom the individual is closer than birth children who don't keep in touch.

A life partner who has never made important financial decisions will usually welcome the support and guidance of an adviser who is familiar with the family's wealth plan and the various components, in the event of their partner dying or becoming seriously ill. It can take several years to get to know a family and its dynamics and uncover the various issues and this takes investment in time and emotional energy on the part of the adviser. The more your wealth adviser gets to know you as a person, the more that trust and empathy will develop

The financial bodyguard

There are so many people and organisations out there that are keen to get their hands on your money, it is inevitable a large proportion of available financial products and services will be either unsuitable, uncompetitive or both. You would do well to remember that the commercial objectives of organisations seeking to maximise profits are rarely aligned with either your needs or your best interests. Like unhealthy food, just because something is being promoted for sale does not mean that it is good for you! That is not to say you will be worse off because a company makes a profit but the benefits from any transaction are rarely symmetrical between the provider and consumer.

Poor products and services, the constant barrage of media 'noise' and human emotions can conspire to mean sometimes you will need protecting from people, products and services that are not good for your wealth. The role of financial bodyguard is not always one that you might associate with a good financial adviser, particularly if you have used transaction-based firms like private banks, insurance salespeople or brokers who are reliant on commission from product sales. 'Bodyguard' is, however, a key role provided by advisers who do not represent or are in any way tied to a product provider and whose remuneration is paid directly by you through pre-agreed fees.

The financial organiser

Being well organised means knowing what financial assets you own and why you own them. Knowing the location of important paperwork like legal papers and ownership certificates is also essential. A good adviser can help you to make sense of what you have and, where possible, simplify and rationalise things so that you have as few moving parts as possible. Minimising paperwork, information and other administrative tasks is the key to being well organised. The more organised you feel then the more confidence you will have about your wealth. The more confidence you have, the better your decision making will be and the more you'll enjoy life.

Keeping a good audit trail to substantiate certain financial planning strategies and solutions is another key discipline with which the better advisory firms will help you. For example, a very useful but underused inheritance tax planning technique is to make regular gifts out of surplus income. As long as various conditions are met, the amount gifted falls out of the inheritance tax planning net immediately. A key element necessary to prove to the tax authorities that you have met the conditions for the tax exemption is to have copies of an exchange of letters recording gifts made, including dates and names. Decent firms will help you to maintain the necessary records.

Wealth management

The term 'wealth management' has become more prevalent over the past 15 years, but not all firms that profess to provide it offer the same service. A lot of stockbrokers and investment managers call themselves wealth managers when they only focus on the investment assets and have limited understanding of tax and legal issues and no concept of financial planning. Some independent financial advisers, with limited investment or tax knowledge, focus more on advising and arranging tax wrappers such as self-invested personal pensions (SIPPs) and insurance bonds. Some financial planners focus purely on the overall plan and do not provide investment services. A proper wealth management service should be comprehensive and comprise the various different disciplines and areas that go to make up a proper wealth plan.

A typical comprehensive wealth management consulting process is illustrated in Figure 4.6. While every firm will have its own approach and processes, this will give you an idea of the type of approach to look for. A firm that can't explain its process is unlikely to deliver a slick and professional service.

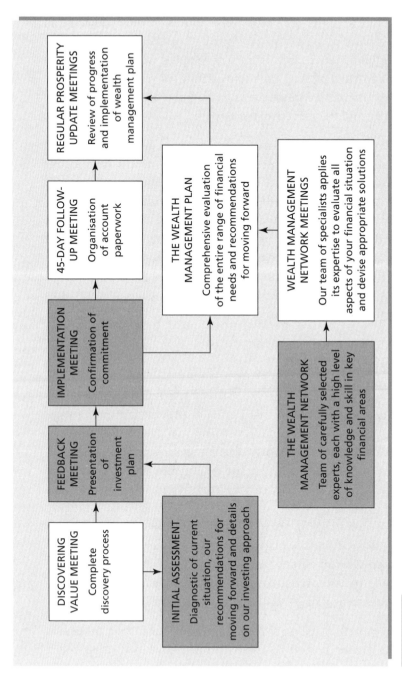

Figure 4.6 A typical wealth management consulting process

Source: Bloomsbury

As illustrated in Figure 4.7 this service should comprise three key elements: investment consulting, advanced planning and relationship management.

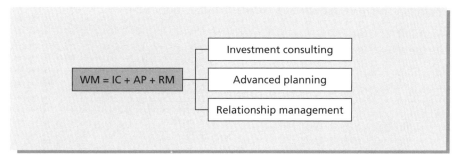

Figure 4.7 **Key elements of a comprehensive wealth management service**
Source: CEG Worldwide

Relationship management (see Figure 4.8) is the ongoing process of ensuring that all advice is complementary and appropriate and action in one area of your wealth planning does not impact negatively on another. If you have existing advisers, for example a tax adviser, then your wealth manager must have both a process and the inclination to engage those other advisers in the wealth management process.

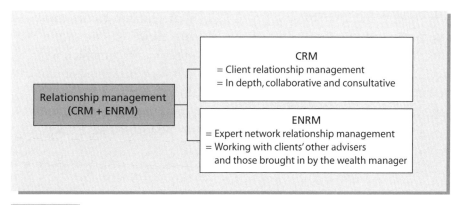

Figure 4.8 **Components of relationship management**
Source: CEG Worldwide

The advanced planning component comprises four strategic areas of wealth enhancement, transfer and protection as well as charitable planning (see Figure 4.9). Each of these strategies usually involves several tactics that enable sophisticated wealth planning to be carried out and will usually be set out in a wealth management plan.

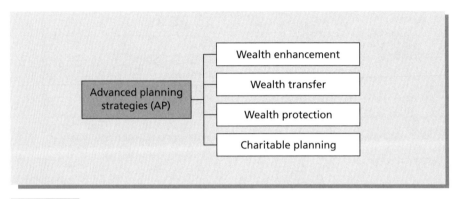

Figure 4.9   **Key elements of a wealth management plan**

Source: CEG Worldwide

The expert network

A good wealth manager will have a very good knowledge of you and your family and a broad understanding of strategies and tactics that you may need to adopt to achieve your goals. However, due to the sheer complexity of the financial and tax environment in which we live, it is unlikely that any wealth manager can be expert in all areas. Sometimes larger firms have different departments and seek to offer a 'one stop shop', while others have a panel of outside experts in different disciplines on whom they can call to provide focused advice and service as necessary (see Figure 4.10).

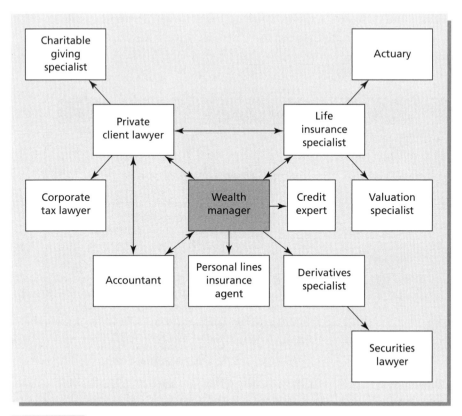

Figure 4.10 Wealth manager's expert network

Source: CEG Worldwide

Experience and professional qualifications

From January 2013 all individuals who provide regulated investment and financial advice to individuals in the United Kingdom will need to have attained a level of professional qualification equivalent to that of the first year of a degree course. In reality a number of areas of advice, like pension transfers, have always required higher levels of qualification but the new standard will apply across the board to insurance salespeople, bank advisers, financial advisers, stockbrokers and private bankers.

Figure 4.11 illustrates the levels of different types of designations and where they sit on the educational ladder, to give you an idea of the quality and difficulty required in attaining different levels of qualification. My view is that you need to be dealing with a lead adviser who is at level 6 or above.

Academic	Level	Vocational
PhD	7	Diploma in Wealth Management (CISI) Diploma for Chartered Banker (CCN)
MSc/MA/MBA	6	Chartered Financial Planner (CII) Advanced Diploma in Financial Planning (CII) Private Client Investment Advice & Management (CISI) Certified Financial Planner (IFP)
BSc/BA	5	
1st year foundation degree	4	Diploma in Accounting & Business (ACCA) Diploma in Accounting (AAT) Diploma in Regulated Financial Planning (CII) Diploma in Investment Advice (CISI) Investment Management Certificate (new, CA Institute) Certificate in Paraplanning (IFP)
International Baccalaureate	3–4	Certificate in Investment Management
A Level/City & Guilds	3	Certificate for Financial Advisers (IFS) Certificate in Financial Planning (CII) Diploma in Financial Service (Chartered Banker) (CNN)
AS Level	2–3	NVQ in Retail Financial Services
GCSE	1–2	Foundation Certificate in Personal Finance Award in Personal Financial Planning

Figure 4.11 Summary of financial services qualifications

Source: Financial Services Skills Council

Qualifications are necessary to act as a barrier to entry, so that those with a low intellect or of an opportunistic nature are weeded out. However, in addition to qualifications, you need to deal with a lead planner who has at least ten years' experience of actually working with and advising people like you. In many good firms the lead planner works alongside colleagues with less experience and a lower level of qualifications (or possibly with similar qualifications but in a complementary specialism) and this blend ensures that you get good advice and attentive service.

To use a medical analogy, I wouldn't want the rookie doing his first heart operation on me until he has stood next to the consultant surgeon, watched how to do the job and been closely supervised by the expert as he learns all the key procedures. That way the chances of a mishap in the operating theatre are low! The same factors apply to your wealth. Make sure that any junior professional staff who work on your affairs are properly supervised by those with wisdom and experience.

Fees and other costs

There are numerous ways that wealth managers charge for their services:

- fixed fee for initial project or annual retainer
- hourly charge
- percentage of assets invested
- proportion of tax saved
- product commissions received on investments, tax shelters, insurance products and tax wrappers implemented via them.

Sometimes these charging methods are combined. The key point is to know what you are paying and why. Regardless of what the rules say and no matter how convenient it might be, I think that you should agree the fees for the advice and services you use and pay them yourself and ideally avoid commission at all costs. An adviser who agrees and charges explicit fees rather than relying on payments from transactions or from product providers has less of a conflict of interests in the advice that they give. It is also easier for you to determine whether or not those fees have been good value for money.

Private banks, insurance representatives and a large proportion of independent financial advisers usually accept commissions and arrangement fees for products like insurance, tax wrappers, structured products, investment funds and alternative investments, whether they agree an explicit fee for planning services or not. Do not accept these terms of business because, quite apart from the impact on returns of higher costs, the likelihood of their advice being totally objective can be compromised. The more complicated the product or solution, the more likely it is to be expensive and to pay a large sales commission to the adviser. This is like your doctor earning a commission every time he prescribes you drugs; in such a situation you can expect most diagnoses to need medication!

If you use a good wealth manager then you should expect to pay a fixed planning fee for the initial work and this might vary between £2,000 and £30,000 depending on the complexity and value of your wealth, as well as where the adviser is located. Ongoing management fees should be a little less than the initial fees but make sure that you know what you are paying, what you are getting for those fees and you have a means of assessing value for money.

Low advice fees are not usually linked to good advice and service because either the work will not be carried out in sufficient detail and to a high enough standard or the wealth manager will probably be subsidising their fees with product commissions. As a corollary, expensive fees do not guarantee good advice either. The box below lists questions to ask a prospective adviser and sources of good advice can be found in the Useful websites and further reading section at the end of the book.

Checklist

Full service wealth management firm – due diligence
- Do you provide structured financial planning as the core service before offering investment or tax advice?
- Do you offer a transparent 'fee for service' charging structure that is not linked to the sale of products?
- Do you offer products, funds and financial solutions from the whole marketplace or do you offer only a restricted range from a few companies?
- Do you have experience of dealing with people like me in terms of personality, family situation, level of wealth and wealth issues?
- Do you and your colleagues hold advanced-level professional financial advice qualifications and, if so, what are these?
- What arrangements do you have to bring in expertise from outside of your firm if needed, such as legal or tax planning, and how is this integrated into your own service?

■ If you receive a sales commission from any source will you rebate this either back into the product or directly to me?

■ What is your investment philosophy and have you a comprehensive document that sets out your approach and rationale?

■ How are the professional staff in your firm remunerated?

■ Would you be able to allow me to speak to one of your clients in a similar situation to myself before committing to using you?

■ Do you offer any form of value or satisfaction guarantee and, if so, what does this entail?

■ Could you show me example outputs of the way that you document the work you do so I can have an idea of what to expect?

■ How many meetings and discussions can I expect to formulate the initial strategy and how long is this likely to take?

■ What is the minimum commitment required from me in terms of time and fees?

■ What level of resources does your firm have in terms of financial planning, investment and tax expertise?

■ Who are the actual people with whom I and my family will be dealing on a day-to-day basis?

■ If something goes wrong with the service or your advice, to whom do I complain?

■ What are the key financial results for your company in terms of balance sheet strength, revenue and profits?

■ Do you think that I am the type of customer you are looking for and could service well?

part

2

The investment engine

5

Rules of the investing 'game'

While cash has historically been a poor store of value, particularly over the medium to long term, it is the best home for capital that may be needed within three to five years to meet any planned and unplanned expenditure. We refer to such capital as 'savings' because it is earmarked for short-term needs and as such we are less worried about inflation and more concerned that the value won't fall in nominal terms (i.e. excluding the effects of price inflation). There is no point in committing capital to a diversified investment portfolio, only to find that you need to sell some of it when the portfolio might have fallen in value – as it invariably will – because you need to spend it on something in the short term or your nerves are fraying due to downward movements in the value of your investments! Your savings capital will be secure, if you are a UK resident and invest no more than £85,000 with a UK-registered financial institution (this is the current limit for the Financial Services Compensation Scheme), otherwise you will be dependent on the financial strength of the deposit taker to ensure that they can repay your capital.

Whilst before tax it should be possible to at least match inflation by holding cash over the long term, most individuals are unlikely either to be non-taxpayers or obtain the most competitive interest rates on a consistent basis. Consumer organisation Which? carried out research[1] that found almost half of the 1,250 easy access and notice

---

[1] 'The great British savings scandal', *Which?* magazine, November 2010.

savings and cash ISA products available in the UK pay interest at or below 0.5%. Just to ensure that your savings maintain their value relative to inflation of 3% you would need to earn 3.75% if you are a basic rate taxpayer, 5% if you are a higher-rate taxpayer and 6% if you are an additional rate taxpayer.

The term 'investing' means the process of allocating your capital in such a way as to protect against inflation and fund your desired life-style, however long that might last, as well as any other objectives. This involves exchanging capital security, to a greater or lesser extent, in return for higher returns than are likely to be produced from sav-ings. To be successful at investing, all you need is a sound intellectual philosophy, a functional and practical process for implementing and managing the investment portfolio and a framework to provide context and discipline to stay the course. The benefits of this approach are:

■ It has a high probability of meeting your defined lifetime required rate of return

■ It is robust and able to withstand a range of economic and investment conditions

■ It delivers you, the investor, a fair share of the market returns that are due to you for the risks you take

■ It helps take much of the wealth-destroying emotion out of investing

■ It will help you to stay focused on your long-term strategy.

In formulating your investment strategy, whether you work on your own or with professional advisers, you need to:

■ review the available evidence and decide what works

■ decide on a route that offers the highest probability of a successful investment experience

■ build a functionally robust portfolio

■ implement the portfolio in the most efficient manner possible

■ monitor the progress of the portfolio on an ongoing basis against your lifestyle goals

■ maintain the balance of risk and reward.

Speculating is not investing

It is easy to confuse speculating with investing. Speculating is trying to second-guess what investment markets will do with the intention of exploiting those expected movements for financial gain. Speculating is win–lose in that if you make the right choice you win and if you make the wrong one you lose. Investing is not win–lose because capitalism will provide a return on your capital over the long term. You only lose if your belief in capitalism fails! Most retail investment advice is actually speculating advice. While speculating might be exciting, the available evidence suggests that it is like all gambling and is seriously bad for your wealth. History is full of examples of wealth destroyed by those two powerful human emotions of greed and fear.

Speculation is what fuels an investment 'bubble', whether that is equities, property, gold or tulips! As more and more people see the easy money others are making, they start speculating until eventually the whole thing collapses and this is well illustrated by Figure 5.1. The sad thing about bubbles is that, in seeking abnormal investment returns, speculators miss out on the meaningful and worthwhile reasonable investment returns there for the taking.

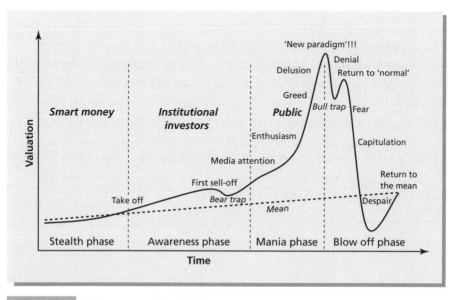

Figure 5.1 **Main stages of a bubble**

Source: Reproduced by kind permission of Dr Jean-Paul Rodrigue, Department of Global Studies and Geography, Hofstra University

Capitalism and markets do work

For all its faults and shortcomings, the capitalist system is the only economic system that has actually stood the test of time. Capital and resources (both human and physical) are the two essential ingredients for economic activity, which arise directly from the human race's desire to maintain and improve its standard of living. In a perfect world all capital and resources would be used in the most efficient manner and the maximum return would be achieved for the minimium effort. However, we don't live in a perfect world and, as such, capital and resources are not always allocated efficiently. This does not mean that the capitalist model is wrong, just imperfect.

Over the past few decade we have seen major changes in the world economic order and this came to a head with the start of the last global financial crisis in 2007–2009. There is no doubt that many things went seriously wrong with regulation, product innovation and world economic policy but that is not to say capital markets failed. In proper open capital and labour markets, with no political interference and rigorous and credible pricing and clearing/settlement mechanisms, returns would be properly allocated in the most efficient way.

The accumulated empirical evidence, research and theory suggest we should trust in capitalism as this is the only system that creates wealth and allocates capital effectively enough over the long term, as illustrated in the chart in Figure 5.2. In addition, capital markets are generally efficient and provide an effective equilibrium (self-levelling) system. The aggregate current market view is the best gauge of the value of an investment and represents the value of expected future dividends and earnings for companies and interest payments for fixed income investments.

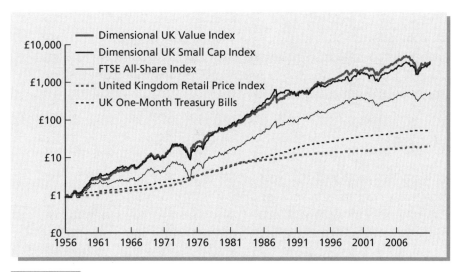

Figure 5.2   **Growth of wealth (January 1956–December 2010)**

Source: Dimensional Fund Advisors, FTSE, Office for National Statistics, UK Debt Management Office, Data Stream

Risk and return are linked

Risk and return go hand in hand and if you want higher returns you have to take higher risks. There are no shortcuts and if an investment offers more than the risk-free rate (generally defined as very short-term government deposits) then it comes with higher risks, in terms of capital loss and the possibility that the investment return will turn out to be lower than anticipated. Diversification means allocating your capital across different asset classes (not having all your eggs in one basket) and it can help reduce the various risks associated with investing. In this regard diversification can be viewed as just about the only 'free lunch' available in investing, in that no one else has to lose to enable you to benefit.

The next step is to identify the various investment risks and how they are compensated, then decide whether (or not) to take them. Once you've decided on how much exposure you will have to the various risk factors, you (or your adviser) need to manage that exposure closely to ensure it doesn't increase over time.

Equity risk

William Sharpe shared the Nobel Prize in Economics in 1990 for his pioneering contribution to asset pricing theory. Sharpe developed the Capital Asset Pricing Model (CAPM) to try to explain, using simplifying assumptions, that an equity's expected return was a function of its volatility (price movements) relative to the volatility of the universe of risky assets. The expected higher returns from equities come with associated risks. These risks are a combination of 'systematic' or 'unsystematic' risk.

- **Systematic risk** includes macroeconomic conditions affecting all companies in the stock market. Systematic risk cannot be diversified away.

- **Unsystematic risk** includes company (the specific risk of owning shares in, for example, Barclays, GlaxoSmithKline or Rolls-Royce) and industry risk (such as pharmaceutical, banking or telecom shares) specific to individual securities. The effect of these can be reduced through sufficient diversification (i.e. allocating capital across a number of different securities).

Sharpe's conclusion was that the most efficient portfolio, from a risk return perspective, is one containing the entire universe of risky assets. The CAPM model is the intellectual foundation of the total stock market index fund. The lesson for investors is they should not expect markets to reward them for risks that can be diversified away. They should expect compensation only for bearing systematic risks. Figure 5.3 illustrates this concept visually.

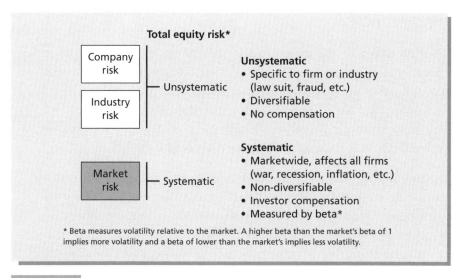

Figure 5.3   Total equity risk

The multi-factor model

Sharpe's CAPM model was developed further in the early 1990s by two eminent US finance academics, Professors Eugene Fama and Kenneth French. They developed a framework, known as the **multi-factor model**,[2] for explaining two more systematic risk factors relating to equity investment. Fama and French found that 96% of the variation in returns among equity portfolios can be explained by the portfolios' relative exposure to three compensated risk factors:

1 market factor – equities have higher expected returns than fixed income securities

2 size factor – small capitalisation equities have higher expected returns than large capitalisation equities

3 value[3] factor – lower-priced 'value' equities have higher expected returns than higher-priced 'growth' equities.

---

[2] Fama, E. F. and French, K. R. (1993) 'Common risk factors in the returns on stocks and bonds', *Journal of Financial Economics*, 33(1): 3–56.

[3] The proper term for this risk factor is 'book-to-market' (BtM) factor or ratio.

The market factor

The first factor in the model relates to how much of a portfolio is allocated to the stock market, i.e. equities, which are defined as the complete universe of companies on a market value-weighted basis. Because equities have a higher risk than fixed interest investments and cash deposits, they have to have a higher expected return. This higher expected return is known as the equity risk premium (ERP).

The ERP is not a static amount and will rise and fall with changes in economic conditions and the supply of and demand for capital by companies. Intuitively we know that an ERP must exist otherwise investors would invest in less risky investments like cash and bonds. There is no definitive or universally accepted way of measuring the equity risk premium but it is reasonable to say that the long-term ERP has a floor of circa 2% pa, being the real yield on index-linked gilts. If this were not the case then no investor would take more risk for a lower return.

Historical analysis of the ERP of 17 countries from 1900–2009 reveals a compound rate of return, i.e. geometric mean, across these markets of 4.4%. The UK and US ERPs to the end of 2009 were 4.2% and 5.2% respectively. Some academics expect the ERP in the next 10 years or so to be lower, about 3%, whereas others think that it will be about 4%, which is just below its long-term historic average. See Figure 5.4.

There are periods when equities experience very extreme negative and positive returns. The impact of these extreme returns, but not the probability of them occurring, reduces with longer time horizons. For example, over 25 years or more even the worst returns from UK equities have still generated positive purchasing power growth, but that isn't to say this will necessarily be repeated in the future. If you have a time horizon of, say, 35 years, the chances of losing money in real terms (i.e. after inflation) over that period are about 5%.[4] This possible risk needs to be weighed up against the potential upside and the consequences of not receiving that upside had you never invested in equities in the first place. See Figure 5.5.

---

[4]   Hale, T. (2009) *Smarter Investing*, Pearson Education, p. 149.

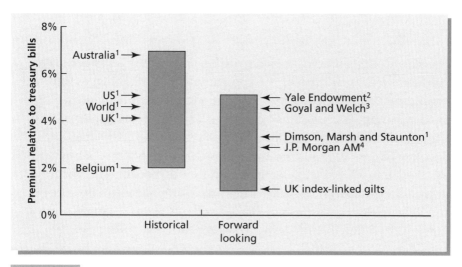

Figure 5.4 The equity risk premium in developed markets

Sources: Dimson, E., Marsh, P. and Staunton, M. (2006) 'The worldwide equity premium: A smaller puzzle', 7 April. EFA 2006 Zurich Meetings Paper; Swenson, D. F. (2000) *Pioneering Portfolio Management*, Free Press; Goyal, A. and Welch, I. (2006) 'A comprehensive look at the empirical performance of equity premium prediction', 11 January, Yale ICF Working Paper No. 04–1; J. P. Morgan Asset Management (2010) Long-term Capital market assumptions', 20 November 2010.

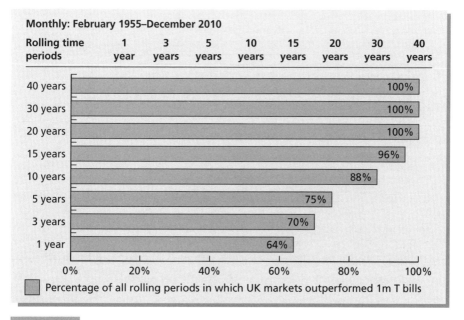

Figure 5.5 Equities verses cash over the past 55 years

Source: UK one-month T-bills provided by Datastream; prior to January 1975, UK three-month T-bills. UK market is the FTSE All-Share Index. FTSE data published with the permission of FTSE.

The size factor

The second risk factor that Fama and French identified as impacting on returns is the size of the company. Smaller companies have lower capitalisation than larger ones and tend to be more vulnerable to adverse trading conditions. As such, even if such companies have high growth prospects, they are more risky than big companies and therefore have to pay more for their capital. This higher cost of capital translates into additional potential return for the investor. The smaller companies' premium (the additional return) fluctuates all the time and sometimes larger companies outperform (see Figure 5.6). However, Fama and French's multi-factor research indicates that there is a higher probability of higher returns from smaller companies to compensate investors for these additional risks.

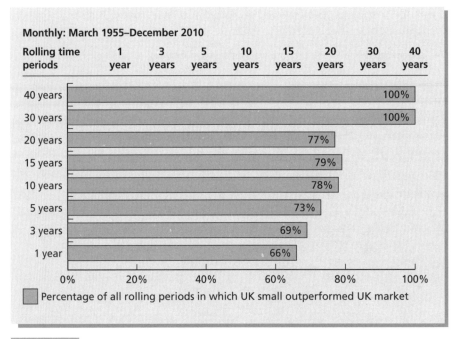

Figure 5.6   Smaller companies' premium – UK small v UK market

Source: UK small simulated from StyleResearch securities data; prior to July 1981, Hoare Govett Smaller Companies Index, provided by the London School of Business. UK market is the FTSE All-Share Index. FTSE data published with the permission of FTSE.

The value factor

The third factor that Fama and French identified was the value factor. Some companies are viewed by the market as 'unhealthy' and this can arise for a number of reasons, such as having poor growth prospects, being involved in a risky trading activity or having suffered continued falls in profitability. As a result, these companies have to pay more for their capital to compensate investors for the additional risk to their capital, which translates into the investor's additional potential return over that available from the main equity market. These financially unhealthy companies are known as 'value' companies because they have what is known as a high book (balance sheet) to market (share price) ratio. Put another way, the share price is low compared to the net assets of the company.

Some of the few successful active fund managers, those who have achieved significant outperformance of the stock market, have actually been value company investors. Once the risk factors associated with value companies are stripped out we can determine that the investment manager's skill had little influence on the outperformance. Risk really is the source of additional returns! But just as the equity risk premium fluctuates all the time, so does the value premium. There have been periods when growth companies (those that the market views as healthy and less risky) have outperformed value companies. However, the research suggests that the value premium does exist and has a higher probability of being delivered over long time periods. See Figure 5.7.

Various research papers have confirmed that the small companies' and value companies' risk premiums exist in both overseas developed markets and emerging markets and are of the same quantum as for UK markets. See Figure 5.8.

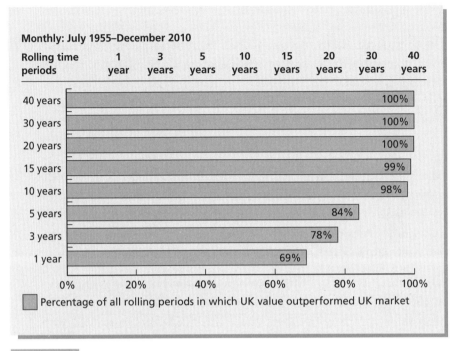

Monthly: July 1955–December 2010

Figure 5.7 The value premium – UK value v UK market

Source: UK market is the FTSE All-Share Index. FTSE data published with the permission of FTSE. UK value simulated Bloomberg securities data; prior to 1994, data provided by London Business School.

The multi-factor model therefore helps us to decide how to allocate a portfolio to the different asset classes based on risk and expected returns. It also supports the contention that making further distinctions between different sectors such as industrials and mining are unlikely to add much value because they are merely components of equities as an asset class and don't have sufficiently different risk and return attributes from equities as a whole. In the same way, geographical distinctions in overseas developed or emerging markets are probably less important than one might expect because it is the risk of the asset class as a whole that is the main determinant of returns.

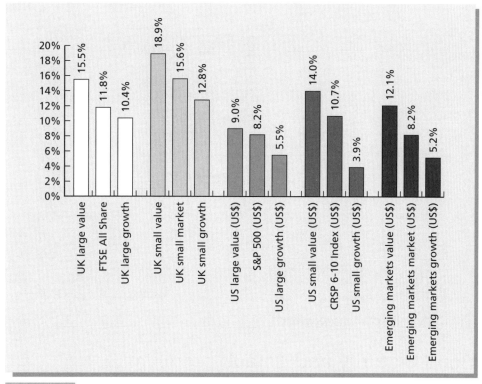

Figure 5.8 Size and value effects across global equity markets

Source: Value stocks are above the 30th percentile in book-to-market ratio. Growth stocks are below the 70th percentile in book-to-market ratio. Simulations are free-float weighted both within each country and across all countries. UK and Europe data provided by London Business School/StyleResearch. US value and growth index data (ex utilities) provided by Fama/French. FTSE data published with the permission of FTSE. The S&P data are provided by Standard & Poor's Index Services Group. CRSP data provided by the Center for Research in Security Prices, University of Chicago. MSCI Europe Index is gross of foreign withholding taxes on dividends; copyright MSCI 2011, all rights reserved. Emerging Markets Index data simulated by Fama/French from countries in the IFC Investable Universe.

Taken together, the three equity risk factors of market, size and value account for around 96% of the variation in returns between portfolios. Using a multi-factor approach, you have the potential to earn higher expected returns by increasing exposure to compensated risk factors rather than trying to market time either your asset allocation or the underlying equity or bond holdings (see Figure 5.9).

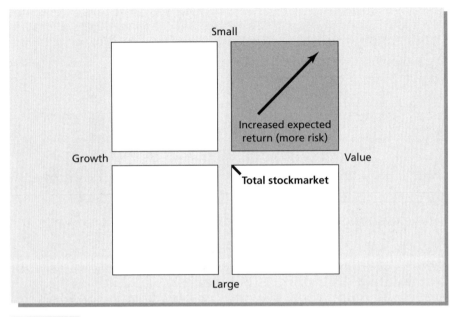

Figure 5.9   **Risk factor exposures**

Bond maturity and default premium

The real return from government bonds has averaged about 2.5% pa compounded over the past 50 years.[5] Bonds with a longer time until they mature usually pay a higher return than cash or bonds with a shorter time until maturity. Although not identified by them, Fama and French's multi-factor research also referred to two other factors that related to bonds, those being duration (the time that a bond has to be held until maturity) and credit quality (the credit rating of the company issuing the bond). (See Figure 5.10.)

Bonds issued by companies and governments that are perceived to be more risky, as they may not repay some or all of the bond interest or capital on maturity, pay a higher return than less risky companies or governments. However, if the role of fixed income is to lower the risk of a portfolio then if you invest in longer-term bonds and/or those with a lower credit quality you are unlikely to be sufficiently compensated for the risks taken. We'll go into more detail about bonds in Chapter 6.

---

[5]   Barclays Capital (2011) 'Equity gilt study 2011', p. 92.

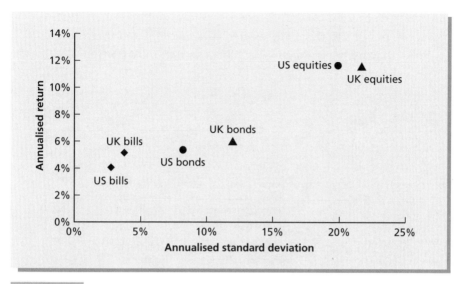

Figure 5.10 Risk and return of UK and US bonds, 1900–2000

Source: Dimson, Elroy, Paul Marsh and Mike Staunton, *Millennium Book II: 101 Years of investment Returns* (ABN AMRO and London Business School, 2001). This publication defines the data used for the above chart and matrix as follows: UK Bills are UK One-Month Treasury Bills (FTSE). UK Bonds are the ABN AMRO Bond Index. UK Equities are the ABN AMRO/LBS Equity Index. US Bills are commercial bills 1900–1918 and One-Month US Treasury Bills (Ibbotson) 1919–2000. US Bonds are government bonds 1900–1918, the Federal Reserve Bond Index 10–15 Years 1919–1925, Long-Term Government Bonds (Ibbotson) 1926–1998, and the JP Morgan US Government Bond Index 1999–2000. US Equities are Schwert's Index Series 1900–1925, CRSP 1–10 Deciles Index 1926–1970, and the Dow Jones Wilshire 5000 Index 1971–2000.

Focus on the mix of assets

'Let every man divide his money into three parts, and invest a third in land, a third in business, and a third let him keep in reserve.'

Talmud, c. 1200 BC–AD 500

Asset allocation is the process of dividing up your capital and allocating it to one or more different types of asset classes. An asset class is the term given to a group of investments that share similar risk and return characteristics and includes cash, equities, fixed interest, property and commodities. In addition, there are a number of investment types that are known as 'alternative' asset classes, because they fall outside of the mainstream asset classes. Figure 5.11 shows the main investment characteristics of the three key asset classes – cash, fixed interest and equities – that are the main building blocks used in most portfolios.

Asset class	Cash	Bonds	Equities
Returns	Low but volatile	Medium and more stable	High but more volatile
Inflation	Real risk of devaluation over long term	Some risk of devaluation over long term if not short dated or inflation linkes	High inflation protection over the long term
Return mechanism	Purely through interest	Primarily through interest/yield	Dividends and growth
Key role in portfolio	Liquidity	Stable but low returns over long term or to reduce risk of volatile assets	Core real return generator

Figure 5.11 Characteristics of main asset classes

Because asset allocation is the principal determinant in the variation and/or volatility in returns in a broadly diversified portfolio[6] it is critical to get the right strategic asset mix in place at the outset and to maintain that mix. At the high level you need to determine the overall split to risky (equity-type) and defensive (bond-type) assets. Think of risky as whisky and defensive as water. If you like a strong drink you may not add any water but be prepared for a big kick! If you don't like alcohol or can't hold your drink then water will probably be all you need. The same goes for investing, in that you need to determine the right blend

---

[6] There have been numerous academic studies on this subject, the most respected and well-known of which include: Brinson, G. P., Hood, L. R. and Beebower, G. L. (1986) 'Determinants of portfolio performance', *The Financial Analysts Journal*, July/August and (1991) 'Determinants of portfolio performance II: An update', *The Financial Analysts Journal*, 47(3); Ibbotson, R. G. and Kaplan, P. D. (2000) 'Does asset allocation policy explain 40%, 90%, or 100% of performance?', *The Financial Analysts Journal*, January/February; Statman, M. (2000) 'The 93.6% question of financial advisors', *The Journal of Investing*, 9(1): 16–20.

of assets, taking into account the return you need and the risks you can cope with. Equities are expected to generate higher returns than cash or bonds (fixed income) over the long term. This makes sense as equity owners are taking the highest level of capital risk.

Income-type assets provide most if not all the return in the form of income. Income investments include cash, bonds and certain equities. Returns tend to be more stable but lower over the long term and are more vulnerable to the effects of inflation. Growth-type investments provide most of the return in the form of capital growth over time. Examples of growth investments include UK and international equities and property. Because growth investments have the potential to pro-duce higher real returns over the long term, they tend to have much more volatile returns over the shorter term.

Investment risk

The main (although not the only) way that risk is measured in invest-ment terms is called standard deviation. This is a way of measuring how investment returns have varied from the average[7] over a series of time periods. As illustrated in Figure 5.12, the higher the standard deviation figure, the more the returns have varied from (both above and below) the average. As a general rule, higher average returns usu-ally come with a higher standard deviation (as risk and return are related); such investments can and do experience big swings in returns above and below the average!

The magnitude and likelihood of the return varying from the average is expressed as a multiple of the standard deviation number. Assuming that the data set is large enough to be representative, a particular period's return will fall within 1 standard deviation either side of the average about 65% of the time, while it will fall within 2 standard deviations about 95% of the time and within 3 standard deviations about 99% of the time.

---

[7] The 'average' referred to here is the arithmetic mean.

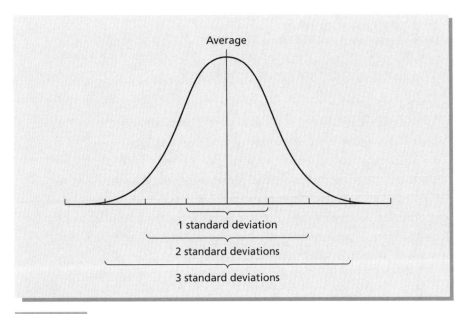

Average

1 standard deviation

2 standard deviations

3 standard deviations

Figure 5.12 Standard deviation

To help you to understand standard deviation, consider the following two investments set out in Figure 5.13. Investment X has a lower average annual return than investment Y but it also has a much lower range of higher and lower annual returns. So, 65% of the time (1 standard deviation) we can see that investment X delivered a return as low as 2% (3% – 1%) and as high as 4% (3% + 1%). By comparison, investment Y delivered a return as low as –7% (8% – 15%) and as high as 23% (8% + 15%).

Investment	Average annual return	Standard deviation	65% certainty annual return between	95% certainty annual return between
X	3%	1%	2% and 4%	1% and 5%
Y	8%	15%	–7% and 23%	–22% and 38%

Figure 5.13 Investment returns and risk

However, if we want to include a wider range of outcomes, we need to look at the range of returns that fall within 95% of the sample period (2 standard deviations). In this instance, we can see that investment X delivered as low as 1% (3% – 2%) and as high as 5% (3% + 2%) in 95% of the sample period. Investment Y, on the other hand, delivered as low as –22% (8% – 30%) and as high as 38% (8% + 30%) in 95% of the sample period.

Think of standard deviation like temperature. The long-term average temperature for the UK in July might be 20°C but there is a possibility that it might be as high as 30°C and as low as 10°C although it is highly unlikely ever to go below 0°C. Perhaps in October the long-term average might be 10°C but it could be as high as 22°C and as low as –2°C (a standard deviation of 12°), thus it could go below zero.

Standard deviation is a statistical measure that can be used in a wide variety of applications not limited to financial planning. It is therefore important not to imbue it with magical predictive value as it is entirely dependent on the data set used to calculate it. If the future is different from the past, placing reliance on historic standard deviation to forecast future volatility could prove dangerously costly. The evidence from the historical record of investment performance is that standard deviations do vary over time.

Slow and steady wins the race!

Focusing on average investment returns is a bit like focusing on how many buses left the bus station in the morning and returned in the evening. Due to unforeseen factors (traffic delays, breakdowns or delays boarding passengers), passengers might wait ages for a bus only to have three turn up at once. The fact that ten buses left the bus station in the morning and then returned in the evening is of little consolation to the passenger who waited an hour for his bus along the route!

If two portfolios have the same expected return but one suffers higher volatility than the other, then over the medium to long-term, the portfolio with the lower volatility will produce a higher return than the more volatile portfolio. This is because the long-term average investment return masks the fact that investment returns are not delivered in a straight line but vary from one year to the next. The previous year's return impacts on the current year's return and this effect is known as compounding. The value of your wealth will be determined by the **compound returns** achieved each year, not the average return.

The greater the portfolio loss in any given year then the higher the level of future growth required to recover from that loss. For example a 35% fall in portfolio value requires 54% growth to recover whereas a 5% fall in portfolio value requires only 5.3% growth to recover. Minimising portfolio volatility, therefore, should be one of your key objectives, and will prove its worth *when* we experience the next market downturn.

Table 5.1 shows a simplified example of how this concept applies in practice. Two portfolios have the same average annualised return of zero over a two-year period. However, Portfolio 1 has a much higher level of volatility than Portfolio 2 and as a consequence the compound annualised returns are –13.4% and –0.50% respectively. This translates into an end value of £75,000 for Portfolio 1 and £99,000 for Portfolio 2. Portfolio 1 needs to generate growth of over 33% to get back to £100,000, whereas Portfolio 2 only needs to generate growth of 1%.

Table 5.1 Impact on a hypothetical £100,000 portfolio

	Year 1 return	Year 2 return	Average return	Compound return
Portfolio 1	50.0%	–50.0%	0.0%	–13.4%
Portfolio 2	10.0%	–10.0%	0.0%	–0.5%

What's right for me?

There is no 'perfect' portfolio and you need to take into account your life goals, income need, life expectancy and risk profile in helping to determine your asset allocation strategy. A prudent approach for most investors will be to diversify capital across the major asset classes. Figure 5.14 shows a range of possible portfolio allocations, ranging along the risk–return spectrum, which might provide you with a reasonable starting place. If you are looking for your portfolio to provide a regular and rising income throughout your lifetime then your asset allocation policy will also need to take that into account.

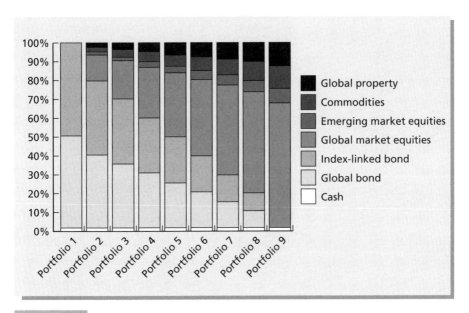

Figure 5.14 Range of asset allocations

Figure 5.15 shows historic risk–return simulations for a range of asset allocations, which allocate the equity between UK and international markets for the period 1956–2010, to give you an idea of how they performed. However, do remember that the past is unlikely to be repeated and I suggest you assume much lower investment returns in the future.

		Portfolio 0	Portfolio 20	Portfolio 40	Portfolio 60	Portfolio 80	Portfolio 100
	Defensive:	100%	80%	60%	40%	20%	1.5%
	Growth:	0%	20%	40%	60%	80%	98.5%
Defensive							
Cash		1.5%	1.5%	1.5%	1.5%	1.5%	1.5%
Short-dated global bonds		49.3%	39.3%	29.3%	19.3%	9.3%	0.0%
Index-linked bonds		49.3%	39.3%	29.3%	19.3%	9.3%	0.0%
Growth							
UK core		0.0%	7.5%	15.0%	22.5%	30.0%	36.9%
International core		0.0%	6.0%	12.0%	18.0%	24.0%	29.6%
Emerging markets core		0.0%	1.5%	3.0%	4.5%	6.0%	7.4%
UK property		0.0%	1.3%	2.5%	3.8%	5.0%	6.2%
Global property		0.0%	1.3%	2.5%	3.8%	5.0%	6.2%
Commodities		0.0%	2.5%	5.0%	7.5%	10.0%	12.3%
Returns (simulated, net of all costs)							
One-year ending 31/12/2010		3.6%	6.3%	8.8%	11.3%	13.6%	15.6%
Three-year annualised ending 31/12/2010		4.7%	4.1%	3.3%	2.4%	1.3%	0.2%
Five-year ending 31/12/2010		4.0%	4.0%	4.0%	3.8%	3.4%	3.1%
10-year annualised ending 31/12/2010		3.5%	3.6%	3.6%	3.4%	3.0%	2.6%
15-year annualised ending 31/12/2010		4.0%	4.4%	4.7%	4.9%	5.0%	4.9%
20-year annualised ending 31/12/2010		4.6%	5.4%	6.1%	6.7%	7.2%	7.5%
Annualised 01/1956 to 12/2010		6.2%	7.4%	8.4%	9.3%	10.1%	10.7%
Annualised standard deviation 01/1956 to 12/2010		1.9%	3.6%	6.5%	9.5%	12.6%	15.4%
Lowest one-year return		0.0%	-6.0%	-15.3%	-26.4%	-36.4%	-44.3%
		Feb 2006	Mar 2008	Oct 1973	Oct 1973	Oct 1973	Oct 1973
Lowest annualised three-year return		1.8%	-0.6%	-4.6%	-8.6%	-12.6%	-16.1%
		Jul 2001	Apr 2000	Apr 2000	Apr 2000	Apr 2000	Apr 2000
Highest one-year return		15.2%	23.8%	39.4%	56.0%	73.5%	89.6%
		Nov 1979	Jan 1975	Jan 1975	Jan 1975	Jan 1975	Jan 1975
Highest annualised three-year return		13.5%	15.4%	21.7%	27.9%	34.3%	39.9%
		Jun 1979	Aug 1984	Oct 1974	Oct 1974	Oct 1974	Oct 1974
Growth of £1 01/1956 to 12/2010		£ 28	£ 50	£ 85	£ 135	£ 199	£ 265

Due to the effect of rounding, some allocations may not total 100%

Figure 5.15 Historic risk-return simulations, 1988–2010

Source: Bloomsbury – calculated using Dimensional Returns 2.2. Asset class data have been used that represent close proxies for the asset classes included in the portfolio strategies. 1956 marks the starting point of this asset class data providing a reasonably informative proxy. As later asset class data becomes available, they are added into the calculation. Includes allowance for fund, custody and advice fees.

6

The investment building blocks

As we identified in the last chapter, equities and fixed income are the key asset classes used in most personal investment portfolios. In this chapter we'll take a more detailed look at these two asset classes so you can gain a better understanding of the risks and rewards and how you might deploy your capital.

Fixed interest investments

Fixed income (which from here on we'll refer to as 'bonds') are loans by investors to governments and companies that will be repaid at a pre-agreed date in the future (although a small number of bonds are undated). In return for lending their capital, bondholders are paid a fixed amount of interest, referred to as the 'coupon'. Corporate bonds (those issued by companies) usually rank ahead of normal sharehold-ers in the event of the wind-up or failure of the company, but behind other creditors such as the tax authorities and banks.

The principal uses of fixed interest investments in most long-term portfolios is to provide a reliable source of cashflow and to lower risk by dampening the volatility (the degree to which the value of an asset moves up and down) of risky assets like equities. This is because bonds have lower correlation to and lower volatility than equities. This means that the price of bonds changes at different times and to a dif-ferent degree than those of equities. See Figure 6.1.

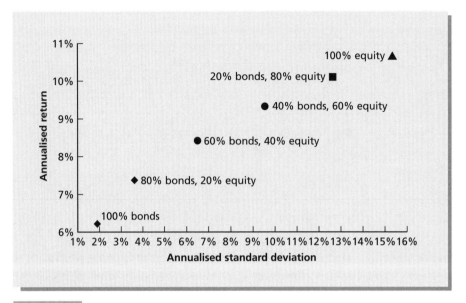

Figure 6.1 **Risk and return**

Source: Bloomsbury: Simulated returns using Dimensional Returns 2.2 after all costs

No surprises

Fama and French's multi-factor model referred to the two key risk factors associated with fixed income as being: the default (credit quality) premium, being the additional return provided to investors lending money to companies with lower credit ratings; and the maturity premium, being the additional return for holding bonds that have a long time period until they mature. Many investment experts have concluded that the return premium for these two risk factors, when bonds are being used to reduce equity risk, are not sufficient compensation for the risks involved.

One way to avoid these unnecessary fixed income risks is, therefore, to:

■ reduce maturity risk by holding shorter-term bonds, i.e. those with less than five years to maturity

■ reduce default (credit) risk by holding only high-quality bonds, i.e. those with AAA/AA investment grades

■ eliminate currency risk through hedging a basket of global bonds back to the currency in which you expect to spend any portfolio withdrawals.

Replacing long-term fixed income with short-term bonds of higher quality reduces volatility of those bonds and thus enables a portfolio to pursue higher expected returns in equities. Where the role of fixed income is to lower risk and provide cashflows, it doesn't make sense to take any more risk with this asset class than is absolutely necessary.

Figure 6.2 shows four ways that one might allocate the fixed income element of a portfolio with 60% equities and 40% bonds. Portfolio 2 reflects a move from long-term to short-term fixed interest. A reallocation to short-dated bonds improved annualised compound returns and reduced annualised standard deviation (risk) during this time period.

If the small expected additional reward does not justify the higher risk of longer maturity and lower credit quality, an investor may be better served holding shorter-term bonds, then 'spending' the risk on greater exposure to equity risk factors (small cap or value), where the expected return premiums are potentially increased.

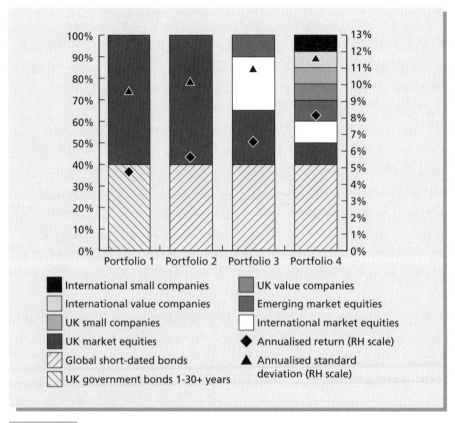

Figure 6.2   Use of fixed income in portfolios

Source: Citigroup UK Government. Bond Index 1–30+ Years (hedged) provided by Citigroup.
FTSE All-Share Index published with the permission of FTSE. Global short-dated bond index
data simulated by Dimensional. MSCI World ex UK and MSCI Emerging Markets data provided
by MSCI. MSCI data copyright MSCI 2011, all rights reserved. UK Value Companies, UK Small
Companies, International Value Companies and International Small Companies data compiled
by Dimensional from StyleResearch and Bloomberg securities data.

Global short-dated bonds (currency hedged)

Recommended for between 50 and 100% of bond exposure.

High-quality, short-term bonds (or a fund that invests in them), i.e. those with less than 5 years to maturity, have lower volatility and lower correlation to equities than long-term bonds, i.e. those with 20 or more years to maturity. In addition, short-term bonds have a much lower probability of suffering a large loss than long-dated bonds. If your equity allocation is less than 70% then the additional risks associated with long bonds don't seem worth it. Even if you have a higher equity allocation the evidence suggests that the possible additional return of long bonds probably isn't worth pursuing given the disproportionate associated risk.

Currency hedging in a bond fund makes more sense with bonds that are being used to dampen portfolio volatility, because short-term currency fluctuations can have a negative impact on the value of the bond holding. The cost of a fund manager hedging short-dated bonds is relatively low (unlike equities where it is expensive) and although it will reduce the returns achieved on the bonds it will also reduce risk.

Intermediate index-linked gilts

Recommended for between 50 and 100% of bond exposure.

Index-linked gilts have been in existence since the 1980s, as a direct result of the hyper-inflation of the 1970s, and are government-backed, fixed income investments that pay a guaranteed and fixed return plus inflation. The actual yield to maturity will depend on the actual inflation rate arising over the period the gilt is held, although the real return (the amount over inflation) will be locked in at the outset as long as the gilt is held to maturity. The historic real return on index-linked gilts has typically been in the range of 1–2% pa and a risk of about 12%. However in the mid-1990s it was as high as 4% and at the time of writing it is actually negative for all maturities up to 2024. New issue index-linked gilts are issued with a real yield of circa 0.50%.

If the real yield on new index-linked gilts rises to reflect changes in demand, i.e. more competition for capital from other asset classes, then the value of existing index-linked gilts will fall to reflect these new investment conditions. Although this will not adversely affect the investor who holds their existing gilts to maturity, it does mean that they can't easily switch from the lower real return to the higher one without suffering a loss before maturity. Index-linked gilts are, therefore, not risk-free and highly sensitive to demand from investors (like pension funds) and the inflationary outlook. Intermediate index-linked gilts, i.e. those with a time to maturity of between 10 and 15 years, have about half the amount of risk of longer-duration issues but have a very similar expected return. Therefore, it makes a lot of sense to invest in intermediate issues or a fund that does so.

Conventional long-dated gilts

Not recommended for risk-averse investors with long-term horizons or moderate equity allocations.

As I've already explained, and particularly at the more aggressive, equity-orientated end of the risk spectrum, fixed income's role is primarily that of a diversifier of equity market trauma and financial crisis. In this role, and despite normally positive correlations to equities, at times of equity market trauma high-quality bonds (such as UK gilts) have the potential, although not the certainty, of acting as havens of safety and liquidity, with commensurate positive consequences for yields (downwards) and prices (upwards). Gilts with a long time to maturity (known as long duration) magnify this positive effect.

When the market anticipates mild positive inflation in the future, then the yield on gilts usually rises as the time until maturity (known as duration) increases. Thus gilts with six months to maturity should normally yield less than those with five years to maturity. This makes sense as investors require a higher return to compensate for the potential risk of higher inflation. Thus if we plotted on a graph the redemption yields (the total return that arises by holding the gilt until maturity) on all gilts, starting with the shortest duration to the longest duration, and joined up the plots we would see a line that slopes upwards over time. This is referred to as a normal yield curve (see Figure 6.3).

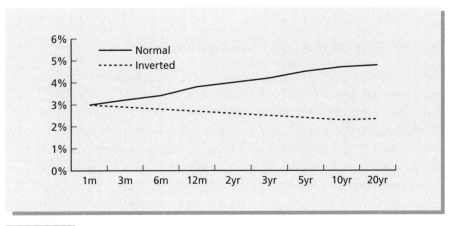

Figure 6.3 **The bond yield curve**

If the market anticipates a fall in inflation in the future, perhaps because a recession is expected, then the yield on longer-dated gilts will fall, possibly below those of the shorter-dated ones, which will rise. This is known as an inverted yield curve and is characterised by interest rates on accessible deposit accounts yielding much more than long-term gilts, as happened in 2007–2008. Investing in conventional long-term gilts when the yield curve is inverted would be a very imprudent thing for an investor to do if they had other alternatives.

Sometimes technical factors can cause the yield curve to move in a way that is not in line with the inflation outlook. For example, several years ago, due to changes in the rules on how certain big pension funds calculated their liabilities, such schemes were forced to invest a lot more in long-term gilts to match their long-term liabilities, thus causing a fall in the yield on long-term gilts, even though long-term inflation was still a threat.

Long-term bonds experience higher volatility than short-dated bonds and the distribution of annual returns on the downside means there is also a higher likelihood of suffering a large loss. These factors, together with the poor inflation protection provided, mean that long-dated conventional gilts are not recommended for risk-averse investors with limited human capital (the ability to earn income or generate wealth), who are looking to preserve their investment capital in real terms.

National Savings Certificates

Recommended as proxy for cash or short-dated fixed income.

National Savings products are 100% backed by the UK Treasury and, as such, offer the highest level of capital protection available. The range and competitiveness of products available changes from time to time based on market conditions and the level of funds required by the UK government. In the autumn of 2010 National Savings withdrew most of its most attractive savings products as they had been too successful in attracting funds for the government. Existing maturing products are permitted to be reinvested and new products can be expected to be launched early in each financial year as the government resets its borrowing targets.

Index/LIBOR-linked high-quality corporate bonds

Not recommended for risk-averse investors due to equity-type risks.

A recent innovation is the launch, by big companies like Royal Bank of Scotland, Barclays and Tesco, of corporate bonds that pay the higher of a minimum yield (typically 3–4% pa) or the increase in either the Retail Prices Index (RPI) or the London Inter-Bank Offered Rate (LIBOR – basically the variable interest rate banks charge each other for lending each other funds).

While on the face of it these issues appear to offer the best of both worlds, a minimum fixed rate of interest and protection against rising inflation or interest rates, you are effectively taking on the risk that your capital could be wiped out if the issuing company goes bust or seeks to reorganise its balance as a result of financial difficulties. Remember that risk and return are related. If something pays a higher return – in this case higher than index-linked gilts – then it comes with higher risk.

While the risk of a large quoted company going bust or suffering financial pressures is likely to be low, it is much higher than for UK gilts. In addition, the bondholder will only obtain the original capital back as and when the bond matures, which is likely to be between 10 and 15 years from issue. If the holding is sold in the market before maturity the price will be determined by the yield on the bond, which is influenced by both the economic conditions at the time and the financial strength of the company behind the bonds.

Permanent interest-bearing shares (PIBs)

Not recommended due to capital risks.

These are securities issued by building societies, usually at relatively high fixed rates of interest (although a small number of issues pay variable interest), which are quoted on the stock market. PIBS have no maturity date, although with some issues the building society can redeem the PIBS early on a certain specified date. The two principal risks of PIBS are that the investor may not get all or any of their capital back if the building society gets into financial difficulty or goes bust. In addition, the capital value of the PIBS will fluctuate in line with supply and demand for the holding based on prevailing economic and investment conditions. Gains and losses arising on disposal are not chargeable or allowable for capital gains tax purposes. If a building society demutualises with PIBS in issue then these become perpetual subordinated bonds (PSBs).

We've seen earlier that there is insufficient return premium to compensate for the additional risk of holding one company's bonds. This point was starkly illustrated by the emergency nationalisation of Bradford & Bingley plc in September 2008. Under the terms of the nationalisation interest to bondholders, i.e. those holding PSBs, interest payments were cancelled and no repayments of capital will be made until the bank has fully repaid the £14 billion owed to the Financial Services Compensation Scheme and the £4 billion owed to the government, with interest. It is likely to be many years before bondholders will know how much, if any, payment they will receive.

Convertible preference shares, high-yield bonds, convertible bonds, emerging market bonds

Not recommended due to uncompensated equity-type risks.

Because risk-averse investors in a diversified, multi-asset portfolio allocate capital to bonds to reduce risk, it doesn't make sense to include in the portfolio any of the above bond-type investment, because they represent a similar risk to equities but without the same level of upside. Any available risk 'capacity' would be better allocated to equities for a higher expected return. For this reason these bond investments are not recommended.

Equities

> *'If inflation continues to soar, you're going to have to work like a dog just to live like one.'*

George Gobel, American comedian

The role of equities in your portfolio is as a core return genera-
tor, which manifests itself through dividends and earnings growth.
Equities have historically offered the highest long-term return and
inflation protection of all the asset classes. However, this higher
return comes with high volatility and uncertainty, which has a greater
impact over shorter time periods, i.e. less than 20 years (see Table 6.1).

Table 6.1 Post-inflation investment returns by asset class

	2010	10 years	20 years	50 years	111 years
Equities	8.9%	0.60%	6%	5.4%	5.1%
Gilts	4.4%	2.4%	5.8%	2.5%	1.2%
Corporate bonds	3.9%	2.1%	N/A	N/A	N/A
Index-linked	5.3%	2.4%	4.3%	N/A	N/A
Cash	−4.1%	1.1%	2.5%	1.7%	1.0%

Source: Barclays Capital (2011) 'Equity gilt study' 2011

Equities represent ownership in businesses and, as such, offer the
opportunity for investors to participate in current and future profits
generated by those businesses. Profits are either paid out by way of dividends or retained by the company to reinvest to grow profits further.
Either way, over the long term, investors expect to earn a significant
premium over and above the return that they could earn from risk-free
assets, like cash. As I explained in Chapter 5, this extra return is known
as the equity risk premium (ERP). Figure 6.4 sets out the probability of
equities outperforming cash and bonds over various time periods, with
18 years having the highest probability of outperformance.

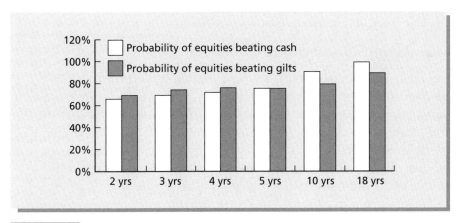

Figure 6.4   **Probability of equities producing higher returns than cash or gilts**

Source: Barclays Capital (2011) 'Equity gilt study 2011'

International developed markets equities

Recommended as a core return provider and diversifier.

There should be no excess return available from international developed markets over the UK stock market as there is no additional systematic risk. Those overseas countries should experience similar rates of economic growth to the UK and that should lead to similar rates of earnings growth by overseas companies in developed markets. In addition, international companies have a similar cost of capital to UK companies. The primary reason to allocate some of the equity exposure to overseas developed markets is to provide additional diversification.

> 'In the long run, stock markets in Germany, Japan and the United Kingdom ought to generate returns similar to those of the United States, while exposing investors to similar risk levels.'[1]

David F. Swensen, Chief Investment Officer, Yale University

---

[1] Swensen, D. F. (2000) *Pioneering Portfolio Management: An unconventional approach to institutional investment*, Free Press, p. 113.

Emerging markets equities

Recommended as a return enhancer and diversifier.

Emerging market companies are those located in parts of the world that are still rapidly developing and are characterised by young and growing populations, rising living standards, increasing access to education and development of infrastructure. While some emerging countries have established democracies, many have less stable regimes or controlled economies. Emerging countries include big states like Russia, China, Brazil and India, and small states like Vietnam, Malaysia and South Africa. Although the growth rates of these countries has been, and is expected to be, higher than developed countries like the USA and UK, they are also much riskier. Sometimes governments impose restrictions on investors accessing their investments, seize ownership of industrial assets or impose unexpected tariffs or taxes. This higher risk is compensated by the higher expected returns compared to developed markets.

Emerging market equities offer two key benefits. Firstly, investors expect higher long-term returns from these markets to reflect both the higher levels of growth generated by countries that are developing from agricultural to industrial and service-based economies, and as compensation for the higher level of risks involved (i.e. political, currency, legal, liquidity and higher costs). The second benefit is that emerging markets provide additional diversification because the economies of many emerging countries, and as a result their stock markets, often move out of synch with the UK. Although this lower level of correlation (the degree to which an asset class acts more or less like another asset class) has been narrowing. Recent research[2] confirms that the benefits of diversification remain.

With Western countries' economic growth lagging and populations ageing, some commentators have suggested that investors should allocate a lot more of their capital to the faster-growing economies like Brazil, Russia, India, China and South Africa (the so-called 'BRICS') and reduce their weighting to the US and other main developed markets. The investment industry has certainly been busy launching new funds investing in the BRICS and the story certainly sounds compelling.

---

[2] Christofferson, P., Errunza, V. R., Jacobs, K. and Jin, X. (2010) 'Is the potential for international diversification disappearing?', available at **http://papers.ssrn./sol3/papers. cfm?abstract_id=1573345.**

However, the investment opportunity is not the same as the economic opportunity. Take a look at Figure 6.5, which ranks the top 20 countries by gross domestic product (GDP). The US is currently ranked number 1 with China ranked 2, India ranked 4, Russia 6 and Brazil 9. The UK is currently clinging on to 7th place but predictions[3] are for this to slip to 15th place by 2020 while the BRICS countries will all be within the top 7 positions, behind the US in first place.

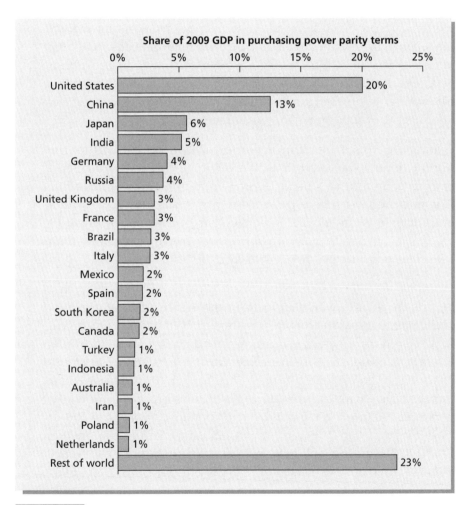

Figure 6.5 Top 20 countries by gross domestic product

Source: World Bank

---

[3] Centre for Economics and Business Research (2010) 'Global prospects report'.

Let's now look at the country weights of the MSCI World All Countries Investable Markets Index in Figure 6.6. This illustrates the true investment opportunities for global investors, taking into account any restrictions imposed locally on foreign share ownership. The actual investment opportunity is somewhat different for emerging economies from their economic output. The UK market, by contrast, offers a much larger investment market than the BRICS countries combined. This is logical because with faster growing countries the economies grow much faster than the financial markets that support them. Emerging economies are not a clearly homogeneous group. For example India and China are big importers of commodities, whereas Brazil and Russia are big exporters of those commodities. China is a big exporter of finished goods whereas India mainly exports services like call centres and computer programming.

If you weight your investment portfolio based on the GDP of the world economy you'll end up with a very high exposure to emerging markets compared to a market capitalisation-weighted basis. While that might offer a higher potential return it will also come with a much higher risk profile. For some investors that higher risk might be acceptable, but for the majority of investors, seeking to preserve their wealth, such an elevated risk is unlikely to be desirable.

Emerging markets are a separate asset class that complement, not replace, developed investment market exposure. In addition, exposure to these faster-growing economies is also achieved through investment in developed market stock markets, to the extent that those companies derive revenue from activity in emerging market economies. Recent estimates suggest that around 20% of earnings in FTSE 100 companies come from emerging markets. For example BHP Bilton, which is listed on the UK's FTSE 100 Index, is the world's largest mining company and 20% of its global revenue in 2009 came from China. Imperial Tobacco, another FTSE 100 listed company, now derives a large amount of its revenue from the faster-growing markets of China and the Far East.

Although in times of extreme market turbulence, as happened in 2007–2009, emerging markets experience similar falls, over longer time periods they can be much more volatile than developed markets. For this reason your allocation to emerging markets should be moderate in the expectation, but not the guarantee, that there may be additional returns and a lowering of overall risk to the portfolio.

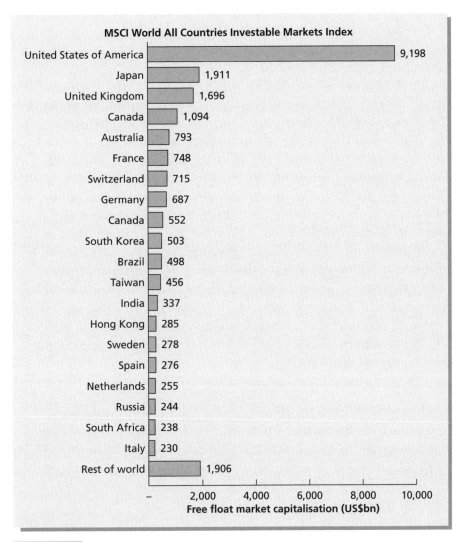

Figure 6.6 Country weights of MSCI World All Countries Investable Markets Index

Source: Bloomberg Securities, as at 31.12.10

Collaterised commodities futures index fund

Recommended for investors prepared to give up some investment return for lower risk.

Commodities include things like energy, precious metals, gem stones and basic foodstuffs. Commodities have no expected return and no mechanism (like dividends) for distributing one. They merely represent the supply and demand at any given time for these materials. Although equities provide an implicit exposure to commodities by virtue of the trading activities of the companies that are represented by equities, it can be more attractive for risk-averse investors to allocate some of their portfolio equity exposure to a fund that invests in commodity futures. This is because, historically, commodity futures returns and equity returns have had a very low correlation, i.e. they react differently to news and economic conditions. This low correlation provides a lowering of risk and, as a consequence, a lowering of expected future returns, compared to a portfolio that does not have an allocation to commodity futures. The available data suggests that commodities futures provide more risk-reduction benefits than other diversifiers like international equities.

A collaterised commodities futures fund is not an investment directly in commodities but, rather, an investment in a fund that continually buys futures in an index of commodities. As such it presents the expected future price of commodities. Those prices can and do change rapidly to news and events and there can be periods of significant positive and negative returns to investors.

Commercial property

Recommended as a core return provider and diversifier.

As the Talmud pointed out a few thousand years ago, property has always been an integral part of a sensible investment strategy. As an asset class, property has a low correlation with equities and bonds. In addition it provides an effective hedge against unexpected inflation. It is also easier to borrow to fund property investment, which can increase (and decrease) overall returns.

The expected return from property is somewhere between bonds and equities. This is because rental income provides regular cashflow like bonds and, as that rent rises, so should the capital value, similar to equities. However, this generalisation masks the fact that there is a range of different types of property, with differing risk–return profiles.

Property that is let to a very high-quality tenant on a very long, upward-only, lease will act more like a bond. Property that is let on very short tenancies, such as hotels, will act more like equities in that the capital value fluctuates in line with rental income based on the demand for rooms. That demand in turn is affected by economic conditions.

If commercial property as a whole has a risk–return profile that is between a bond (with a 2% pa real return) and an equity (with a 5% pa real return), then the mid-point is half the difference between them, i.e. 1.5%. Adding 1.5% to the 2% real return from bonds gives a reasonably conservative estimate of future expected returns from unleveraged commercial property of circa 3.5% pa over inflation.

Ethical equity investing

Not recommended due to insufficient data on returns and risk factors, but may be suitable for inclusion for those with strong ethical views.

Over the past 20 or so years there has been a growing interest in ethical (or socially responsible) investment. Ethical investment is the incorporation of social, ethical and/or environmental factors into the process of selecting companies in which to invest. Investment in some of the developed equity asset classes can also now be done on an ethical passive basis, since the introduction of the FTSE4Good indices in 2001 (see Table 6.2). There is not, however, long-term data from which we can draw any conclusions about the efficacy of using passive ethical funds for equity exposure. In addition, there are no ethical index funds that cover all the asset classes to make this approach viable if you require evidence to support your investment decisions.

Table 6.2 Performance of FTSE4Good indices

	1 year	3 years		5 years	
	Return %	Return %	Risk %	Return %	Risk %
UK FTSE4Good	10.1	−5.1	23.1	16.7	16.5
Global FTSE4Good	4.3	−23.4	26.3	7.4	20.8
FTSE All-Share	12.5	−3.1	23.1	24.7	16.8
FTSE Developed Markets	7.4	−20.7	25.2	11.3	19.9

Source: FTSE.com factsheet Q3 2010

7

Alternative investments

There are a number of asset classes other than cash, bonds and equities that you might consider as part of your wealth plan. In this chapter I'll explain the main types and whether or not I recommend their inclusion in your portfolio.

Gold

Not recommended in a multi-asset portfolio held for the long term because its expected return does not cover its risk as a portfolio asset.

Gold has been a store of value for thousands of years and has as much emotional appeal as it does potential for investment. Some investors view gold as the ultimate protection against rampant inflation and corrupt or profligate governments, with its appeal and, thus, value rising as confidence in governments' economic policies declines. In many Middle Eastern and Asian countries, particularly those with less-developed banking infrastructures and less stable political institutions, gold is still a trusted form of exchange for goods and services. In addition, there are strong cultural traditions that perpetuate the allure of gold. For example at Indian weddings it is usual for the bride and groom to be given gold as a wedding present.

The capital return from gold can only come from a rise in the price due to increasing demand. A large part of the demand for gold arises from its use in jewellery and other goods, known as the 'consumption dividend'.[1] This consumption dividend pushes up the price of gold and as such lowers its expected capital return. If you invest in gold bullion or a gold fund as part of your investment portfolio all you will receive is the expected capital return as you are not receiving the consumption dividend. The expected capital gain return is, however, insufficient compensation for the risks associated with the asset class. Figure 7.1 shows the return from gold after adjusting for inflation over the past 30 years compared to the S&P 500 and FTSE 100. These two key arguments suggest that the average historic return on gold is probably higher than we can expect in the future. Although gold has diversification characteristics, because it has very low correlation with equities and bonds, its expected return should be low because of its role in reducing risk in the portfolio overall.

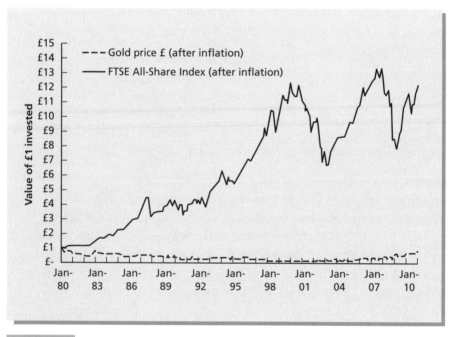

Figure 7.1   Historic after inflation return from gold compared to FTSE All-Share Index

Source: FTSE, Dimensional Fund Advisors

---

[1] The term 'consumption dividend' means the utility value that comes from actually using gold in products or owning gold for pleasure or status. Owning gold bullion or a gold fund does not provide this consumption dividend to the investor.

Hedge funds/fund of hedge funds (FOHFs)

Not recommended due to their complexity, high costs and unsubstantiated risk/reward characteristics.

Hedge funds are not an asset class as such but a class of active investment management that covers a wide range of different investment approaches and styles. On the face of it hedge funds appear to provide attractive characteristics to investors, including low correlation to equities and bonds, high returns and low risk. Investment can be by either a fund that invests in a number of other hedge funds (known as a fund of hedge funds) or as individual funds. The hedge fund industry claims that, in aggregate, their funds generate returns over and above the market due to the skill of investment managers. However, because we know that there are no high-return low-risk investments, such claims should be treated with a high degree of scepticism.

The most commonly available risk and return databases for hedge funds contain a number of biases that overstate returns and understate correlations (against other asset classes) and volatility. In addition, the data conceals the fact that there is usually an increased probability of very large losses. Recent research suggests that returns from hedge funds may in fact be systematic exposure to alternative sources of market-based returns (beta) rather than manager skill.[2] During the period November 2007 to March 2009, when the UK equity market fell almost 40%, diversified FOHFs failed to live up to their diversification and skill-based returns sales pitch, losing over 20% in dollar terms.[3] This suggests that such products are simply the result of taking directional market bets, for very high fees. Over the long term these high fees will have a very detrimental impact on investor returns, even if a manager gets those directional bets right (there is no evidence that those who do so can repeat their success in a way that can reliably be attributed to skill rather than luck).

---

[2] Géhin, W. and Vaissié, M. (2005) *'The right place for alternative beta in hedge fund portfolios: An answer to the capacity effect fantasy'*, EDHEC and Journal of Alternative Investments, 9(1): 9–18; Jensen, G. (2005) 'Hedge funds selling beta as alpha', Daily Observations, Bridgewater Associates.

[3] HFRI Fund of Funds Diversified Index in US$.

Assessing hedge funds is an expensive, time-consuming and complex task, which involves trying to understand the underlying strategies, selecting truly skilful managers and performing the necessary due diligence. (Bernie Madoff fooled a number of wealthy professional investors and large private banks with his US-based fraud, so it is not as easy as it might appear.) In addition, the costs of a typical hedge fund are very high, with a typical fund charging 2% annual management charge and 20% of any gains, plus 1% and 10%, respectively, on top of that for a fund of funds. In addition, the costs incurred by the manager in buying and selling holdings are likely to add significant additional costs, which will be at least as much as traditionally managed funds, but most likely much higher, given the typically higher level of buying and selling within hedge funds.

Investing is a zero sum game before costs (for every winner there must be a loser) and over the medium to long term hedge funds have a very high hill to climb in obtaining investment returns just to cover their increased costs. In order to do this, they need to take more risk (with your money). Synthetic hedge funds, which replicate underlying market risk factors at far lower cost and with greater liquidity, could be a possible option for investors in the future, but it is still too early to establish their efficacy in delivering the desired characteristics and there is still a lack of available funds of this type.

Structured products

Not recommended for long-term investors due to high costs, additional provider risks and loss of return upside but may be suitable for very short-term investors who accept the downsides.

Structured products, created by investment banks and enthusiastically promoted by their private banking divisions, started gaining popularity with European retail investors in the 1990s and with US retail investors in the mid-2000s. In simple terms a structured investment pays a return based on the performance of an underlying asset, such as an index, commodity or equity according to a pre-set formula, usually over a set time period of up to six years. In some issues it is possible to encash the investment early but this may be subject to certain penalties and even then will depend on the market price of the underlying asset.

On the face of it these products can be useful to investors who desire a specific payoff structure linked to the performance of the underlying asset(s) at apparently lower risk. Certainly the promise of capital protection with market upside participation looks appealing to the average investor. However, behind the sales message is usually a complex payout mechanism that even the most mathematically minded would struggle to fathom out and risks that may be neither immediately obvious nor quantifiable.

The combination of a simple investment proposition supported by extremely complex financial engineering means that most retail investors buy structured products on the advice of 'experts' such as private banking advisers and independent financial advisers (IFAs). As I've stated previously there are no high-return low-risk investments. Therefore as an investor you know intuitively that a fixed income product that pays a high yield and offers additional upside potential must carry some form of downside risk. A financial institution will not offer more benefit without getting something in return! The usual price of capital protection is giving up part of the return from the underlying index, security or commodity on which the structured product is based. In addition, the guarantee of the return of principal is only in nominal terms (invest £100, get £100 back) and a period of high inflation could seriously erode purchasing power.

> 'They are horrible investments for retail investors… Simple portfolios of bonds, stocks or the S&P 500 will beat structured products 99.5% of the time because of the heavy profit built into the pricing.'
>
> Craig McCann, former SEC economist

A common feature of these products is high, but rarely quantifiable, costs. It is in the issuer's interests to make the product as complex as possible so that it is hard for investors and advisers to quantify the costs and the profits accruing to the issuing bank. Many investors wrongly equate complexity with high returns, to their detriment. While the return payout may appear to be passive in nature, being linked to an index or other asset class measure mean that many structured products are simply gambles on the direction and magnitude of the movement of a market or a basket of markets.

In addition, a key risk is that of the counterparties providing the downside protection. Investment bank Lehman Brothers backed $900 million of structured products in 2009, before filing for bankruptcy in September of that year. As a consequence, investors in Lehman Brothers-backed structured products have sustained big losses and some are expecting to recover only 20% of their investment.[4]

Private equity

Not recommended due to high costs and poor return characteristics.

Private equity, i.e. leveraged buy-outs and venture capital, appear to provide exciting opportunities for higher returns than the public market and additional diversification benefits. In reality, capturing these higher returns comes at the price of illiquidity, higher risk and higher costs. A recent study by former banker Peter Morris found that private equity managers often charge excessive fees (typically a 2% annual fee and 20% performance fee) and overstate potential returns. 'Calculating returns on private equity is not a trivial issue,' Morris says. 'The most widely used measure, the internal rate of return, is misleading and often overstates realised returns. This creates room for uncertainty, at best, and, at worst, manipulation.'[5]

Morris questioned the extent to which the returns that the managers do deliver relate to their own skill and the extent to which they come from what the market would have provided anyway and from the leverage involved. For instance, his study analysed the returns on 110 deals in the UK and Europe over a decade from 1995 to 2005. The average internal rate of return in those deals was 39%, of which debt accounted for 22% and a rising stock market 9%. The other 8% was the contribution of the private equity managers. Given that the average annual fee in private equity was at least 8%, this meant the investors who provided the bulk of the money would have done just as well investing in the market directly and borrowing from the bank. See Figure 7.2.

---

4   Light, L. (2009) 'Twice shy on structured products?', *Wall Street Journal*, 28 May.
5   Morris, P. (2010) 'Private equity, public loss?', Centre for the Study of Financial Innovation, July.

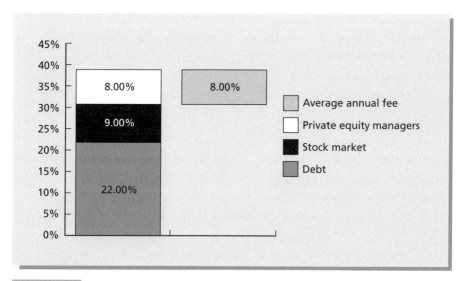

Figure 7.2   Return composition of private equity deals

Source: Morris, P. (2010) 'Private equity, public loss?', Centre for the Study of Financial Innovation, July

Another recent European study[6] looked at cashflows from more than 4,000 liquidated private equity investments and found the 'alpha, or return unexplained by risk factors to which investors could have obtained low cost exposure anyway, was zero'. This study inferred an historical risk premium from private equity of around 18%, of which about 10% was the market premium, 5% was the value (or book-to-market) premium and the remaining 3% was the premium from liquidity risk – the risk of not being able to sell out of the asset sufficiently quickly to avoid a loss.

> *'...private equity is simply public equity with additional layers of leverage; it is therefore likely to be a good deal more risky than quoted equity markets, while several orders of magnitude more expensive in management fee structures... From an accounting perspective, private equity might appear to be a lower risk investment than quoted equities, while delivering historical returns that display low correlations with equities. In the real world, nothing could be further from the truth.'*

> Barclays Capital, *'Equity gilt study 2007'*

---

[6]   Franzoni, F., Nowak, E. and Phallippou, L. (2010) *Private Equity Performance and Liquidity Risk*, Swiss Finance Institute, 17 June.

Leading finance academics Eugene Fama and Kenneth French recently expressed their view that, to the extent private equity managers add value through the application of their skills, the evidence indicates this additional return tends to go to the managers themselves.[7] Fama and French also dispute that private equity is a diversification tool, because the types of targets chosen by private equity – small companies and start-ups – tend to be highly sensitive to the market.

There is a wide range of possible outcomes for the returns from private equity when compared to those from the quoted stock market. However, these returns are driven by chance, which makes it hard for investors to discern whether the returns they are paying for are due to skill or luck. So while private equity can generate good returns, once these returns are adjusted for market risk, value and size risk and liquidity risk, there is little sign of the managers adding any further value through their own skill. In any case, the size of the fees involved suggests that what additional spoils are on offer tend to go to the managers, not the investors.

Life settlement funds

Not recommended due to poor upside and lack of transparency.

Life settlement funds purchase life insurance plans from individuals with impaired life outlooks at a discount and then receive settlement on the death of the original policyholder. Given that returns are uncorrelated to financial markets and some existing funds have delivered returns in the region of 8% per annum with low volatility, they are, at least superficially, attractive.

There are four main points to consider when weighing up whether or not to use life settlement funds. First, returns are based on someone else's misfortune, which may not be acceptable to some people. Second, the risk exists of a misselling scandal, not only of life policies, but the fact that there may well be alternatives to selling a policy, which may not have been properly explained to the policyholder

---

[7]   Fama, E. F. and French, K. R. (2010) 'Q&A: *Public vs private equity*', Fama/French Forum, Dimensional Fund Advisors 7 July.

and would be financially more attractive to them. Third, you need to remember that high returns may be arbitraged away as more players enter the life settlements marketplace. Finally, you need to understand the various risks associated with this type of investment.

You are relying on the skill of the manager to make the correct assumptions about the life expectancy of the policyholders from whom policies are purchased. If they underestimate how long policy-holders will live, the overall return from the fund will be much less than anticipated as they will need to find cash to pay ongoing pre-miums and this may require the forced sale of other policies at a discounted price. In addition, like structured products, life settlement funds have a rather opaque product structure that combines relatively high costs with multiple counterparties including the manager, life policy adviser, policy administrator and custodian. For all these rea-sons the UK's main financial regulator has also made it clear that it sees a very limited audience for life settlements.[8]

Zeros

Not recommended due to equity-type risks.

Investment trusts are quoted companies that exist solely to invest in other companies and they have been in existence for well over 150 years. Zero dividend preference shares, known as 'zeros', are a class of investment trust share issued by split capital investment trusts that provide a predetermined return on the maturity of the zero, similar to a zero coupon bond (a fixed income investment that pays all its return at maturity rather than regular interest payments throughout its term). The zero is assured of being repaid as long as the trust's assets grow by a fixed amount, which is defined at the launch date of the trust. At the time of writing, most zeros are sufficiently well covered that the value of the assets in the company can fall each year and still be sufficient to repay the value of the zero at maturity; however, the majority of these trusts wind up in 2012 so there is limited scope for investors.

---

[8] Speech by Peter Smith, Head of Investments Policy, Conduct Policy Division, FSA to the European Life Settlement Association, London, 24 February 2010.

In the early 1990s some investment trusts invested in each other and also took on debt to boost returns further, thus increasing risk beyond that which would have applied in a fully diversified market portfolio. In the early 2000s, with equity markets in free fall, the impact of those market falls was amplified by the cross-holdings and debt, and banks started calling in their loans. Like the proverbial deck of cards, this led to a number of trusts becoming insolvent and defaulting on payouts to their shareholders at maturity. In the mid-2000s the investment trust industry agreed a compensation package to provide limited compensation to those who lost out in this situation.

Convertible bonds

Not recommended due to equity-type risks.

These are fixed income securities issued by companies that also offer the holder the option to convert to ordinary share capital of the issuing company at a predetermined price in the future. The concept is that the investor receives a known return through the interest paid and capital security, with the potential to share in the upside of the company. As a result convertible bonds act more like bonds when they are issued and gradually take on more and more equity risk characteristics as they near maturity. As I explained in Chapter 5 there is no extra return benefit from taking the risk of investing in one company's securities and the equity-like nature of convertibles is incompatible with the principal role of fixed income in most portfolios – that of reducing the risk of risky assets.

Residential buy-to-lets

Not recommended for most investors due to lack of liquidity; potential for rent 'voids' and rental hassles cutting yields rapidly, unless a significant amount of capital can be allocated to build a diversified property business.

In the UK we have an obsession with property and for various reasons we seem to think that it represents a type of investment 'get out of jail' option. Let me explain why I think this attitude is misplaced for most investors. Although a gross average annual yield of 7% (the consensus at the time of writing) would appear to make residential property an attractive alternative asset class for your long-term wealth plan, when you take into account maintenance costs, arrears from bad tenants and **void rent** (where no rent is received due to the property being empty), you'd be lucky to get 3% net and that's before tax and inflation! While there are clearly a number of people who have made money out of residential buy-to-let property, as the market has grown over the past 15 years, most of this arose from unsustainable growth in capital values fuelled by cheap money and lax lending activity by financial institutions.

There are a number of factors that will affect whether residential buy-to-let makes sense as a viable long-term investment. Tenant demand reached new heights in the third quarter of 2010, rising 19% from the previous quarter to more than 61,000 new tenants registering for rental accommodation.[10] Estate agents would have us believe that tenant demand will continue to grow in the future. Currently, there is a shortage of UK rental property but a glut of property for sale. The last time this happened in 2008, sellers decided to hang on to their property and rent it out instead of taking what they perceived to be low offers from purchasers. The outcome was a sharp fall in rents as more rental property became available.

Notwithstanding the potential for more rental property to become available as the buying and selling market stalls, the impending reforms to housing benefit are also likely to have a negative impact on overall rent levels. It is undoubtedly the case that high rents paid for some social tenants, particularly in London, have been pushing up rents across the board. Therefore cutting State funding of the most expensive social housing must have a negative impact on overall rents.

Even if rents can be maintained at current levels, it still looks challenging to make a decent return once the true costs of repairs and maintenance are accounted for. Add in the strong probability of loan interest costs rising in the medium term, the potential for rent voids and having a bad tenant and the chances of experiencing negative cashflow looks likely.

---

[10] Countrywide press release, 'Over 61,000 new tennants enter the rental market', 27 October 2010, **www.countrywide.co.uk/media**

Perhaps if you had a large diversified portfolio of, say, 30 properties and a full-time property manager you might be able to withstand the occasional negative cashflow on a small proportion of properties and derive economies of scale on running costs. But the reality is that most buy-to-let investors have relied on capital gains to provide the bulk of their returns. Once those capital gains evaporate and negative cashflow kicks in, property equity can quickly be wiped out.

One of the key problems with property, and one usually glossed over by investors when comparing it to a fully diversified investment portfolio, is that property is an illiquid asset class. If you want to realise your investment (and any accrued capital gains who will arise in a single tax year) you need to find someone else willing to buy it from you. Putting aside the issue of whether UK residential property is over- or undervalued, the fact is that the number of buyers who are willing and able to buy residential property for investment purposes has been falling consistently since 2008 due to the continuing lack of mortgages for investors in residential property.

If you want to run a business and you have an interest in property then by all means invest in residential rental property, but make sure that you understand the significant risks you will be exposed to compared to the potential returns, you can handle the lack of liquidity and ensure you do it on a big scale!

8

Active or passive?

Once you have a good idea of your overall wealth plan and asset allocation policy you will need to make a third key decision: should you pursue an active or passive investment approach or a combination of the two? Figure 8.1 sets out the key characteristics of each approach.

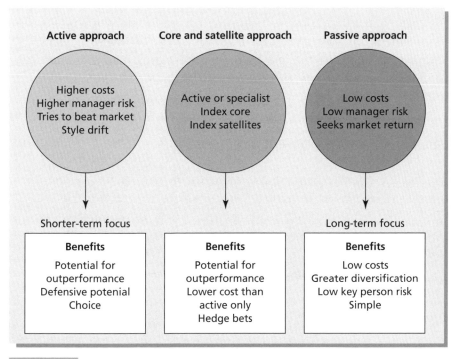

Figure 8.1 The three investment management approaches

Source: Vanguard

Active investment management

Active investment management is where a manager (or investor) aims to beat, rather than simply match, the return of an investment market or agreed benchmark. Active investment management can be at the asset allocation or stock selection level or a mixture of the two.

Market timing is where an investor makes bets about whether to place more or less in a particular asset class at any given time. For example, the manager might believe that UK equities are likely to provide a higher return over the next year than, say, UK gilts and as a result might increase their allocation to UK equities and reduce the allocation to UK gilts. In the past few years more and more investors have been attracted to gold and have added or increased exposure to this asset class because they think it offers better return prospects than other asset classes such as equities and property.

Active stock selection is where the investor makes bets on whether to invest in certain sectors or individual holdings within an asset class. For example, banking shares versus drug companies or Merck versus GlaxoSmithKline. Over the past few years a lot of investors were attracted to companies that pay high dividends rather than those that pay little or no dividends, as a result of the turmoil that has arisen in world markets since 2008.

Passive investment management

Passive investment management is where the manager aims to closely match the returns of a market, benchmark or risk factor. This is achieved by either buying a representative sample of the underlying holdings or all the holdings in an index so as to replicate, as far as is possible, the market. This approach is called indexation and is the most common form of passive management.

A smaller proportion of the passive management sector follows a slightly different approach, which is known as asset class investing. Asset class funds do not attempt to replicate or follow traditional indices but, instead, seek to hold shares that reflect a particular risk characteristic. For example, a fund investing in smaller companies may use a different definition of what is a smaller company compared to the established indices and also may adopt a more flexible approach to trading than an index fund that has to rigidly follow the bench-mark index.

Core and satellite investing

This approach aims to deliver the benefits of passive and active man-agement. The portfolio comprises a core of long-term investments and a periphery of specialist or shorter-term holdings (see Figure 8.2). Core investments are usually represented by long-term, low-cost index funds that closely track an index such as the FTSE All-Share. Satellite

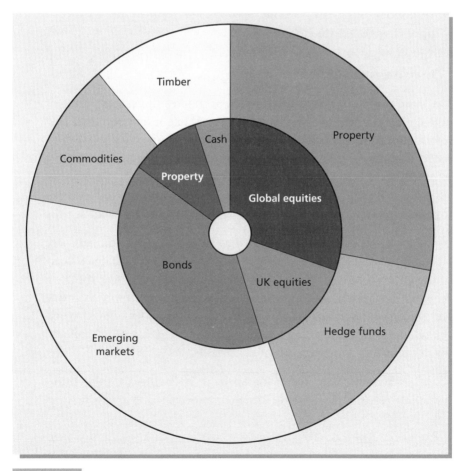

Figure 8.2 Example of core and satellite allocation

Source: Vanguard

investments usually include specialist investments that are not highly correlated with core investments. Examples of satellite funds include hedge funds, commodities, timber and emerging market equities.

The efficient market hypothesis

A key concept to understand is what is known as the efficient market hypothesis. This is a model that was developed back in the 1960s to understand how investment markets behave.

Basically, the efficient market hypothesis[1] states that:

■ current prices incorporate all available information and expectations

■ current prices are the best approximation to intrinsic value

■ price changes are due to unforeseen events

■ 'mispricings' do occur but not in predictable patterns that can lead to consistent outperformance.

The basic principle is that in an efficient market the current price of underlying securities reflects all publicly available information. As new information (news) comes to the market, prices immediately adjust to reflect that news, whether positive or negative. The implications of this hypothesis are that active management strategies cannot consistently add value through security selection and market timing, while passive investment strategies reward investors with capital market returns.

In 2008, when Lehman Brothers went bust, investors immediately changed their view of risks and returns, fearing an immediate collapse of the entire financial system, and prices adjusted to reflect this new scenario. By March 2009 investors had become even more negative and stockmarkets around the world had fallen to all-time lows. When the financial meltdown didn't turn out as expected, investors' appetite for risk returned and prices adjusted upwards.

So unless investors can predict the future or have (illegal) inside information, it is extremely difficult for them to do better than the market,

[1]   Fama, E. F. (1970) 'Efficient capital markets: a review of theory and empirical work', *Journal of Finance*, 25, (2): 383–417; Fama, E. F. (1977) 'Foundations of finance', *Journal of Finance*, 32(3): 961–964.

certainly not consistently over any period of time. Traditional investment managers strive to beat the market by taking advantage of pricing 'mistakes' and attempting to predict the future. Too often, this proves costly and futile. Predictions go awry and managers miss the strong returns that markets provide by holding the wrong stocks at the wrong time. Meanwhile, capital economies thrive – not because markets fail but because they succeed.

As we discussed in Chapter 5 investment markets throughout the world have a history of rewarding long-term investors for the capital they supply. Companies compete with each other for investment capital and millions of investors compete with each other to find the most attractive returns. This competition tends to drive prices to fair value, making it difficult for investors to achieve greater returns without bearing greater risk. The futility of speculation is good news for the investor. It means that prices for public securities are generally fair and persistent differences in average portfolio returns are largely explained by differences in average risk. It is certainly possible to outperform markets, but not, in general, without accepting increased risk.

Testing times for the efficient market hypothesis

Behavioural scientists have been critical of the efficient markets hypothesis, contending that investors' irrational behaviour causes greed to lead to asset price bubbles and fear to lead to price crashes. However, the behavioural school seems to now agree that the most practical solution for most investors is to hold a diversified portfolio based on one's own lifestyle goals and tolerance for risk. Professor Richard Thaler is a leading member of the behavioural school and now thinks that the recent financial crisis has strengthened the efficient markets hypothesis. In an article in the *Financial Times*, Professor Thaler explained his view:

> *'While markets could make mistakes, it was still impossible to profit from how they were wrong... Lunches are not free. Shorting internet stocks or Las Vegas real estate two years before the peak was a good recipe for bankruptcy, and no one had yet found a way to predict the end of a bubble.'*[2]

---

[2]   Professor Thaler (2009) 'The price is not always right', *Financial Times*, 5 August.

Concentrated risks can and do have big payoffs and so if you do want the highest returns possible, and can live with the highly probable consequences of failure, put all your eggs in the same basket, but watch that basket! The problem is that most concentrated risks are unlikely to be compensated. In other words, you are unlikely to be adequately rewarded for the risks that you take with such investments.

'The four most dangerous words in investing are, It's different this time.'

Sir John Templeton, legendary investor

Some comentators suggested that diversification failed during the financial crisis and 'this time it is different' and active asset allocation and stock selection are now key to investment success. All that the global credit crisis of 2008–2009 has proven is that markets can and do experience extreme price flucuations in response the rapid changes in economic conditions. The problem is a large body of investors started to believe an outcome that was, statistically, likely to happen once in a lifetime, would happen in someone else's lifetime, not their own! For example in the 12 months ended 31 December 2008 American Express returned –63.67% while Wal-Mart returned +19.95%. So even in a market meltdown some companies will do much better than others. The problem is correctly, and consistently, picking the winners in advance.

In the summer of 2009, just a few months after world stock markets hit their historic lows, Professor Eugene Fama – the man widely considered the father of the efficient market hypothesis – had this to say:

'The market can only know what is knowable. It can't resolve uncertainties that are unresolveable. So there is a large amount of economic uncertainty out there, there's going to be a large amount of volatility in prices. And that's what we've been through. As far as I'm concerned, that's exactly what you'd expect an efficient market to look like.'[3]

---

[3]   Fama, E. F. (2009) 'Fama on market efficiency in a volatile market', Fama/French Forum, Dimensional Fund Advisors, 11 August, **www.dimensional.com**

Harry Markowitz, an academic and Noble Laureate who is considered the father of modern financial economics with his theory of the efficient portfolio in the 1950s, had this to say about portfolio theory during the recent financial crisis:

> *'During a crisis almost all securities and asset classes will move in the same direction. This does not mean that individual securities are no longer subject to idiosyncratic risks. Rather it means that the* systematic risk swamps the unsystematic risk during this period.'[4]

Even large and apparently prosperous firms can fail. Take Enron for example, which was, for many years, a star performer of the stock market and appeared to have a very bright future. Within a matter of months the company imploaded and filed for bankruptcy. Shareholders in Enron suffered a total loss of their capital. BP is another example of a massive company that got into difficulty when it suffered a major accident at one of its oil wells in the Gulf of Mexico in 2010. As a consequence of suspending dividends and uncertainty about the eventual compensation costs arising, the share price fell from around £6.50 before the accident to just over £3 within six weeks of the accident, as investors reassessed the risks associated with holding BP shares. One year later the shares stood at only £4.50 as more information became available and BP resumed paying dividends, albeit at a lower level.

The folly of market timing

If it were possible to avoid the worse-performing investment days and capture returns from the best-performing days then it would be possible to produce both postive returns all the time and significant outperformance of the market as a whole. It is the allure of these potential high returns that causes many investors, both professional and non-professional, to ignore the reality of market efficiency and to speculate on the future direction of markets. The evidence shows that markets experience gains often in short, unpredictable bursts. This

---

[4] Markowitz, H. M., Hebner, M. T. and Brunson, M. E. (2009) 'Does portfolio theory work during financial crisis', **www.ifa.com/pdf/Does%20Portfolio%20Theory%20Work%20 HMM%20mbedits%205-19-09.pdf**

means that it is easy for an investment trader to enter and leave the investment market at the wrong time. Sometimes missing just a few – usually the best – days in the stock market can result in significant long-term underperformance. Taking the 15-year period (1990–2011) we can see in Figure 8.3 that missing the best 40 trading days would have cut the FTSE All-Share Index annualised compound return from nearly 7% to –4.69%.

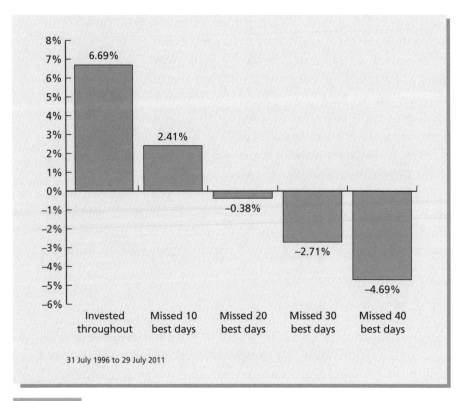

Figure 8.3   **Missing the best days in the UK stock market**

Source: Fidelity, FTSE. FTSE data published with the permission of FTSE.

Market timing is very challenging, as identified by a research study that looked at the US and UK stock markets from 1871 to 2004 and 1899 to 2004 respectively. The researchers compared a range of market timing approaches to a simple buy-and-hold strategy. While market timing techniques were found to work in identifying cheap and expensive markets resulting in a return differential over a buy-and-hold strategy, investors are still better off with a buy-and-hold approach. This is what the authors had to say:

> *'Our findings are not encouraging for proponents of active management using very long-run mean reversion: we find investors are inevitability better off with a simple buy-and-hold equity strategy rather than trying to time the market using moving average rules.'*

> *'The returns from equities, even during the sub-optimal periods when they are expensive, have been markedly better than cash.'*[5]

Bulls and bears

Investment markets have been described as voting machines in the short term, reflecting current sentiment based on news and other economic data, but weighing machines in the long term, reflecting the value of current and future earnings and dividends generated by companies. When stock markets are experiencing strong increases in valuation they are described as a bull market. When they are experiencing severe reductions in value then they are described as a bear market. When markets are not moving either up or down much they are described as 'range bound'. History suggests that bull market cycles last longer than bear market cycles and produce cumulative gains that more than offset losses experienced in bear markets. Figure 8.4 shows the time and magnitude of those rises and falls for the UK stock market over the past 55 years.[6]

---

[5] Gwilym, O., Secton, J. and Thomas, S. (2008) 'Very long-term equity investment strategies', *The Journal of Investing*, 17(2): 15–23.

[6] The graph in Figure 8.4 documents bull and bear market periods in the FTSE All-Share Index from February 1955 to December 2010. The market cycles are identified in hindsight using historical cumulative monthly returns. Monthly index returns are total returns, which include reinvestment of dividends. All monthly observations are performed after the fact. A bear market is identified in hindsight when the market experiences a negative monthly return followed by a cumulative loss of at least 10%. The bear market ends at its low point, which is defined as the month of the greatest negative cumulative return before the reversal. A bull market is defined by data points not considered part of a bear market. The rising trend lines designate the bull markets occurring since 1955, while the falling trend lines document the bear markets. The bars that frame the trend lines help to describe the length and intensity of the gains and losses. The numbers above or below the bars indicate the duration (in months) and cumulative return percentage of the bull or bear market.

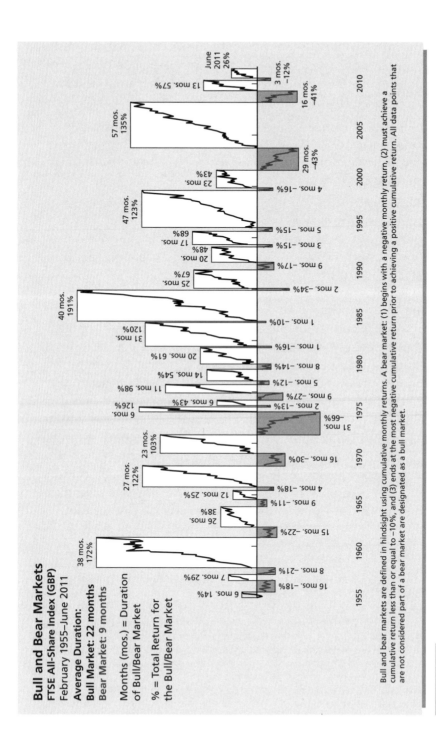

Figure 8.4 The past 55 years of bull & bear stock markets

Source: Dimensional Fund Advisors. FTSE data published with the permission of FTSE.

The chart in Figure 8.4 does not show total compounded returns or growth of wealth. Once the cycle is established in retrospect, the first month of that cycle resets the performance baseline to zero. Fluctuating performance within each trend illustrates that volatility and uncertainty occur even within established market cycles: bull markets may have short-term dips and bear markets may have short-term advances. The immediate trend is not readily apparent to market observers and may become clear only in hindsight. This analysis highlights the difficulty of accurately predicting and timing market cycles and the importance of maintaining a disciplined investment approach that views market events and trends from a long-term perspective. If you react emotionally to short-term movements you are likely to make bad decisions that compromise long-term performance.

Do managers beat markets?

There is no credible evidence of persistence of success of active investment management and that success outperformance cannot, in the vast majority of cases, be explained by exposure to risk factors. One study examined 115 US equity mutual funds between 1945 and 1964 and found 'very little evidence that any mutual fund was able to do significantly better than that which we expect from mere random chance'.[7] Another study examined 4,686 US equity mutual funds between 1965 and 1998 and found 'none of the styles included in the study are able to generate positive abnormal returns, compared to the Fama/French (1993) benchmark'.[8]

> 'All the time and effort that people devote to picking the right fund, the hot hand, the great manager, have in most cases led to no advantage.'[9]

Peter Lynch, ledgendary US fund manager

A report prepared for the Norwegian government found that: 'The average active return from January 1998 to September 2009 generated by Norges Bank Investment Management has been statistically

---

[7] Jensen, M. (1968) 'The performance of mutual funds in the period 1945–1964', *Journal of Finance*, 23(2): 414.

[8] Davis, J. L. (2001) 'Mutual fund performance and manager style', *Financial Analysts' Journal*, 57(1): 19–27.

[9] Lynch, P. (1993) *Beating the Street*, Simon & Schuster, p. 60.

indistinguishable from zero.'[10] Recent research[11] into the results arising from both passive and active investment management examined
active manager outperformance (known as 'real alpha') in five full
investment market cycles over the past 30 years. It concluded that in
68% of the sectors, time frames and investment cycles under analysis, passive investment strategies were either better than or the same as
active investment strategies. It also made the point that where active
funds did outperform passive ones, those funds tended to have below
average fees and charges. In other words, most outperformance was
dissipated by high costs in the majority of cases.

Another paper examined the empirical evidence and logic for investing using a passive approach in the UK by reviewing UK-based equity
and bond funds over the 15-year period through to 31 March 2010.
After deducting the results of all the funds that were closed in that
period only about 30% of UK large cap equity funds beat the market
and virtually no funds beat the market for UK-government bonds over
ten years. The authors came to the following conclusion:

> 'Active managers fight against the tide of higher costs... We believe that the
> evidence supports the case for investing using an asset allocation model that fits
> an investor's needs, objectives and risk tolerance, rather than trying to pick best
> performing funds.'[12]

Time after time, analysis of past performance shows that the majority
of active investment managers deliver returns below that of the market
as a whole. Figure 8.5 shows the returns from over 130 UK equity
funds that existed during 1990 to 2009. We can see that the majority of managers (and don't forget that this excludes all the funds that
never survived 20 years) underperformed the market as represented by
the FTSE All-Share Index, which is consistent with the principles of
efficient markets.

---

[10] Ang, A., Goetzmann, W. N, Schaefer, S. M. (2009) 'Evaluation of active management of
the Norwegian Government Pension Fund – global', Ministry of Finance, Norway, p. 65.

[11] Li, J. (2010) 'When active management shines vs. passive: Examining real alpha in 5 full
market cycles over the past 30 years', Fund Quest White Paper, pp. 11–12.

[12] Molitor, J. S., Philip, C. and Cole, C. W. (2010) 'The case index fund investing in the
UK', Vanguard Research, December.

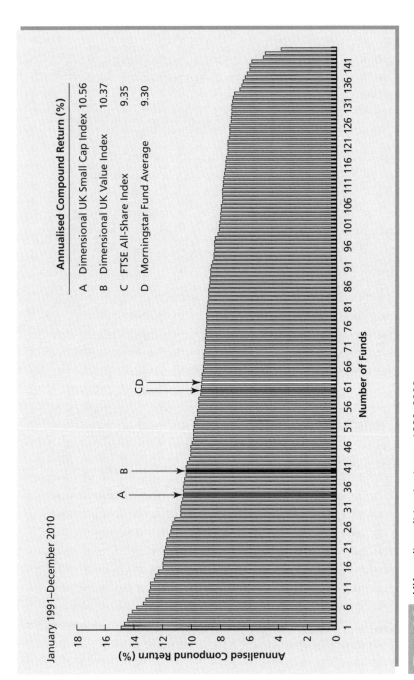

Figure 8.5 UK equity unit trust returns: 1990–2009

Source: Dimensional Fund Advisors, Inc. Morningstar data provided by Morningstar Inc. Includes all equity funds in the Morningstar categories UK Large Cap and UK Mid/Small Cap with 20-year returns, oldest share class only, as at 31 December 2010. FTSE published with the permission of FTSE. Dimensional index data simulated by Dimensional from Bloomberg and StyleResearch securities data; not available for direct investment. Past performance is no guarantee of future results.

'There are two kinds of investors, be they large or small: those who don't know where the market is headed, and those who don't know that they don't know. Then again, there is a third type of investor – the investment professional, who indeed knows that he or she doesn't know, but whose livelihood depends upon appearing to know.'

William Bernstein, US financial theorist and author

Random chance dictates that at any one time we would expect a small number of money managers to outperform the market average. The problem is they are rarely the same managers each time and picking the winning managers in advance is virtually impossible to do consistently. A large group of chimpanzees throwing darts at the share pages of the *Financial Times* has more chance of picking winning shares than a group of experienced equities analysts!

The issue of luck verses skill is rarely addressed in academic studies. A recent working paper[13] from the respected finance professors Fama and French, however, looked at whether or not individual fund performance was distinguishable from luck. The key findings were that active managers show no statistical evidence they can enhance returns and they do not have enough skill to produce risk-adjusted returns which cover their costs. Only the top 3% of funds perform as well as might be expected if their true alpha (excess return) was down to luck. A key conclusion of the authors was that 'Some [funds] do extraordinarily well and some do extraordinarily poorly just by chance.'

In his book[14], *The Wisdom of Crowds*, James Surowiecki gives a very good example of why the aggregate view is generally right more often than not. He cites an ox weight-judging contest held at the 1906 West of England Fat Stock and Poultry Exhibition. The average weight guessed by the 797 contestants was 1,197 pounds compared to the actual weight of 1,198. In another example, a Professor Treynor asked his finance class students to guess how many beans were in a jar. There were in fact 850 beans in the jar compared to the group estimate of 871. Only one of 56 students made a more accurate guess.

---

[13] Fama, E. F. and French, K. R. (2009) 'Luck versus skill in the cross-section of mutual fund returns', Tuck School of Business Working Paper No. 2009–56, Chicago Booth School of Business Research Paper and Journal of Finance, LXV(5): 1915–1947.

[14] Surowiecki, J. (2005) *The Wisdom of Crowds*, Anchor.

'People are overly impressed by the performance of money managers... It's difficult to realise that you would get very similar patterns if there was no skill at all.'[15]

Daniel H. Kahneman Nobel Laureate 2002

Winning the loser's game

Active investment management is a zero sum game before costs and a loser's game after costs – for every winner there has to be a loser and costs reduce returns. In aggregate the maths does not support the proposition that there is a credible, reliable and replicable way of consistently outwitting the investment marketplace. None of us is smarter than all of us. Every penny that you save in costs is either more returns for you or you can take less risk to obtain the same level of return. See Figure 8.6.

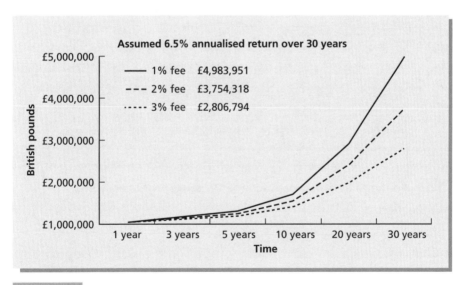

Figure 8.6 Impact of different annual fund costs on investment values over 30 years

---

[15] Kahneman, D. and Riepe, M. (1988) 'Aspects of investor psychology', *Journal of Portfolio Management*, Summer.

There are two main costs associated with investment funds, total expense ratios (TERs) and turnover. TERs include ongoing costs like trustee and custodian fees. Turnover costs include the hard costs to the fund of buying and selling investments as well as the impact that buying and selling has on the price of the investments. Recent analysis (Figure 8.7) shows that the average annual expenses ratio charged on UK equity investment funds is 1.63.

> *'After costs, the return on the average actively managed dollar will be less than the return on the average passively managed dollar for any time period.'*[16]

William F. Sharpe, 1990 Nobel Laureate

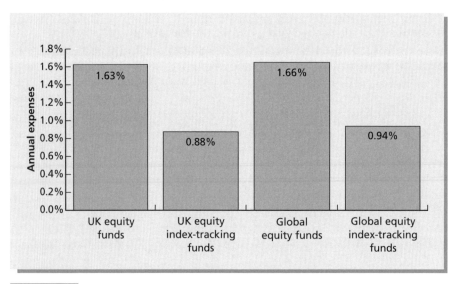

Figure 8.7   Average annual expense ratios on UK equity investment funds

Source: Fitzrovia, 2010.

A summary of the most recent research papers on the issue of portfolio turnover and trading costs suggests that 'an argument could be made for the straightforward, yet conservative assumption of trading costs attributing to performance drag of 1% (for 100% annual turnover)'.[17]

---

[16] Sharpe, W. F. (1991) 'The arithmetic of active management', Financial Analysts' Journal, 47(1): 7–9.

[17] Ed Moission, Head of Research, Lipper Fitzrovia, suggested this view in correspondence with the author.

The odds in terms of costs are so heavily stacked against active management it is no surprise that persistency of outperformance is so low. If you have to recoup an annual cost of 2.6 per cent (comprising the annual charges and the effect of turnover within the fund) just to break even then failure seems assured.

Charles Ellis, in his seminal book *Winning the Loser's Game*, explained how to be an investing winner:

> 'The objective of beating the market is in fact a loser's game and that most people striving to beat the market actually have very unhappy experiences. They do not succeed. And, when I say most I'm not talking about 52% or 55%, I'm talking about 85 or 90%. So, the first part is do not play the game you will not win, which is I'm going to beat the market, here I go. There's an alternative where you can easily win and, therefore I would call it a winning game. And, the winner's game is what is it you're really trying to accomplish, what would work really well for you? And, then go about that specific objective. And, each of us has different characteristics of what we're trying to do. Sometimes the characteristics have to do with how long you're going to stay invested. If you're investing for the very, very long time… I have a three year old, a six year old and two three year old boys as my grandchildren. Any investments that they're making are investments for 80 years – that's a long time. And, they can invest differently than could someone who was saving to buy a home or saving for college or saving for some other specific purpose that's going to come up in a year or two. So, your time horizon's number one.'[18]

Even the State doesn't recommend active management

In 2011 the UK government launched the National Employment Savings Trust (NEST), a new government-controlled, compulsory pension savings scheme aimed at low-to-moderate earners and their employers who do not currently have pension savings in place. There are five investment asset classes available: global equities; conventional gilts; index-linked gilts; cash and diversified global growth. The tendering process for appointing investment managers for these asset classes made it clear that only passive fund managers could apply for the first three catagories.

---

[18] Ellis, C. (2009) *Winning the Loser's Game: Timeless strategies for successful investing*, McGraw-Hill.

In the case of the last two categories there is still a presumption in favour of passive approaches. The management fee on the cash component is so low that it might as well be passively managed, with the main function of the manager being to manage the risk of a capital loss from a deposit taker. As for the diversified global growth asset class, NEST's chief investment officer Mark Fawcett stated at the time of the fund manager tendering process that this will be a core of passive holdings but with a small element of non-tactical active management. Given that the annual management charge will initailly be capped at 0.30% per annum, it is unlikely that many hedge fund managers will be queuing up to manage the diversified growth!

The passive detractors

This chapter would not be complete without highlighting research that puts the case for active management. A recent research paper[19] that, on the face of it, gives some support for active management analysed 31,991 UK mutual funds (excluding index funds) in 73 categories over 30 years through to February 2010, representing $7 trillion of assets. Returns before costs (which has the effect of flattering active management returns) were then compared to the appropriate indices (after removing obsolete funds) to identify whether or not active managers had delivered excess return over the market (known as alpha). The findings were that, of the 73 categories, active management was recommended in 23, passive in 22 and in 28 the case was neutral.

The author's main conclusion was as follows:

> 'Our studies have found that both types of investing have their strengths and weaknesses. It depends on the market segments and the economic climate. We believe investors should utilize a blend of both active and passive investing with the goal of optimizing their portfolio.'[20]

The first observation is the staggering fund selection choice faced by investors – nearly 20,000 funds, of which 12,000 failed to survive! Also it is interesting to note that even on a gross performance basis

---

[19] Li, J. (2010) 'When active management shines vs. passive: Examining real alpha in 5 full market cycles over the past 30 years, FundQuest White paper.

[20] Ibid, p. 2.

(i.e. before deduction of costs), active management was not the preferred approach in many major categories: inflation-protected bonds, government bonds, world bonds, foreign equities, global real estate and commodities. If costs had been taken into account, then the proportion of cases when active management would have been recommended would have been even lower. The conclusion that active and passive investing are not rivals but complementary is not justified by this paper and its somewhat biased approach.

Making a choice

Having looked at a range of the available evidence there are several key questions that you need to answer.

- Do you believe that an active manager can, after adjusting for risk factors like the value and smaller companies premiums, beat the market after costs from skill?
- If a manager can show that they have demonstrated skill in the past that has caused outperformance of the market rather than exposure to risk factors, do you think that they can consistently do so over time?
- How confident are you that you can predict which manager will have the skill to provide this outperformance?
- How will you manage the risk of style drift?
- How will you manage your emotions and make rational decisions if the manager is underperforming?
- What will you do if the manager leaves (and managers move around quite a lot)?

My view is that a non-predictive, index/asset class strategy should be your default investment approach unless you have a high conviction an active investment approach will be successful; you disbelieve the evidence; or you need to believe active investment management works.

> 'Most investors, both institutional and individual, will find that the best way to own common stocks is through an index fund that charges minimal fees.'[21]

> Warren Buffett, Chairman, Berkshire Hathaway Corporation

Diversification is the only free lunch (don't put all your eggs in one basket!) Because we don't know which asset classes will produce the best return or the lowest risk at any given point in the future, by combining them in varying proportions, we can avoid or reduce the probability of big losses and participate in the returns that markets do deliver.

---

[21] Chairman's letter, Berkshire Hathaway 1995 annual report **www.berkshirehathaway.com**

9

Options for investing

Whatever investment approach you follow, you and/or your adviser will need to use investment funds to gain access to the various investment asset classes. Investment funds provide effective diversification as your capital is pooled with that of other investors to gain exposure to the underlying investment holdings. In the UK, investment funds are either regulated or unregulated. Unregulated funds may not be promoted to most investors, unless the investor is assessed by someone authorised under the Financial Services Act as being exempt from the prohibition. Unregulated funds do not have to comply with any of the regulatory rules that cover things like diversification, pricing, gearing and security.

Unregulated funds, therefore, have additional risks over and above pure investment risks, which are associated with how they are operated. You should avoid unregulated funds because carrying out effective due diligence is difficult and in most situations there are plenty of suitable alternative regulated funds.

Only regulated funds may be promoted to members of the public in the UK because they are subject to detailed rules on how the fund must be operated and administered. There are three main types of regulated investment fund:

- unit trusts, open-ended investment companies (OEICs) and Société d'Investissement à Capital Variable (SICAVs – open-ended collective investment schemes)
- exchange-traded funds (ETFs)
- investment trusts.

Unit trusts, OEICs and SICAVs

These are open-ended funds in that investors purchase units from the fund manager who then invests their capital in a range of investments according to the mandate of the fund (e.g. UK smaller companies). When investors want their money back they sell their units back to the fund manager. If more money is received from new investors than is being repaid to investors who are leaving the fund then the manager can just create more units, and vice versa. In most open-ended funds the manager usually holds some of the fund in cash to meet day-to-day redemptions from investors. Over the long term, holding any of the funds in cash will serve to reduce investment returns compared to a fund that is always fully invested. In addition, if large numbers of investors all require their money back at the same time, then the investment manager can be forced to sell some of the fund's more liquid and favoured holdings to meet those redemptions, thus potentially having an adverse impact on long-term performance.

A majority of open-ended funds also tend to be relatively expensive, with a range of internal costs that are not easy to identify, which will dampen long-term returns. The total expenses ratio (TER) measures the cost of annual management fees and a range of other fixed costs such as custody, trustee and audit fees. The TER does not, however, measure the cost of trading incurred within the portfolio. As explained in the previous chapter, transaction costs have a direct impact on the level of investment returns. TERs are, however, falling and it is now possible to buy an OEIC that tracks the FTSE All-Share Index with a TER of 0.15% pa.

Open-ended funds are usually traded once a day at 12 p.m. based on the underlying portfolio value the previous day. This is not usually a problem for long-term investors but it can be very restrictive for investors who want to trade at other times in the day or when markets are moving very quickly.

In terms of investor protection, most OEICs and unit trusts will be subject to supervision by the UK regulator and covered by the Financial Services Protection Scheme, in the event of financial failure of either the fund manager or the fund being unable to meet its obligations.

Exchange-traded funds (ETFs)

These are a relatively recent development in the retail investment world, although they originate from the institutional investment world, where they have been used for many years to gain investment exposure to different asset classes. The market for ETFs has grown from just over $50 billion in 2005 to $750 billion in 2010[1] and this is expected to continue to grow (see Figure 9.1). There are ETFs covering almost every type of asset class, from the largest and most liquid asset classes like US equities to the smallest and most esoteric ones like Mexican smaller companies!

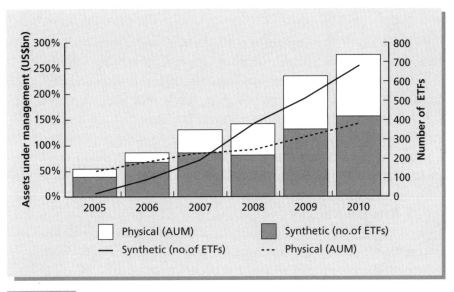

Figure 9.1 Growth of funds held within ETFs

Source: BlackRock

An ETF fund is represented by shares that are listed on the Stock Exchange, with the share price reflecting the value of the underlying investment portfolio. The manager of the fund acts as the marketmaker and ensures that there is a liquid market in the shares so that buyers and sellers can be matched. If there are more buyers than sellers in the

---

[1] Financial Services Authority (2011), *Retail Conduct Risk Outlook*, March, p. 70.

market then the fund manager can create more shares and if there are more sellers than buyers they will buy those shares and cancel them to reflect the redemption of those funds.

ETFs are used to provide access to a range of asset classes, the majority of which are passive, although some are actively managed. Some funds obtain investment exposure by buying all or some of the underlying holdings in proportion to the index it is seeking to track – known as 'physical replication'. Other funds use what are known as 'swaps' (where the fund manager pays another counterparty, such as an investment bank, to provide the return of the index or market to which exposure is desired) to obtain such exposure. This is also known as 'synthetic replication', more of which later.

ETF costs tend to be competitive but are often higher than other nil commission collective funds. For most long-term investors, however, ETFs hold no particular benefit over traditional, low-cost, open-ended funds, other than where the desired asset class is only available via an ETF. A final point worth making about ETFs is the position of investor protection in the event of the failure of the fund manager causing a loss to investors. In many cases ETFs listed on the London Stock Exchange hold funds that are domiciled elsewhere in the EU, such as Luxembourg and Ireland, and as a result are neither supervised by the UK financial regulator nor covered by the UK Financial Services Protection Scheme. Non-UK-domiciled ETFs are supervised by their own regulator and covered by investor compensation protection that may be different from that provided to UK domiciled funds.

Investment trusts

Investment trusts are listed companies that invest in other companies. The underlying portfolio is managed by a professional fund manager, usually on an active basis but a small number of investment trusts are run on a passive basis. Investment trusts are described as closed-ended because there are a set number of shares in issue and investors buy shares in the trust through the stock market. The value of the underlying portfolio of the trust is called the net asset value (NAV).

Most of the time the share price of investment trusts trade below their NAV to reflect the fact that there are usually more sellers than buyers (institutions are long-term sellers of investment trusts). The typical discount is about 5% but some trusts trade at much higher discounts. This means that with, say, a 5% share price discount to the NAV the investor obtains 100% of the investment returns for only 95% of the cost. If the discount doesn't change or it narrows (i.e. the share price increases more than the NAV) then this is a good deal. If, however, the discount widens then this has a negative impact and the share price can fall even if the underlying investment portfolio hasn't.

When a trust trades at a very large discount to its NAV it can be a sign that there is low confidence in the underlying investment manager or the trust's investment approach. For example Alliance Trust plc is one of the oldest and largest international general investment trusts and it has traded at a significant discount for some years (15% at the time of writing). Over the past few years hedge fund investors have built up large stakes in the trust and have been lobbying the manager to make changes to the way the trust is managed in the hope that this will cause a narrowing of the discount of the share price to NAV.

When demand for shares in a trust is very strong and/or the manager buys back and cancels shares in issue, the share price will rise quicker than the NAV and will trade at either a very small discount, the same as the NAV or, in some cases, a higher value to the underlying NAV (see Figure 9.2). A share price above the NAV is known as a premium and is effectively an additional charge for accessing the underlying portfolio.

Historically, investment trusts have had lower costs than open-ended funds, but this is mainly because most do not pay sales commission to brokers and advisers. This advantage is being eroded by the growth of investment platforms and the introduction of nil commission open-ended funds ahead of the banning of adviser commission in 2013. Investment trusts are covered by the same regulatory oversight and investor protection as open-ended funds. In general, investment trusts do not represent the most efficient means of obtaining investment exposure over a low-cost, open-ended fund, mainly due to the issues around discounts and premiums to the NAV potentially distorting returns.

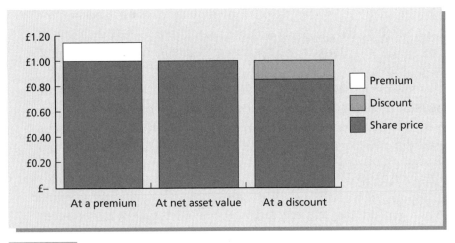

Figure 9.2   Investment trust pricing

Passive management approaches

As explained in the previous chapter, I recommend that you use passive funds to obtain asset class exposure. The question then arises as to what type of passive funds you should use.

Most ETFs and tracker funds aim to replicate the performance of a basket of securities by reference to an 'official' index like the MSCI World or FTSE UK All-Share Index. The problem with most of the official indices is that they include many securities that either dilute or skew the return of the required asset class. Take for instance the FTSE All-Share, which includes investment companies and foreign companies that have a listing in London. Investment companies invest in other companies and so represent a dilution of the asset class. A South African mining company, for example, isn't really representative of a UK equity but is, in fact, more an emerging market equity, which would be better held within an emerging market fund.

In the case of the FTSE 100 Index, each quarter the index is reconstituted based on the market prices and number of shares in issue and this inevitably leads to companies being added and removed from the index. Because such changes happen on pre-set dates, other market participants can take advantage of a traditional index managers' need to buy shares that have been added to the index or to sell those that have left it, because an index portfolio manager needs to maintain a portfolio that matches the index composition as closely as possible. The consequence is that prices rise prior to a company's inclusion in the index and then decay shortly afterwards (see Figure 9.3). Over the longer term this can have the effect of reducing (or dampening) returns from a traditional index fund. However, the phenomenon is a bit like high cholesterol; you don't notice it at first and it is not explicit but the effect compounds over time to have a significant negative impact on the returns you receive.

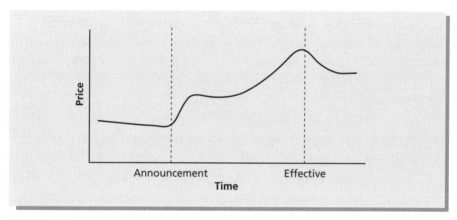

Figure 9.3   Price impact when an equity joins the index

When a company is first listed on a stock market, its initial listing value is determined by the sponsoring investment bank and broker based on what they think the market will pay for the shares. Several pieces of research[2] suggest that most initial public offerings (IPOs) go on to experience relatively poor performance over the next five years or so. Clearly some companies experience price rises after they are listed but a significant majority does not. Traditional index funds and ETFs must buy into these new IPOs as they enter the index, causing them to buy shares that more often than not will experience a decline in value while investors determine the true market value.

---

[2] Loughran, T. and Ritter J. R. (1995) 'The new issues puzzle', *Journal of Finance*, 50(1); Ritter, J. R. (2009) *Some Factoids About the 2009 IPO Market*, University of Florida; Gregory, A., Guermat, C. and Al-Shawawreh, F. (2010) 'UK IPOs: Long run returns, behavioural timing and pseudo timing (2009–11)', *Journal of Business Finance & Accounting*, 37(5–6): 612–47.

A good example of an IPO that entered the FTSE 250 Index is Betfair plc. The company was listed on the London Stock Exchange in October 2010 with an opening price of £13 and by the end of its first day of trading it had risen 20% to close at £15.50. The sponsoring banks – Barclays Capital, Goldman Sachs and Morgan Stanley – all hailed the float a success and more than justified their £15 million of arranging and underwriting fees. Sadly the share price has drifted down since then and six months later was trading at just under £9, representing a fall of over 30% from the offer price for a company that is profitable and seems to be recession-proof!

Some companies that make up the index can be in extreme financial distress and might be near to receivership. Until the shares are suspended an index manager is compelled to buy shares in that company in proportion to the index, even if it is evident that the company is in dire financial condition.

Is the index an appropriate representation of the market?

Stock market indices are not designed as an optimal investment proposition (the first index funds only appeared in the early 1970s, long after indices were introduced). Consequently, some indices are less useful than others when it comes to representing the market they measure. The levels of the US Dow Jones Industrial Average and the Japanese Nikkei 225 Index, for example, are determined solely by the prices of the constituents, so a movement in a single security can give rise to a large index movement; the market capitalisation of the constituents is not considered.

There are four main ways that passive funds obtain returns on the various asset classes as follows.

1 Full replication

This is where the manager chooses an appropriate index, e.g. the FTSE All-Share Index and then buys all the underlying holdings that make up that index in as near to the same proportions as the index as possible. Consequently this method is mostly used to track the largest and most liquid markets. As well as the price effect explained previously, full replication usually generates relatively high trading costs (dealing commissions and the spread between buying and selling prices) and market impact costs (the tendency of prices to move against the investor when they place large trades). Almost all index managers who use this approach carry out stock lending – lending their investments to other investors in return for a fee.

2 Stratified sampling

This is where the manager uses a sophisticated computer program to buy a range of holdings that represent a reasonable proxy for the index being followed and that can be expected to display almost the same risk and reward characteristics. This approach usually gives the manager more flexibility on what is bought and sold (thus reducing market impact costs) and should also have lower explicit costs than full replication. It does, however, also have a higher likelihood of having performance that is different from the index that it is seeking to track, as the portfolio itself will differ from the index. Such funds also engage in stock lending.

Stock lending – who benefits?

Stock lending gives rise to two important questions on which investors need to be clear. First, what security is taken by the manager to protect their investors? Some funds accept bank guarantees while others insist upon a third party holding liquid securities that are at least twice the value of the securities lent. Second, how much of the stock lending fee is passed back to investors in the fund? BlackRock, for example, which owns the iShares range of ETFs, retains 40% of such income and passes 60% to investors in its funds, whereas Dimensional Fund Advisers and Vanguard pass 100% back to investors in their funds.

---

3 Synthetic or swap-based replication

This is where the fund manager uses 'swaps' or other derivatives to obtain exposure to the chosen asset class, rather than physically buying the underlying investments. The manager gives the ETF's capital to an institution that undertakes to deliver the index return on that capital. In exchange, the ETF manager takes security over or possession of other assets of at least equal value to the capital given to the institution, so as to provide protection in the event the institution goes bust. The contractual undertaking from the third party (such as an investment bank) to provide the return of the asset and security, in the form of other assets from the bank, introduces what is known as *counter-party* and *collateral* risk.

Sometimes, the assets pledged as security to the ETF manager can be illiquid and this can introduce additional problems if the counterparty providing the index goes bust and the EFT manager needs to liqui-date the assets that were provided as security. Selling illiquid assets in a hurry invariably involves some compromise in terms of the price that the seller must accept! Funds that use 'synthetic replication' may, therefore, represent a higher risk than physical replication as they rely on the financial security of the various counterparties (the participat-ing investment banks) and their ability to honour their obligations associated with the 'swaps' contract as well as the quality of the col-lateral held as security.[3] Lehman Brothers is a recent example of what can happen when a counterparty fails. It is estimated by its admin-istrators that when the bank failed in 2008 it had nearly a million contracts worth around $45 billion of swaps outstanding, of which nearly 90% still remained unsettled in March 2011.

4 Pure asset class (PAC) or rules-based funds

These were originally developed in the 1980s to provide a low-cost and more effective exposure to US smaller companies. Such funds seek to avoid the key problems associated with tracking an index and have the following features.

■ They create their own definition of the asset class and which holdings can and cannot be included, for example removing investment companies, utilities or other restricted securities and avoiding recent IPOs.

■ In addition to having a more flexible approach over which holdings may be included in the asset class, the manager has a flexible trading policy that does not force them to buy or sell specific securities on set days.

■ Because the manager has a flexible trading policy, they can take advantage of difficult trading conditions by being able to buy, at a discount to normal market price, securities that others need to turn

---

[3] Financial *Stability* Board (2011), 'Potential financial stability issues arising from recent trends in exchange-traded funds (ETFs)', April.

into cash. Recent research[4] suggests that this could add between 0.60 and 0.80% per annum to the asset class return alone.

■ The unit price is the same for buyers and sellers and there is no need for complex and costly trading activity to achieve this.

■ All stock-lending income is passed back to investors in the fund.

■ Some PAC funds have a slight exposure (known as a tilt) towards smaller and financially depressed companies (known as value companies) and this provides an expected return premium over the main stock market due to the higher risk of these companies.[5]

■ Management fees on PACs are generally much lower and trading costs a fraction of those incurred by actively managed funds on average and generally at the lower end of traditional index funds, as illustrated in Figures 9.4 and 9.5.

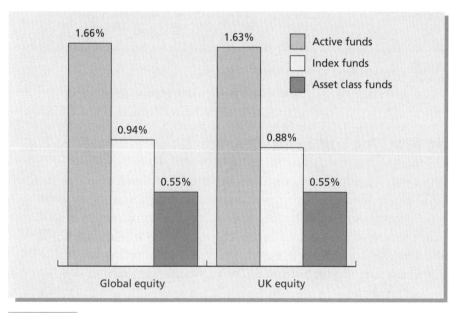

Figure 9.4 Average fund total expense ratios

Sources: Fitzrovia UK Fund Charges January 2011; Dimensional OEIC TERs per Report and Acounts December 2010, audited; Dimensional UCIT TERs per Report and Accounts, November 2010, audited

---

4   Wahal, S. (2010) 'Trading advantages of flexible portfolios', **www.dfa.com**, p. 1.

5   Expected return premium on DFA UK Core Equity Index of 0.97% pa and risk of 2.25% compared to return drag on FTSE 100 of –0.41% pa and risk of 2.52%. This is based on simulated index data from January 1993 to December 2010. (*Source*: Dimensional Fund Advisors.)

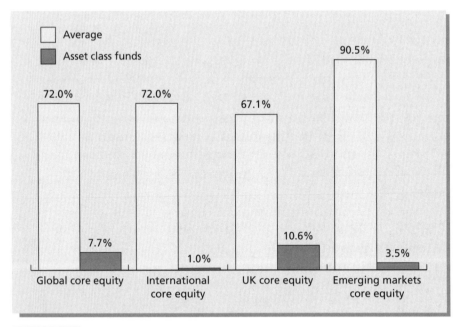

Figure 9.5 Average fund turnover data

Sources: Fitzrovia Portfolio Turnover of UK Funds December 2010; Dimensional internal information, December 2010, audited

What are the *full* costs?

Any portfolio, index fund or ETF that slavishly follows an index (as its mandate requires), whichever method of replication it uses, will have to carry out regular buying and selling of holdings and this generates *turnover* costs. Obviously, actively managed portfolios and funds also experience portfolio turnover, which is also usually considerably higher than for passive portfolios. The higher the turnover, the higher the trading costs.

Trading costs come in two forms: **hard** trading costs include dealing charges, spreads between buying and selling prices and stamp duty, while **soft** costs such as market impact costs (which are a function of the liquidity of a security) are largely hidden but still erode the investor's return.

Based on several independent studies over a period of ten years, Fitzrovia,[6] a respected financial research organisation, suggests it is reasonable to assume that a fund experiencing 100% turnover in a year leads to an annual performance drag of around 1%.

> 'We estimate trading costs for a large sample of equity funds and find that they are comparable in magnitude to the expense ratio'.[7]

Another difference between ETFs and open-ended index funds, such as unit trusts or open-ended investment companies (OEICs), is how the share or unit price is calculated to represent the value of the underlying index. With an open-ended fund the manager sells and buys back units based on the value of the underlying securities, known as the net asset value (NAV). ETF shares are traded on a stock exchange and as a result supply and demand can cause the share price to deviate from the NAV. To keep the ETF share price in line with the NAV, the ETF manager relies on what is known as a 'spread arbitrage mechanism'. This means that institutional investors (usually the bank sponsoring the ETF) undertake complex trading that has the effect of allowing them to profit from positive or negative differences in the share price compared to the NAV of the ETF after accounting for trading costs.

This arbitrage mechanism usually works very well in the largest and most liquid markets such as US or UK large companies, as the costs incurred have a negligible impact on the accuracy with which the fund tracks the index. However, in smaller and less liquid markets, such as international smaller companies or emerging market companies, the transaction and execution costs are much higher and, as such, the ETF will usually produce a return quite a bit lower than the index (known as a negative tracking error). Over the long term this tracking error adds up to a loss of return to the investor and is one that many ETF enthusiasts rarely mention.

---

6   Moisson, E. (2011) 'Trading costs: research review', Lipper Fitzrovia, April.
7   Edelen, R. M., Evans, R. and Kadlec, G. B. (2007) 'Scale effects in mutual fund performance: The role of trading costs', Working Paper, 17 March.

Other types of investment funds
Fund of funds (FOFs)

This is an investment fund that invests in other investment funds. The idea being that the investor obtains access to several managers who are all specialists in their respective areas, overseen by the main professional manager who does all the initial and ongoing due diligence. The manager of the main fund decides which funds/managers to invest in and when to move money to other managers based on their performance.

FOFs are often used to obtain alternative investment strategies like hedge funds, where due diligence and fund costs can be prohibitive for most individual investors. They are, however, extensively used to provide standard investment exposure, particularly by financial services companies that do not offer their own, in-house, investment management service. The manager of the FOFs levies an annual management charge on top of the annual charges levied by the underlying fund managers. The additional costs involved in most FoFs make them unattractive for most investors although if you are keen to obtain exposure to alternative investments they might be useful.

Target/lifestyle funds

Target funds are a type of FOFs managed with the intention of meeting a known objective or liability at a specific date in the future. Target funds have a range of dates with the minimum being ten years. Initially the manager pursues capital growth through exposure to risky assets such as equities. As the target date approaches, the manager gradually reduces exposure to equities in favour of increased exposure to more defensive assets like bonds and cash. The change in asset allocation takes place over several years so that by the time the fund meets the target date the fund holds no risky assets and, as such, it cannot fall in value. This is shown graphically in Figure 9.6.

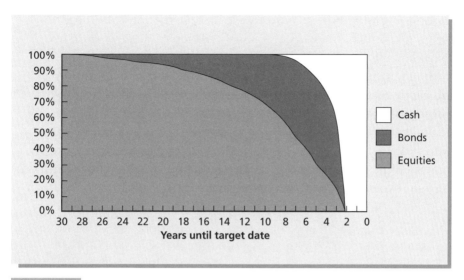

100%
90%
80%
70%
60%   Cash
50%   Bonds
40%
30%   Equities
20%
10%
0%
30 28 26 24 22 20 18 16 14 12 10 8 6 4 2 0
Years until target date

Figure 9.6   How target funds work

While target funds do, on the face of it, appear to offer an attractive and hassle-free way of investing a lump sum for a specific need at a known date in the future, particularly for modest amounts or those investing in retirement funds, they suffer from a number of drawbacks that make them unattractive for most affluent and wealthy investors including:

■ higher costs due to active management charges and/or duplication of fund costs

■ may not capture all available returns by reducing exposure to risky assets (which have a higher expected return) too soon

■ accessing funds before the target date may be either not permitted or subject to penalty

■ requires the investor to commit to having their funds managed by the chosen target fund provider for the term until the chosen target date (great for the fund manager but not so good for the investor who is unhappy with performance and wants out).

In choosing what type of fund to use in your portfolio you need to weigh up cost, counterparty risk, asset class return method, liquidity, tax treatment and investor protection. If you are using the services of a portfolio manager or wealth manager then you need to make sure you are happy that these factors have been considered by them. You have a right to expect your adviser to have carefully researched the types of funds that they use and to have a detailed rationale they can share with you. There is no point having a great wealth plan and investment strategy if the funds you use are not up to the job or have hidden risks that go beyond those applying to the asset class in general.

10

Other investment considerations

There are a number of other issues that you need to consider in relation to your investment strategy and these include:

- the impact of dividends on investment returns
- the impact of regular withdrawals from your portfolio
- the importance of rebalancing your portfolio
- the use of debt and investing.

Impact of dividends on overall investment returns

It is regularly stated that reinvested dividends make a big difference to overall equity investment returns over the medium to long term. This is well illustrated by Figure 10.1 that shows the FTSE All-Share Index with and without net dividends reinvested over the past 30 years.

I've heard some investment 'experts' suggest that high dividend-paying shares are better to own because they pay you for owning them and that in difficult investment conditions investors are somehow more likely to retain ownership of dividend-paying shares than those which pay no or a very low dividend. Research[1] suggests that high dividend-yielding stocks may be more risky and indeed the dividend

---

[1]   Miller, M. and Modigliani, F. (1961) 'Dividend policy, growth, and the valuation of shares', *Journal of Business*, 34(4): 411–33.

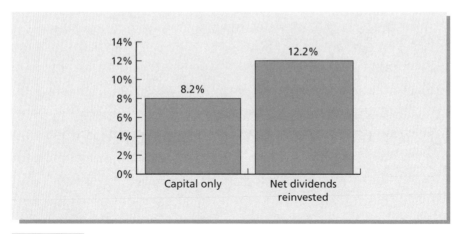

Figure 10.1 Returns of the FTSE All-Share Index with and without dividends reinvested (returns for 30 years to 31 December 2010)

Source: Barclays Capital (2011) 'Equity gilt study 2011'

may be high (when expressed as a percentage yield) because the price of the company has fallen. Dividends do not provide downside protection because current share prices reflect whether the earnings of a company have been paid out or retained. Dividends do not prevent encroaching on your capital because the distribution of dividends is reflected in companies' share prices. The notion that owners of dividend-paying shares are somehow more committed shareholders may have some merit but it is unlikely to be of any material consequence for most long-term investors.

Another downside to focusing on companies that pay dividends, of whatever amount, is that you are highly likely to miss out on significant investment returns from high-growth companies. Microsoft, Starbucks and Cisco Systems are just a few of the massive global companies that never paid any dividends for many years, but their share prices grew much faster than those of many dividend-paying companies. The key point to appreciate is that whether companies pay dividends or not makes no difference to the total investment return, whereas the investment policy of the underlying investee companies will.

The impact of regular withdrawals from your portfolio

If you need your portfolio to fund your lifestyle over the long term, then you need to factor this into your investment strategy. The required amount of regular withdrawals, the portfolio's time horizon (which may be your life expectancy), your risk profile and asset allocation are closely interrelated. If the amount regularly withdrawn from the portfolio is too high, then you might run out of money before you die or not be able to leave a legacy. If the portfolio is too risky and suffers high volatility, then the regular withdrawals may exacerbate the negative returns experienced during market downturns. Figure 10.2 illustrates this point well with the risky portfolio volatility being compounded by the regular withdrawals.

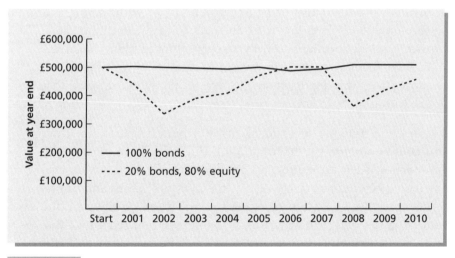

Figure 10.2 Effect of withdrawals on portfolio value – 715,000 p.a.

There are a number of approaches that you could adopt when it comes to taking withdrawals from your investment portfolio and the right one will depend on your spending needs, investment strategy, risk capacity/profile and tax status.

■ **Natural yield**. You take whatever interest or dividends are generated from the portfolio. Although the yield will vary from year to year, you could expect this to increase in real terms if you have made reasonable allocations to short-dated bonds, index-linked gilts, equities and property. This approach is likely to produce a relatively low level of income as a proportion of the portfolio, particularly for riskier portfolios.

■ **Fixed amount**. You take a fixed monetary amount each year (e.g. £50,000) regardless of actual investment yield or overall returns. While this provides a constant level of 'income' it needs much closer monitoring, particularly if you have a reasonable allocation to risky assets and a high amount of withdrawal relative to the portfolio value. You may have to stop or reduce the amount withdrawn during market downturns.

■ **Percentage of portfolio**. The withdrawal is expressed as a percentage of the portfolio, which may be higher or lower than the natural yield or overall return. The actual amount of withdrawals will vary up and down in line with fluctuations in the portfolio value, with higher allocations to risky assets leading to higher volatility in income withdrawals. However, the chances of running out of money with this approach are likely to be quite low, provided that the withdrawal percentage is not excessive.

If you need a stable level of cashflow from the portfolio, then you could combine the fixed amount and percentage of portfolio approaches. Such an approach could combine a fixed withdrawal based on a percentage average of, say, the past three years' annual lifestyle expenditure with a percentage amount based on the portfolio value. You can weight these factors to favour your preference for either more stable cashflow or a greater chance of portfolio survival. This allows you to customise your withdrawals to smooth out consumption while responding to actual investment performance.

Sustainable regular withdrawals from your portfolio

Over the years a number of studies have tried to determine sustainable levels of regular portfolio withdrawals for various scenarios. By sustainable we mean that the portfolio will not be exhausted in your lifetime or a given time horizon. One major academic study found that, over a 30-year time horizon, a portfolio that was allocated 50% to equities and 50% to bonds and with 4% annual withdrawals increasing with inflation, historically, had a 95% success rate, i.e. the investor would not have run out of money in 19 out of 20 times.[2] This approach is commonly known as **the 4% rule**. Other researchers have made similar studies using backtested and simulated market data and other withdrawal systems and strategies and the general approach is widely endorsed, particularly in the United States.

The report's authors, however, made this qualification:

> *'The word planning is emphasized because of the great uncertainties in the stock and bond markets. Mid-course corrections likely will be required, with the actual dollar amounts withdrawn adjusted downward or upward relative to the plan. The investor needs to keep in mind that selection of a withdrawal rate is not a matter of contract but rather a matter of planning.'*[3]

More recent research[4] has highlighted the limitations of the 4% rule and put forward some alternative approaches. The researchers highlighted the obvious mismatch between financing a constant, non-volatile spending plan with a risky, volatile investment strategy and the investment inefficiencies arising from such an approach. The study found that the typical withdrawal rule 'wastes' 10–20% of the portfolio funding future investment surpluses the investor doesn't spend and a further 2–4% is used to fund overpayments in years when performance is lower than the amount withdrawn. Thus those adopting the 4% rule (and the associated risky asset exposure) pay a relatively high, but not always apparent, price for the income they receive. The study concludes that if investors can afford to take lower withdrawals than 4% pa of the portfolio and adopt a less risky portfolio strategy, then they dramatically reduce the likelihood of exhausting the portfolio.

---

[2] Cooley, P. L., Hubbard, C. M. and Walz, D. T. (1998) 'Retirement savings: Choosing a withdrawal rate that is sustainable', *AAII Journal*, 10(3): 16–21.

[3] Ibid.

[4] Scott, J. S., Sharpe, W. F. and Watson, J. G. (2008) 'The 4% rule – at what price?', April, **www.stanford.edu/~wfsharpe/retecon/4percent.pdf**

Example portfolios and withdrawal rates

There are a number of useful tools now available on the internet that enable investors to model various combinations of investment strategy and withdrawal rates. While there are drawbacks to using such tools, they do at least give a useful idea of the tradeoff between risk and reward and the importance of using realistic and cautious assumptions.

Figure 10.3 shows a range of inflation-adjusted withdrawal rates based on historical index returns arising from an untaxed portfolio of 50% UK equities, 40% UK government bonds and 10% cash. As you can see, the 3% withdrawal rate lasts the longest at 25 years. However, a taxed investor would have experienced a worse outcome than this.

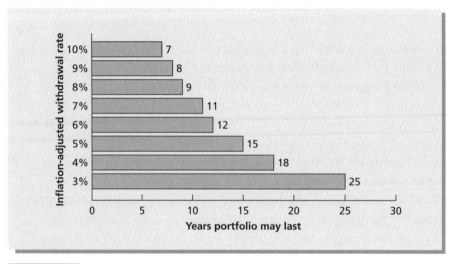

Figure 10.3   **Withdrawal risk**

Source: Fidelity Investments. TIme for hypothetical untaxed portfolio of 50% UK equities, 40% UK Government bonds and 10% UK cash might be expected to last with a reasonable degree of certainty. Rates of return are based on historical index returns for the period 31 December 1969 to 31 December 2005. Actual returns may be higher or lower.

Principles to guide you

While there is no single answer, there are several principles that you can use to help you determine the right portfolio withdrawal strategy.

Determining the right portfolio withdrawal strategy |

- The highest chance of success and most efficient use of capital is likely to arise if regular withdrawals are (and remain) low in proportion to the portfolio value and the investment strategy has a low risk profile (i.e. with low volatility).

- Assuming that the portfolio will be investing entirely in index-linked gilts and a low withdrawal rate will be taken (broadly equivalent to the natural yield) this seems to be a sensible base scenario to compare to other withdrawal strategies, as this represents a low-risk option for an investor whose liabilities (i.e. future expenditure) are expected to increase with inflation.

- If you anticipate your lifestyle spending rising at a rate higher than the official rate of inflation, you are more likely to maintain living standards in relation to your higher **personal inflation rate** if you take withdrawals relative to the portfolio and a significant proportion of the portfolio is allocated to equities. However, this approach comes with a degree of investment 'inefficiency' and the possibility of running out of money.

- If you have a long time horizon and expenditure that rises much faster than official inflation, coupled with a low equity allocation, this will translate into a high probability of declining consumption in the long term (i.e. withdrawals will have to be reduced at some stage) to avoid the portfolio being exhausted.

- For shorter time periods, higher starting spending rates may be justified, irrespective of where your portfolio is on the risk spectrum, but even over these shorter periods, it will increase the probability of a need to reduce withdrawals eventually to avoid the portfolio being exhausted.

- Expected legacies are higher for portfolios with high equity allocations, but so is the likelihood of leaving a small legacy. This is a classic risk–return tradeoff.

- It is imperative to review the withdrawal level periodically in the light of actual investment returns achieved and make adjustments as necessary. This is particularly important for portfolios with higher levels of withdrawals, regardless of their exposure to risky assets and to all portfolios with high allocations to equities regardless of the level of withdrawals.

Adding risky assets to a portfolio is done in the expectation, but not the certainty, that it will generate real returns in excess of those available from cash and index-linked gilts. As an investor you need to weigh up the probability of running out of money in your lifetime against the alternative of a less expensive lifestyle.

The importance of rebalancing your portfolio

As we've already discussed, your portfolio's asset allocation is one of the most important decisions in the portfolio-construction process and is the major determinant of its risk–return characteristics. How the portfolio is taxed can also have a big impact on how much of those returns you keep. With a multi-asset class portfolio that uses collective funds, over time, each asset class will generate different returns, which will cause your portfolio's asset allocation and consequently its risk profile to change. This is known as **portfolio drift** and is unlikely to be consistent with your goals, preferences and tax position. The portfolio will, therefore, require some ongoing management and review to manage both risks and taxes.

Sometimes an asset class can experience significant volatility over a time period but end it at the same value as that at which it started. Take, for example, the Japanese stock market as represented by the Nikkei 225 Index for the 25 years ending 2009. As you can see from Figure 10.4, the ending value was actually below the starting value but in that 25-year period the market experienced many rises and falls of between 30% and over 100%!

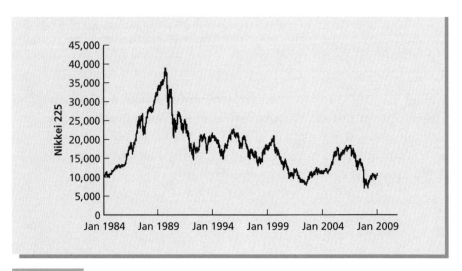

Figure 10.4   Performance of the Nikkei 225 Index (25 years ending 2009)

Source: Dimensional Fund Advisors

A disciplined rebalancing policy forces you to sell high and buy low. This doesn't remove risk but maintains the risk exposure (which is after all the source of additional returns) that you set at the outset. In order to re-establish the portfolio's original risk and return characteristics, it needs to be rebalanced so that each holding reflects the original asset allocation. All other things being equal, a regularly rebalanced portfolio will maintain the risk–reward characteristics of the target asset allocation compared with a portfolio that is never rebalanced. In other words, an optimally rebalanced portfolio is likely to produce a similar return to that of a non-rebalanced portfolio but at a lower level of risk. See Figure 10.5.

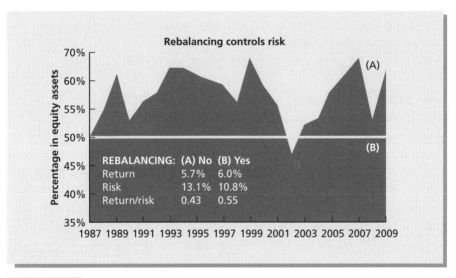

Figure 10.5   Comparison of rebalanced and non-rebalanced portfolios

An additional benefit of rebalancing a taxable portfolio is that it enables gains and losses to be crystallised, which can help with minimising tax. In practice, a sensible rebalancing strategy forces you to reduce exposure to those asset classes that have performed relatively well compared to the others you hold, in favour of asset classes which have performed relatively poorly and/or fallen in value. This 'sell high and buy low' discipline is the opposite of what most retail (and many institutional) investors do, because taking profits and buying more of what could be an asset the price of which is falling is difficult for most people to do, due to their emotional response to losses and gains. However, logically, if an asset has fallen in value, then its expected return increases and if it has risen in value its expected return falls.

In the same way that there is no 'perfect' asset allocation, there is no 'perfect' rebalancing approach. In developing your rebalancing strategy you need to consider three key questions.

1 How frequently should the portfolio be reviewed?

Most of the research on portfolio rebalancing suggests that the risk-adjusted returns are not significantly different whether rebalancing is carried out monthly, quarterly, bi-annually or annually. However, you need to balance the benefits arising from rebalancing against the practicalities of doing so and the associated costs and tax impact arising.

2 By how much should the holdings be permitted to deviate from the original allocation before triggering a need to rebalance?

The reason why you should aim to have a threshold to trigger rebalancing is to minimise unnecessary transactions that may have unwelcome tax and cost consequences, not to mention unnecessary additional work! The most recent research[5] suggests that a threshold of between 5 and 10% of the weight of each asset in the portfolio would be optimum, assuming annual or semi-annual monitoring. In the case of a 10% tolerance an asset the target weight of which is 30% would be rebalanced if its actual weight in the portfolio fell to under 27% or rose above 33%. At a 10% tolerance the portfolio would require only 15 rebalancing events (trades) compared to well over 1,000 events for a portfolio with no threshold.

---

[5]   Jaconetti, C. M., Kinniry Jr., F. M. and Zilbering, Y. (2010) 'Best practices for portfolio rebalancing' Vanguard, July, **www.vanguard.com/pdf/icrpr.pdf**

3 Should the portfolio be rebalanced exactly to the original asset allocation or a close approximation thereof?

If you pay transaction costs that are fixed (e.g. £20 per trade irrespective of size) and small in relation to the value of the rebalancing trades, then exact rebalancing is probably preferable as this reduces the need for further future transactions. However, if costs are a proportion of the transaction – which is usual in the case of commissions and taxes – then an approximation to the target asset allocation is probably desirable to minimise those costs.

The answers to the three rebalancing questions are mostly matters of investor preference. If you have a diversified equity and bond portfolio, pay a flat transaction fee and minimal tax (assuming reasonable expectations regarding return patterns, average returns and risk) then a sensible approach is to monitor your portfolio annually, use a tolerance trigger of 10% of the original allocation for each asset class and to rebalance exactly to the preferred asset allocation. Variations will apply if your personal circumstances are different. Formulating a sensible rebalancing strategy will also provide the discipline to enable you to stick with your investment strategy through thick and thin. Regardless of whether markets are surging or plummeting, rebalancing helps you to avoid misplaced optimism or irrational fear.

The mechanics of rebalancing

The simplest way of rebalancing your portfolio is to use new cash to invest in those assets that are underweight. This cash might come from additional capital being added to the portfolio or, more likely, from accumulated interest and dividends arising from the portfolio holdings. For this reason it is important to avoid investing in any funds that automatically reinvest interest and dividends. By using cash to rebalance you will reduce the number of transactions that you or your adviser will need to carry out and, in the case of portfolios that are taxable, you'll avoid unnecessary crystallisation of taxable capital gains.

The other method of rebalancing is to realise cash from the overweight portfolio holdings to reinvest in the underweight holdings. In the case of taxable portfolios, this might be more attractive than using new cash if you need to crystallise gains to utilise your annual capital gains tax exemption or crystallise losses to offset against current year gains or to be carried forward for use in future tax years.

If a large, taxable capital gain would arise as a result of rebalancing back to the exact allocation, then you might wish to rebalance to as near to the model as you can without crystallising the extra tax. Alternatively you might wish to delay the rebalancing if you anticipate being able to add more capital to the portfolio in the near term or expect to be a basic rate taxpayer in the next tax year, but don't fall into the trap of letting tax overly influence the need to rebalance. The most tax-efficient portfolio is one that makes only losses and if you don't rebalance, particularly when markets have risen sharply, you might see those gains evaporate as we saw earlier with the Japanese stock market. Those with shorter memories than the early 1990s may recall the investors who were unwilling to sell out of their technology stocks in the early part of the twenty-first century because of the tax they would have paid. Although continuing to hold them through 2001 certainly avoided the tax problem, the collateral damage to their portfolios when the sector corrected spectacularly may have given rise to a few regrets.

For most people with reasonable-sized portfolios, they are likely to have taxed and non-taxed elements. It is likely, therefore, that a combination of using cash (whether from interest/dividends or additional investment capital) and releasing cash from other holdings is likely to be necessary to carry out rebalancing.

The use of debt and investing

Depending on your point of view, debt is either something to be avoided at all costs or a useful way of multiplying wealth and opportunity. The two most common questions about debt are these.

1 Should I use capital/income to pay down debt or should I invest?
2 Should I use debt to augment my investment capital to leverage higher investment returns?

Debt is a negative bond (fixed-income) exposure, although the interest costs will invariably be higher than the interest rate earned on bonds. So if you have a £200,000 bond and £200,000 equity exposure in your investment portfolio, e.g. 50% to each asset class and a £50,000 mortgage, your actual bond exposure is £150,000 (the bond of £200,000 less the £50,000 mortgage). The result is that instead of having 50% of your portfolio allocated to risky equities you actually have 57%. This higher risk might be acceptable if you have a need and tolerance for a higher allocation to risky assets.

It is unlikely that you will be able to earn a higher rate of interest from cash or bonds in taxable accounts, particularly for higher- and additional rate taxpayers, than the cost of interest on a mortgage. Repaying debt is a risk-free return whereas a taxable investment would need to deliver a higher return than the risk-free rate and, as such, would be risky. In Table 10.1 you can see a range of mortgage rates and the taxable rate of return that you'd need to obtain at different tax rates just to break even.

Table 10.1 Gross investment returns required to equal mortgage interest costs

Tax rate (%)	Mortgage rate (%)				
	3.00	4.00	5.00	6.00	7.00
20.00	3.75	5.00	6.25	7.50	8.75
40.00	5.00	6.67	8.34	10.00	11.67
50.00	6.00	8.00	10.00	12.00	14.00

In tax-free and tax-deferred accounts like ISAs and offshore investment bonds, the position is more finely balanced. However, on tax-favoured accounts like pensions, particularly where initial tax relief is obtained at a higher rate on the contribution than is payable on benefits and tax-efficient growth is achieved in the intervening period, it can be highly attractive not to repay debt and instead make pension contributions (see Chapter 14 on pensions).

Inflation and deflation

A variable rate loan is fully exposed to inflationary pressures and one would expect rates to rise or remain high in an environment of rising or strong inflation. If you think that deflation is more likely, then a variable rate loan makes more sense as the cost of borrowing is likely to fall to nil. However, in that situation, any real assets, such as property or equities, which the loan may have been used to purchase, are also likely to experience a fall in value. A fixed-rate loan, on the other hand, is protected against rising inflation but will be exposed to deflation unless the loan includes the option to repay some of it or the entire amount early without penalty.

Leverage amplifies gains and losses

Borrowing allows you to leverage returns on investment capital. This is great when the asset or business is going up in value, because the return over the cost of the debt is added to the investor's capital as 'free' excess return. However, debt can also amplify losses, as many people and companies have found out since the financial crisis of 2007–2009 began to unwind. Figure 10.6 illustrates the impact on returns in a positive and negative return environment.

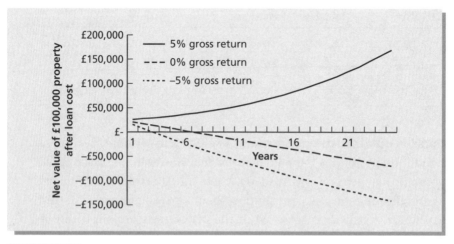

Figure 10.6 The effect of debt on property equity – loan of 75%

For those with significant wealth, the most common use of debt is as investment in property, because fractional ownership of physical property is not feasible in most cases in the same way as it is with equities and bonds. In addition, debt can be introduced to a property portfolio, for example, to allow capital to be extracted tax-efficiently with the rental income servicing the interest. If you want to retain the property as an investment but have a better use for some of the equity then this could be a good idea.

There are a multitude of packaged investments that come with inbuilt leverage, which serves to increase the relative risks compared to unleveraged investment in, say, an equity index fund. Examples of such investments are as follows:

- property funds
- property partnerships and syndicates
- enterprise zone property syndicates
- business premises renovation allowance syndicates
- affordable housing partnerships
- film partnerships
- carbon/clean energy funds
- long/short 130 equity funds.

In some cases, the debt is required to obtain a tax effect, such as with enterprise zone syndicates, whereas with others, like the long/short 130 equity fund,[6] it is required to generate the expected return. The key point to remember is that once you adjust the expected return for the additional risk of debt, you are likely to end up with a return similar, or in some cases lower, than that from an unleveraged investment.

---

[6] A very simple explanation of a long/short 130 equity fund is as follows: the fund typically borrows £30 for every £100 of investors' cash and then invests the combined amount, £130, in equities. At the same time the fund sells £30 of equities that it doesn't currently own, i.e. it goes 'short', in company shares that the fund manager thinks will suffer a fall, with the intention of buying the shares more cheaply to settle the short sale.

Later life needs

Debt can also be used as part of later life planning. Those who need to fund lifestyle expenditure and/or care fees funding, but who have insufficient liquid assets and/or income, could use what is known as a lifetime mortgage secured against their property. In most cases the interest is rolled up and added to the loan until the borrower's death, when the loan is repaid from the proceeds arising from selling the property. Most lenders active in this market give a guarantee that the loan and rolled-up interest will never be more than the value of the property, known as a 'no negative equity guarantee'. For this reason the maximum loan is usually less than 50% of the property value but the actual amount depends on the borrower's age and the lender's interest rate.

Lifetime mortgages are a relatively expensive way of funding later life needs but can be a viable option for individuals who wish to remain in their own home, have no other assets on which to call and don't wish (or are unable) to borrow funds on similar terms from other family members.

In addition to your willingness and need to take risks, using debt in your wealth plan boils down to your need to 'sleep well'. Those at the beginning of their earning capacity and those nearing the end of their life can usually cope with debt more than those with other age and wealth profiles. However, if you are looking to preserve what you have in real terms and want as few moving parts as possible in your investment approach then avoid debt as far as possible.

Other financial planning issues

11

Minimising portfolio taxation

If your portfolio is not held in a tax-free or tax-deferred account like an individual savings account (ISA), self-invested personal pension (SIPP), small self-administered scheme (SSAS) or offshore portfolio bond (OPB), then tax will be due on interest, dividends and capital gains to the extent that they exceed your individual personal allowances.

To determine if total capital gains are taxable you need to first deduct all capital losses arising within the same tax year. Net capital gains in excess of the annual exemption, regardless of how long the investment has been held, are then taxed at either 18% or 28% depending on whether or not there is any unused basic rate income tax band available.

While your total taxable income now determines the rate of capital gains tax you pay, capital gains do not impact on the amount of income tax you pay. Therefore, it is now important to carefully manage taxable income, as far as possible, to allow any taxable capital gains to benefit from the lower 18% tax rate, to the extent that taxable capital gains fall below the higher-rate income tax threshold of £35,000 in excess of the personal income tax allowance.

The way that investments are taxed can have a significant impact on overall returns. This is particularly relevant where the differential between income tax and capital gains tax is wide, with the top rate of income tax currently 50% compared to capital gains tax of up to 28%.

Investment funds are deemed to be either 'reporting' or 'non-reporting' for tax purposes. A reporting fund declares the income arising within the fund, whether this is paid out to investors or not. The investor is then responsible for paying income tax, at their highest rate, on that income arising. Depending on the nature of the underlying holdings this income will be taxed as either interest or dividends. When the investor comes to dispose of their holding, any increase or decrease in value is then subject to capital gains tax treatment.

A non-reporting fund declares neither income arising within the fund nor any capital gains. As such no tax is payable by the investor until the holding is disposed of. If they are a UK resident domiciled person then they will pay income tax on the entire uplift in value of their holding, although no allowance is provided for losses. Many ETFs and most alternative investment strategies such as hedge funds and structured products are offered through non-reporting funds. This adverse tax treatment makes non-reporting funds unsuitable for most taxable investors. The tax distinction between reporting and non-reporting funds is not an issue, however, if the fund is held within a **tax wrapper** like a pension or an offshore bond.

Investment returns can take the form of interest, dividends or capital gains and most portfolios will usually have a combination of all three. Understanding the composition of these returns helps us to consider how the returns will be taxed using different tax structures, which I refer to as tax wrappers. Although there have been major changes to investment taxation over the past few years, for UK-resident and domiciled individuals these apply at the investor level, not the tax wrapper level, and relate to the income and capital gains tax arising. All companies (including UK life insurers) continue to be taxed under the existing rules and, in particular, will qualify for indexation allowance on capital gains.

The other factors that need to be considered when considering investment location are as follows:

- use of your personal capital gains tax (CGT) exemption
- whether or not you have any unused basic rate income tax band
- your need for regular withdrawals to meet expenditure needs
- the amount of periodic rebalancing likely to arise to keep your portfolio within the agreed risk exposure

- if the portfolio is to be held within a trust or pension structure, perhaps as part of other tax planning components
- the ability for CGT to be 'washed out' on your death, i.e extinguished
- the product or tax wrapper charges incurred
- the type of investment held, i.e. deposit, fixed-interest, equity income or equity growth
- the type of investment required – some types of investments and funds are not permitted within certain tax structures
- the administrative work and professional costs associated with tax reporting
- if you also wish to include inheritance tax planning with your investment capital.

The individual savings account (ISA) allowance

This allows a UK resident to hold cash, fixed interest or equity investments in a tax-free environment, although withholding tax on dividends may not be reclaimed. The limit is £10,680 so couples can shield £21,360 from the taxman if both invest in an ISA. If you only ever invest in cash then the limit is £5,340. An ISA makes most sense for those who pay higher-rate income tax and who would generate capital gains of more than £10,600 per tax year. Having said that, it is often possible to invest in funds via an ISA at no extra charge, so just from an administration perspective an ISA is likely to be the foundation of your portfolio tax management strategy.

The transfer of an investment into an ISA is deemed to be a disposal for Capital Gains Tax and thus offers a way of using your Capital Gains Tax allowance (or the lower 18% CGT tax rate if the gain would fall within the higher-rate income tax threshold), without having to dispose of the holding. Ordinarily, where a capital gain arises from the disposal of a personally held investment, it must not be repurchased for at least 30 days; otherwise the gain is deemed not to have taken place. This clearly represents a risk of being uninvested for a month and, hence, being able to trigger the gains without selling the investment by transferring it to an ISA is a simple but effective tax planning technique.

The three main non-pension investment tax wrappers

Let's look at the tax effects of three types of tax wrapper most commonly used to hold an investment portfolio (see also Table 10.1):

1 collective funds held via a nominee account or in own name

2 an onshore investment bond

3 an offshore investment bond.

All other things being equal, a portfolio that generates mostly capital gains within collective funds in your own name is likely to be the most tax-efficient way of holding the portfolio. A portfolio that generates reinvested income (particularly for 40% and 50% taxpayers) is likely to be more tax-efficient if held within an insurance bond. However, where a portfolio contains a mixture of capital growth and income-producing investments, the position is not as clear cut and a proper analysis will be required based on your own circumstances.

Collective funds

Unit trusts and investment trusts, as well as reporting offshore funds, are exempt from CGT on disposals arising *within* the fund and generally corporation tax is not payable, providing that income is distributed to investors. At the investor level, a flat CGT rate of 18% or 28% (depending on the investor's *taxable income*) is charged on disposals of units or shares in such a collective fund. CGT is only payable if such gains exceed the investor's annual exemption, after first taking into account any losses arising in the current tax year or those carried forward from previous tax years. Non- and basic rate taxpayers receive dividends from equity-based collectives free of any additional tax liability, although withholding tax on those dividends may not be reclaimed. Higher rate (40%) and additional rate (50%) taxpayers pay an effective tax of 25% and 36% respectively of the net dividend paid.[1]

---

[1] Dividends come with a non-reclaimable tax credit equal to 1/9th of the net dividend paid. So a £9 dividend would come with a £1 notional tax credit, making the gross dividend £10. The non-taxpayer cannot reclaim the notional tax credit, whereas it settles the liability of the basic rate taxpayer. The higher-rate and additional rate taxpayer, on the other hand, is required to pay 22.5%/32.5% respectively of the grossed-up dividend not represented by the notional tax credit. This is equivalent to 25%/36% respectively of the net dividend paid.

Investment bonds

Investment bonds are single-premium life insurance or capital redemption policies issued by either a UK (onshore) or overseas (offshore) life assurance company. Whilst a life insurance bond pays a slightly higher amount than the policy value on the death of the bond life assured, this is usually very small.

Capital gains arising within an onshore bond will be subject to the life company's tax rate (currently a maximum of 20%) after allowing for indexation relief and expenses. Gains arising within an offshore bond will be exempt from tax. UK dividends received inside a UK life fund bear no further tax and the investor has no tax liability on reinvested dividends either. Under an offshore bond the dividends will be received and no further tax will be payable but there will be no reclamation of the tax credit either. Foreign dividends will be subject to tax inside a UK life fund but typically not inside an offshore bond. In practice, however, the average yield on foreign equities and funds tends to be comparatively low and, in any event, there are often non-reclaimable withholding taxes applied before receipt. Interest received by a UK life fund will be taxed at 20% – the life companys' tax rate. Interest received inside an offshore bond will not be subject to tax and the benefits of almost gross roll-up will be most keenly seen in connection with interest.

Unlike collective funds, where the investor suffers income tax on dividends and interest on an arising basis, plus capital gains tax on eventual encashment, the tax treatment of an investment bond means that the investor suffers income tax on *any* gain (whether arising from interest, dividends or capital growth) on encashment. This provides the investor with a fair degree of flexibility over the timing of such liability, although with the disadvantage for higher- and additional rate taxpayers that this may be higher than the new 28% CGT rate if the underlying returns arise mainly from capital growth.

With an onshore bond, because the taxable return is assumed to have already borne basic rate tax at 20%, there is no further tax liability for nil and basic rate taxpayers. The whole *net gain* arising on *encashment* is added to the investor's other taxable income arising in the same tax

Table 11.1 Comparison of tax treatments of main tax wrappers

	Unit trust/OEIC	Onshore investment bond	Offshore investment bond
Capital gains while invested	None	Taxed at insurers' rate (maximum 20%) after indexation relief and expenses	Exempt from UK tax
UK dividends	Investor taxed on an arising basis	No further tax; investor has no further liability	No further tax but no reclamation of tax credit
Non-UK dividends	Investor taxed on an arising basis	Subject to tax but liability may be accounted for by withholding tax in jurisdiction of origin	Typically not subject to further tax
Interest	Investor taxed on an arising basis	Taxed at insurers' rate (20%)	Not subject to tax
Capital gains when encashed	Subject to Capital Gains Tax (CGT) at 18–28% after annual exemption and allowable losses	Subject to Income Tax. No further tax liability for nil and basic rate taxpayers. Entire net gain added to the investor's other taxable income arising in the same tax year and taxed by a further 20% for a higher-rate (40%) taxpayer and 30% for an additional rate (50%) taxpayer. If, however, the addition of the gain to the taxable income of a basic rate taxpayer makes them a higher-additional rate taxpayer, the gain will be subject to 'top-slicing' relief (i.e. the total gain arising on encashment is divided by the number of complete policy years) to determine the 'sliced' gain. The sliced gain is then added to their other taxable income to determine whether it still exceeds the higher-rate income tax threshold. To the extent that each slice does exceed the higher-rate tax threshold, an onshore bond will be taxed at 20% or 30% on the net gain for each 'slice'	Subject to Income Tax. Gross gain taxed at nil, 20%, 40% or 50% for non-, basic, higher- and additional rate taxpayers respectively. If, however, the addition of the gain to the taxable income of a basic rate taxpayer makes them a higher-additional rate taxpayer, the gain will be subject to 'top slicing' relief (i.e. the total gain arising on encashment is divided by the number of complete policy years) to determine the 'sliced' gain. The sliced gain is then added to their other taxable income to determine if it still exceeds the higher-rate income tax threshold. An offshore bond will be taxed at nil or 20% on the amount of the slice that falls below the threshold for higher-rate tax and 40% or 50%, to the extent that it exceeds it

year and taxed by a further 20% for a higher-rate taxpayer and 30% for an additional rate payer. With an offshore bond the gross gain will be taxed at nil, 20%, 40% or 50% for non-, basic, higher- and additional rate taxpayers respectively.

Side by side

The balance between capital gains and reinvested income can have a big effect on the relative merits of the available investment tax wrappers, as well as the investor's rate of tax paid on encashment of the portfolio (if that ever happens in practice). In addition, the charges levied by the tax wrapper provider can have a significant impact, as can sales commission paid to intermediaries that do not work on a fee-only basis. Figures 11.1 and 11.2 show the pre- and post-tax positions of a hypothetical investment portfolio, invested for 15 years in direct collective funds, a UK investment bond and an offshore investment bond.[2] Three investment profiles have been modelled, ranging from 100% fixed income; 50/50 between equities/fixed income; and 100% equities.

In all cases the offshore bond produces the highest, before-tax, portfolio value. However when tax is taken into account the position changes considerably depending on whether the investor is a basic or higher-rate taxpayer at the time of encashment. Where 100% of the portfolio is invested in fixed income, equally between equities and fixed income, then direct collective funds produced the highest net value for a higher-rate taxpayer, whereas the offshore bond was highest for a basic rate taxpayer. Where 100% of the portfolio is invested in equities then direct collective funds produced the highest net value for a higher-rate taxpayer, whereas the UK investment bond was highest for a basic rate taxpayer.

---

[2] The analysis was necessarily simplified for the purposes of demonstrating the different range of possible returns from different portfolios and tax wrappers. Portfolios and tax wrappers were compared on a 'nil commission' charge basis and funds were assumed to be 1% initial and 1.5% annual. In the case of the UK investment bond an additional annual charge of 0.35% was assumed to reflect the typical charge levied on a self-selected version. The offshore portfolio bond was assumed to charge a flat annual policy fee of £400 per annum. The investor's capital gains tax exemption was assumed to be available throughout and utilised through periodic rebalancing. In some of the scenarios capital gains tax would have been incurred during the investment holding period before final encashment and this is reflected in the value before tax amount shown just prior to encashment. Investment return assumptions: 7.5% p.a. for equities (4% income + 3.5% capital gain) and 4.5% for fixed income.

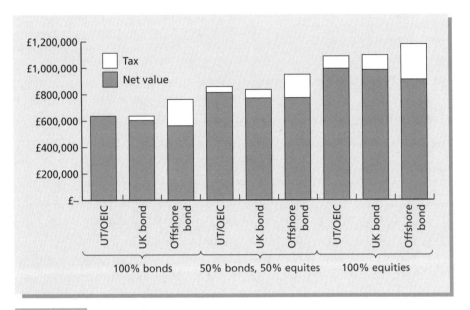

Figure 11.1   Projected portfolio values for 40% taxpayer throughout

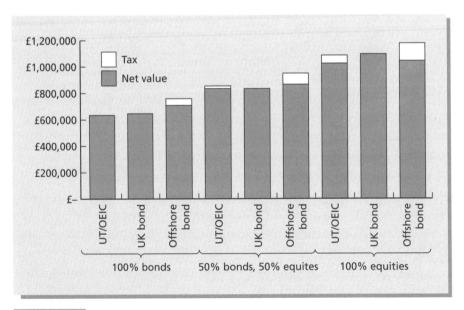

Figure 11.2   Projected portfolio values for 40% taxpayer becoming 20% taxpayer on encashment

A point to bear in mind is the probability of actually paying the tax shown in the examples. A transfer of directly held funds by way of gift to a third party other than a spouse or civil partner will give rise to capital gains tax unless it is to trustees and an election is made to 'hold over' the gain to the trustees. An investment bond, in contrast, may be assigned to a third party as a gift and there is no immediate tax charge on any latent gain. The gain is also gifted to the recipient and subject to their own tax position on eventual encashment. It may be that you are a higher-rate taxpayer during some or all of the holding period of the portfolio but become a basic rate taxpayer prior to encashment. This is where careful management of your taxable income can make a big impact, such as controlling how much income you withdraw from your pension fund, which we will look at in Chapter 15.

It takes five full tax years of non-residence for a previously UK-resident individual to avoid CGT on subsequent disposals of assets acquired while a UK resident, whereas it would currently take them only one complete tax year to avoid the gains on an investment bond. A one-year period of non-residence is often easier to envisage and engineer than five years. Whether the current tax treatment of investment bonds will continue is anyone's guess but it might be vulnerable if lots of people take advantage of the 'anomaly'. In that scenario, having all investment returns classed as income rather than capital gains might turn out to be rather expensive!

Given the many variables to take into account and the inherent uncertainties with regard to the future (e.g. in respect of actual performance, individual investor tax rates and what the tax system will look like), you need to bear in mind that there is an element of risk in choosing how best to hold investments from a tax perspective, given that the assumptions used are highly likely to turn out to be wrong. Asset allocation is the way investors minimise investment risk (for what will always be an uncertain future) by diversifying across different asset classes. This principle of 'spreading' or 'allocation' can also be applied in connection with tax wrapper selection where there is some uncertainty as to the future. Where this uncertainty could make a decision made on an 'all or nothing' basis the wrong one, then it may make sense to diminish this risk by spreading investments across appropriate investment wrappers.

In addition to pensions and ISAs, it may be most appropriate to ensure that high-growth funds are held directly and high-yield/interest funds held within investment bonds. For portfolios that include a mix of equity and fixed interest holdings it will be important to strike a balance and so across a whole portfolio one could see (subject to charges and unnecessary complexity) a range of wrappers being selected. It is also worth bearing in mind the possible need to rebalance the portfolio in the future. This would entail moving capital between different asset classes in order to maintain the required risk exposure, which can be compromised if each asset class is held within a different wrapper type. Choosing the right tax wrapper(s) needs a careful analysis of the facts and your likely future circumstances. The days of building an investment portfolio without consideration of the tax impact or arranging tax wrappers independent of the investment strategy are long gone.

12

General tax planning

The most tax-efficient strategy is to only make losses on your assets, investments and businesses or to spend all your money in your lifetime. If, however, you can reduce, defer or avoid tax, it means that you can spend more, take a lower amount of risk in pursuing your objectives or leave a larger legacy. Over the past few years the rhetoric from the Treasury and Her Majesty's Revenue and Customs (HMRC) has seen tax-avoidance planning (which is legal) described in a similar vein to tax evasion (which is illegal). There has been a lot of talk about taxpayers paying their 'fair' share of tax and the 'immoral' nature of those who seek to exploit legitimate tax-planning opportunities for personal gain.

It is an accepted principle of English law that a taxpayer is permitted to arrange their affairs in the most tax-efficient manner. That is to say, you end up paying the lowest level of tax possible by exploiting the rules and regulations set by Parliament. However, over the years there has been a distinction made between tax mitigation and tax avoidance, with avoidance being viewed as actions that 'conflict with or defeat the evident intention of Parliament' (*IRC* v *Willoughby*), even if such actions are legal. With the current state of public finances, clearly HMRC are looking to collect as much revenue as possible and they are now targeting planning that they deem was carried out solely with the intention of saving tax. However, that doesn't mean that you have to just roll over and pay more tax than is necessary. Saving tax is a legitimate and rewarding activity, but it needs to be considered in line with your personal objectives, wider wealth plan and tax risk profile.

Intaxication (n.): Euphoria at getting a tax refund, which lasts until you realise it was your money to start with.

The main taxes

The following are the main taxes (and rates for 2011/2012) as they affect UK-domiciled and resident individuals.

- **Income tax** – levied on earnings, rental income, royalties, interest and dividends at rates between 20 and 50%.
- **Value added tax (VAT)** – levied on purchase of most goods and services, mainly at a rate of 20%.
- **Capital gains tax (CGT)** – levied on gains arising on disposal of assets in one's lifetime at either 18% or 28% depending on the income tax rate paid, although the rate is 10% for gains of up to £10 million arising from the sale of certain business interests and assets.
- **Stamp duty and SDLT** – levied on most transactions involving the purchase of equities at a flat rate of 0.50% and transactions involving the purchase and sale of land and property at rates between 1 and 5%.
- **Inheritance tax (IHT)** – a flat rate of 40% levied on death of a UK-domiciled individual (or a non-UK-domiciled individual who has become 'deemed' domiciled) on worldwide assets above £325,000 if not left to a surviving spouse/civil partner or charity/ political party (from April 2012 it is proposed that the rate will be 36% where at least 10% of the taxable estate is left to charity). Non-UK-domiciled individuals who have not been classed as 'deemed' domiciled are subject to IHT on most UK assets. A 20% rate is payable in one's lifetime on gifts to most types of trust above a limit (currently £325,000 every seven years).

Your tax risk profile

Just like we have our own individual investment risk profile we also all have our own tax risk profile. Knowing your tax risk profile is important because it will help you to determine what type of tax planning might be worth considering. Your own tax risk profile will depend on a number of factors.

■ Your desire to save tax – most people understand that they have to pay a fair share of tax. The question is, what's your definition of 'fair'?

■ Your need to save tax – what difference will saving tax make to you and/or your wider family?

■ Your capacity to understand – being successful and making wealth doesn't mean that you are necessarily able to understand complex planning ideas.

■ Your feelings about raising your tax profile – the taxman uses a range of profiling techniques for taxpayers based on information gained from tax returns. Certain transactions and disclosures might increase your chances of an enquiry.

■ Whether or not you invest in professional and personalised advice – employing a professional tax adviser can be a good 'investment', both in terms of avoiding pitfalls and securing tax savings many times the fee paid.

There are different degrees of tax planning, ranging from simple and tested through to highly aggressive and contentious.

■ Low tax risk – standard planning that is non-contentious such as making a pension contribution; offsetting losses against gains; using an investment bond to defer tax on gains; and using a limited liability partnership and a limited company to arbitrage between different legal structures to control business profits.

■ High tax risk – this includes aggressively marketed tax schemes that aim to achieve a tax saving. Examples of previous planning that would have fallen within this definition include: Double Trust IOU Home Schemes – to achieve an inheritance tax saving; Employee Benefit Trusts that used a sub-trust to obtain a corporation tax deduction; Certain Qualifying Recognised Overseas Pension Schemes that offered the ability to obtain access to a 100% tax-free lump sum from UK-sourced pension funds.

Tax planning principles

There are a number of principles that you need to follow to minimise taxation.

1 Know your personal allowances – this is the amount you can earn or capital gains that you can realise without paying tax.

2 Know your income tax band – recent research[1] shows that 26% of people earning more than £50,000 think they only pay the basic rate of tax.

3 Take action – make use of tax-efficient savings schemes, allowances and reliefs.

4 Deferring tax – even if you can't avoid tax, deferring when you have to pay it can enable you to generate additional returns in the meantime.

5 Integrated planning – your spending, earning, investing and lifestyle decisions all need to be taken into account to determine how best to minimise taxation.

6 Too good to be true – if something looks too good to be true it probably is!

7 Know what you are doing – if you don't understand it (having at least tried to) then don't do it.

8 Tax schemes – be wary of expensive tax schemes with large upfront fees from organisations with whom you have no existing relationship and that require a Disclosure of Tax Avoidance Scheme (DoTAS) number to be entered on your tax return.

9 Be wary of any arrangement that involves overseas entities or structures and/or that pass through several entities before ending in a final structure, as your money usually feeds many hungry mouths.

10 Nothing is certain – remember that the rules can and do change, although retrospective changes are the exception and not the rule.

11 Tax isn't everything – be careful not to let the tax tail wag the lifestyle planning dog! Moving abroad, for example, might help you to avoid tax but might have an adverse effect on your family and other personal relationships.

Practical ways of saving tax

For the rest of this chapter I'm going to take a whirlwind tour of a number of tax planning ideas so that you can check to see you are taking advantage of all the key tactics. I have not included any planning that is either a 'scheme' or one could view as 'aggressive', although if you have interest in such planning an internet search can yield many 'opportunities'. That being said you must always bear in mind what is acceptable to the tax authorities today may well be unacceptable to them in the future!

---

[1] Fidelity, 'Learn about tax', **www.fidelity.co.uk/investor/guidance-planning/learn-about-tax/default.page**

Closing interest deposit accounts

These are deposit accounts (usually offshore) that pay interest when you close the account and thus no tax liability can arise until then. Such accounts are useful if you want to avoid incurring taxable interest on cash until a future date, perhaps because you will then have your basic rate income tax band available, you might have allowable capital allowances to offset or you might become non-UK resident.

Use other family members' income tax bands

If your spouse/civil partner pays a lower rate of income tax than you, consider transferring sufficient savings or investment capital to them to enable any taxable income arising to be taxed at a lower rate. The transfer must be irrevocable and with tax saving not as the sole motive. You could extend this concept to using other family members, such as a life 'partner', parents, children, brother or sister who are not using their full income tax band but share the same household. Make sure that your paperwork is in order, just in case you have to justify or substantiate any transfers.

Make maximum use of tax-free accounts

Make sure that you utilise your and your spouse's/civil partner's ISA allowance each tax year. You may each contribute up to £10,680 per tax year to a stocks and shares ISA or £5,340 to a cash ISA and £5,340 to a stocks and shares ISA.

Use National Savings products

Make use of National Savings Certificates when they are available as these provide tax-free, albeit low, returns (both nominal and index-linked) and security of capital. Premium bonds also provide tax-free returns by way of prize draws each month. Although the average return is usually quite low compared to most deposit accounts, the top prize each month is £1 million, so it's a reasonable choice if you have significant capital to place in low-risk holdings and/or you have other taxable income subject to higher- or additional rate income tax.

Make a personal contribution to a pension

A personal contribution to a pension scheme is paid net of basic rate income tax (currently 20%) and has the effect of expanding your basic rate income tax band accordingly. For example an £800 contribution would gross up to £1,000 received by the pension fund and your basic rate income tax band would increase accordingly. This means that, to the extent it falls below the threshold at which higher- and additional rate income tax is payable, taxable income from earnings, savings or investment will be taxed at the basic rate (20%) rather than being taxed at the higher (40%) or additional rate (50%).

A pension contribution can also enable you to:

■ restore the loss of personal allowance where total taxable income is between £100,000 and £114,950

■ enable taxable capital gains arising in the same tax year, in excess of the annual exemption of £10,600, to be taxed at 18% rather than 28%, to the extent that such gains fall below the threshold at which higher-rate income tax is payable.

Have your employer make a pension contribution

If you are employed (including by a company owned and controlled by you) your employer could contribute to a pension scheme for you, funded by you, giving up a right to salary or bonus (this is known as salary sacrifice). If salary or bonus is sacrificed in favour of a pension contribution before it has been contractually earned, then no income tax or employer's or employee's National Insurance contributions will be due. Most employers are prepared to add the National Insurance saving to the contribution on the basis that it costs them no extra than the salary or bonus.

Claim capital allowances on property

It is possible to claim capital allowances on the purchase price of certain types of property including holiday lets, residential (as long as at some stage it has been let to multiple households at the same time) and commercial property. The allowance you can claim will depend on the type of property and varies between 5 and 30% of the purchase price, which may be offset against taxable income arising in the current, previous or future tax years.

Rent a room in your home when you are away for tax-free income

If you rent a room in your home to a lodger you can receive up to £4,250 per annum tax-free. The legislation does not say the room or rooms have to be rented to a lodger staying in your home all year so it would be perfectly acceptable for you to go away for a long summer break and to rent out your home to someone while you are away.

There are four basic rules you must follow in order to qualify for the relief:

1 the room or rooms must be within your 'only or main residence'
2 the letting must be for living accommodation, not for use as an office, for example
3 the relief is limited to £4,250 gross receipts in the tax year
4 the relief only applies to individuals, not to companies or partnerships (although it does apply where individuals share the income other than as a business arrangement, for example husband and wife).

The 'only or main residence' is *not* the same definition as for capital gains tax relief but a simpler interpretation of where your friends would expect to find you. This means you cannot take advantage of the capital gains tax rules that allow you in certain circumstances to treat a property as being your main residence even though you do not currently live there. You do not have to own the property, although subletting rooms in a rented property would need the landlord's agreement. The definition of 'living accommodation' does not have to mean place of permanent residence. It would be permanent in the case of a lodger, but the law does not specify permanence as a requirement. A holidaymaker living there for only one or two weeks would be perfectly acceptable under the law. If your tax inspector *does* try to claim you cannot use the relief for temporary lettings or says you cannot let the whole of your home, as then it could not be your 'only or main residence', point out that nowhere in the legislation[2] does it say your home ceases to be your 'only or main residence' when you go on holiday.

Use a limited liability partnership (LLP) to hold property

Property is usually held either personally or through a limited company. Consider using an LLP to own such property and introduce your own company as one of the members of the LLP. This will offer you the best of both types of structure. The LLP treats assets as taxable on the LLP members, with capital and income being something that the LLP members can agree between themselves each year. Including the company member in the LLP allows, for example, some or all of the taxable income to be paid to the company and taxed at the company rate. This might enable you to avoid higher-rate income tax arising to you personally from other sources.

Additional planning can be undertaken that would enable you to access the profits arising within the limited company LLP member, by requiring the company to introduce capital to the LLP but to fund that over a period of years as it generates profits from the LLP. Specialist advice is required for such planning and its efficacy will depend very much on the asset and your personal circumstances.

Make a gift to charity

Gifts to registered charities expand your basic rate income tax band. This provides higher-rate tax relief on any taxable income above the threshold at which higher-rate tax becomes payable. It may also allow capital gains to be taxed at 18% rather than 28%. For a more detailed explanation of the tax treatment of charitable gifts, see Chapter 19 on Philanthrophy.

Become a non-UK tax resident

If you become a non-UK resident for one complete tax year then no UK income tax is usually payable on income arising while you are non-resident. This also extends to gains arising on life insurance investment bonds and offers an opportunity to rebase the value of the bond

---

[2] Section 784 of the Income Tax (Trading & Other Income) Act 2005 dictates exactly how the rent-a-room relief must be applied.

for future investment purposes. It is usually best to avoid holding UK shares or equity funds that generate income while you are a non-UK resident, due to the imposition of unreclaimable withholding tax.

If you have assets that you acquired while a UK resident and on which you crystallise a capital gain after you become a non-UK resident, then you must remain a non-UK resident for at least five complete tax years to avoid capital gains becoming payable retrospectively. If you acquire an asset after you have become a non-UK resident, you may crystallise any capital gains while you remain a non-UK resident and you will usually[3] avoid UK capital gains tax, even if you return to the UK within five years of leaving.

Offset trading losses against income

Business trading losses incurred personally, whether as a sole trader or as a partner or member of an LLP, can be claimed against your other income, from whatever source, in the same year as the loss or the preceding year. Loss relief can similarly be claimed against capital gains, which is likely to be more useful now that the top rate of capital gains tax is 28%. Trading losses arising in the first four years of a new business may be offset against taxable income going back up to three years on a first in and last out basis. While making losses is not to be welcomed, getting the taxman to help you will at least soften the blow! This illustrates a key benefit of using an LLP (possibly with a limited company member) as the primary structure for business and other investment assets, if you have other income subject to the higher or additional income tax rate.

Invest in a venture capital trust (VCT) or an enterprise investment scheme (EIS)

Although traditionally these were high-risk investments, a number of providers now issue lower-risk funds that invest in cash-generative trades, where the objective is to return the original capital invested through an orderly wind-up and distribution of cash after a set number of years.

---

3 Where an asset has been acquired by an individual when non-UK-resident, but which is classed as a replacement asset for an asset previously acquired while UK-resident, then capital gains can become payable on the disposal of the asset acquired while non-UK-resident.

Up to £200,000 may be invested in a VCT each tax year with income tax relief of up to 30%, subject to holding the shares for 5 years. Up to £500,000 (£1 million from 2012/13) may be invested in an EIS each tax year (and a further £500,000 for the previous tax year), with income tax relief of up to 30% (20% if carried back to 2010/11), subject to holding the shares for 3 years. The income tax relief provided on both a VCT and EIS is limited to the extent of your tax liability.

Employing family

If you run your own business and have a lower tax-paying spouse/civil partner or other family member, then you might consider employing them in your business. As long as you pay them below the thresholds at which income and National Insurance are payable (about £7,000 per annum should be fine) no tax will be payable, but valuable State benefits will be accrued. Make sure, however, that they actually do sufficient work to justify the income.

Share the business

You might also give your spouse/civil partner, and possibly your children, shares in your company or partnership so that profits can be distributed to them but be careful if your business is already worth a lot and make sure you take proper tax advice.

Minimise capital gains tax

- Use your annual exemption to crystallise gains.
- Hold capital growth assets within an ISA.
- If your gains exceed the capital gains tax exemption each tax year then consider crystallising sufficient losses to offset those gains.
- Make an irrevocable transfer of assets to a non-basic rate taxpaying spouse/civil partner prior to realising capital gains so they are taxed at 18% rather than 28%.
- Make a pension contribution and/or a charitable gift. This will expand your basic rate income tax band, so that taxable capital gains are taxed at 18% rather than 28%.

■ If you do crystallise some capital gains, be careful about also realising losses before 6 April. Capital losses made in a tax year first have to be offset against gains made in the same tax year, with any extra losses carried forward to future years. If your gains alone would have been within your annual exemption, the losses are effectively wasted. Losses arising from previous tax years may continue to be carried forward indefinitely.

Overseas property ownership

If you are UK-resident/domiciled and wish to buy overseas property or if you are not UK-resident, ordinarily resident or domiciled and you wish to buy UK property, consider holding this through an offshore company and/or offshore trusts as it might offer advantages compared to direct ownership.

Trading assets

Subject to the normal caveats about risk and liquidity, consider investing in a trading business so that disposal of the business would be eligible for entrepreneur's relief, giving CGT at 10% on up to £10 million of gain.

Business profit extraction

Choose your business entity and method of profit extraction carefully. The choice is between sole trader, limited liability partnership (LLP) and limited company (UK or overseas) and each has a different tax effect. Don't assume that a limited company is the correct choice because this effectively creates an artificial tax barrier around profits and assets that can reduce flexibility. An LLP structure, on the other hand, is transparent for tax purposes but by having a limited company member (like a partner) you can get the best of both worlds.

The need for advice

The UK tax system is intricate and constantly changing so your planning needs to be regularly reviewed in the light of the rules and legislation applying. Depending on the level of your wealth and how complex your affairs are, you may need to employ a tax adviser. Minimising tax usually requires a coordinated approach and a mixture of planning tactics. This has never been more so than in today's taxation environment!

A common mistake is to confuse having an accountant with having a tax adviser. The majority of accountants are not tax advisers but are, in all truth, better described as tax and accounts compliance experts. A decent accountant will make sure that you prepare your tax information, make the correct disclosures and submit your tax return within the appropriate timescales. Because of their personality traits and business model, most accountants are keen to preserve their regular fee income arising from tax compliance and audit work. While some do look to provide added-value services like tax planning, for many it is not their focus and they often see it as a risky activity.

A qualified tax adviser, on the other hand, understands the detail of tax legislation/practice and is constantly seeking out ways to arrange clients' financial affairs to minimise taxation. A tax adviser's business model may include a tax compliance service, but many of the best advisers do not get involved in compliance, preferring to work with clients' existing accountants. The best tax advisers are creative, proactive and generate fee income from delivering real tax savings that repay their fees many times over.

And finally...

Tax is a complex area and not something that any affluent or wealthy person should approach lightly. HMRC's new aggressive approach, together with the demands for tax revenue, are likely to see high-value taxpayers targeted more and more for investigation. It makes sense, therefore, to ensure that you have your tax affairs in tip-top condition.

13

The role of insurance

The extent to which you need insurance will depend on a number of factors personal to your own situation, including available financial resources, lifestyle spending, financial commitments and family health history. Perhaps a more important factor is your own view on insurance and if it is a good use of the family wealth to take the risk of self-insuring. In addition, in the case of inheritance tax, much will depend on your views on wealth succession and if you are concerned to replace any wealth lost to the State in tax upon your demise.

In the context of your wealth plan, there are six possible uses of insurance:

1 to protect against loss or damage to material assets like property, vehicles and possessions using general insurance (GI)

2 to protect against unforeseen but financially significant expenditure on healthcare and/or long-term care using private medical (PMI) and long-term care insurance (LTC) respectively

3 to protect against the loss of earned income as a result of being unable to work due to ill health using permanent health insurance (PHI)

4 to provide protection for your surviving family or business against a known liability such as a mortgage, business loan or business buy-out that may be called in following your death or critical illness

5 to protect against outliving your pension resources by transferring investment and longevity risk to an insurance company through the purchase of a traditional or limited-term annuity

6 to replace the value of your estate that would be lost to inheritance tax (IHT) following death through the use of either whole-of-life insurance or seven-year level or decreasing-term insurance.

Insuring property and possessions

Most people underinsure their property and physical possessions, either because they underestimate the true replacement costs at the outset and/or because they fail to update it against inflation. While price is often a major factor in choosing general insurance, it really should only be one factor. While none of us expects to have to call out the fire service, if we do so we want to know that they haven't gone for the cheapest fire engine that fails to start when they get our call! General insurance is the same in the sense that if you need to claim you don't want to find that either the small print excludes your claim and/or getting paid out takes you ages (not to mention wasted hours dealing with the claims department!)

Higher-value homes, cars and possessions need to be covered by insurers that understand and specialise in providing such cover. I recommend using the services of a reputable and experienced general insurance adviser to assess general insurance coverage needs. A good adviser will be happy to visit you at your home and carry out a proper assessment of your needs and suggest a comprehensive solution. You'd be amazed at the real cost of replacing the contents of even a modestly furnished home and wardrobe.

A number of insurers in the higher-value market can provide a single insurance policy that covers all property (including second homes and rental properties), vehicles (including family members and staff) and travel insurance. I can say from personal experience that having one policy to cover these risks is both much easier to administer and ensures nothing 'slips through the gaps'.

Insuring against ill health

While the National Health Service (NHS) provides comprehensive and generally good-quality healthcare, particularly for acute conditions, many families like the choice, flexibility and speed associated with private healthcare. While it is perfectly possible to pay for private healthcare as it is needed, whether or not this is viable will very much depend on the level of your financial resources and your expected quality of health throughout your lifetime.

For most people it will be preferable to put in place some form of private medical insurance (PMI) to provide protection against large medical costs and, as a result, protect the family wealth. The problem with PMI is that it becomes quite expensive as you get older, given the higher risk of claims arising at older ages. There are several ways that you can minimise the cost of PMI and these include having a high excess; accepting a restricted choice of hospitals; restricting certain medical conditions; and the last and probably most popular option being to restrict private healthcare provision to instances in which care could not be provided by the NHS within a specified time period.

Certain long-term health conditions are not treated by the NHS where the primary need is not nursing care. If you live in England or Wales you will be required to pay for any long-term care, whether this is in your own home or a residential care home. Long-term care is most likely to be required in older age and certain health conditions, which are not necessarily life-threatening, can last for many years, causing a serious drain on the family wealth. Long-term care is covered in more detail in Chapter 16.

Long-term care insurance (LTCI) is similar to PMI in that it pays some or all of the costs of care, but only if the insured is unable to perform a number of 'activities of daily living' (ADLs) or is permanently cognitively impaired (senile). ADLs include washing, moving, dressing, feeding, using the toilet and getting in and out of bed and it is usual for the policy to require the policyholder to fail at least two, but more often three, of these before a claim will be paid. LTCI will continue to pay a claim until either recovery or death.

There are relatively few providers active in the LTC market, compared to other types of insurance, but those that are have a lot of experience and some interesting products. There are three types of LTCI policy.

1 **Immediate care annuity** – this is designed for those who need care immediately and wish to pay a single lump sum to pass the long-term liability for funding care costs to an insurance company. As with all annuities, those who live beyond the average will be better off and those who don't will be worse off. An immediate care annuity can be useful if it is essential to have certainty about being able to afford the cost of care but financial resources are limited. However, this still doesn't mean that all future care costs will be covered, particularly if care costs rise faster than the escalation factor (if any) added to the policy.

2 **Pre-funded standalone cover** – this is a pure insurance policy funded by way of either annual or monthly premiums. Whether this is good value or not depends on how long the premiums are paid before a claim. The cost of this cover over the past 15 years or so has increased substantially and this is likely to continue in the future with increasing longevity. This cover is attractive to those who have adequate income/and or capital to fund premiums and view the certainty of paying those premiums as better value than the possibility of their wealth being required to fund care costs.

3 **LTC investment bond** – this is where LTCI is provided in conjunction with an offshore investment bond. Care insurance premiums are deducted from the investment bond, although the capital remains available to the policyholder in the meantime. In the event of a claim for care fees, the capital held within the bond is either available to the policyholder or is used to meet the initial care fees until it is exhausted, depending on which option was chosen at the outset. These policies are potentially useful for those people who have modest needs and want a single investment and care insurance solution. However, they are usually relatively expensive, particularly the investment element, and investment choice may be limited.

Insuring against loss of income

Permanent health insurance (PHI) is neither permanent nor health insurance (which may explain why it is also referred to as income protection insurance), but provides a regular tax-free (as long as it is an individual and not a group policy) income if you are unable to work until recovery, death or the retirement age selected at the outset. The benefit is paid after a deferred period, which can be between 1 and 12 months, and is selected when the policy is established. Generally the longer the deferred period and the earlier the retirement age, then the cheaper the cover will be. Premiums are either guaranteed throughout the policy term or subject to review periodically, with guaranteed premiums being more expensive at the outset. It is also possible to have the income benefit increasing before and/or during a claim to provide some inflation protection.

The basis on which benefits will be paid will also depend on the definition used to describe incapacity. Incapacity can be described as unable to perform:

■ 'any occupation'
■ 'any occupation for which you are suited or trained'
■ 'your own occupation'.

The first definition is the widest and means that you can't do any work, whereas the last is the narrowest definition and means that if you can't do the job you were doing prior to the incapacity, the claim will be paid. If you have a very skilled or specialist occupation, 'own' occupation is preferable, but it is more expensive.

PHI is arguably one of the most underused types of policy, for reasons which have been attributed to the perceived time taken to underwrite benefits, complexity and a lack of awareness by individuals of the likelihood of needing to make a claim. Nevertheless, if you are dependent on earnings for your current and future lifestyle, it is the only insurance that can provide prolonged protection against their loss.

If you are already financially independent but still generating income from employment or self-employment, then there is no need for you to worry about insuring against the loss of that income in the event of ill health or disability. However, if you are using that income to make regular gifts to a family trust or one or more individuals, and you want to continue that in the event of ill health or if you are not quite financially independent and are relying on future earned income to add to your financial resources, then insuring against loss of income should be a priority.

Some professional advisers advocate using LTCI policies to provide for loss of income for younger clients who are happy to accept that benefits will only be paid if they fail two activities of daily living (ADLs), rather than the occupation definitions used in PHI policies. The benefit is that the cost is lower and the claim will potentially be paid for longer, although probably only for serious conditions. It is certainly worth comparing the cost of PHI against LTCI if you only need the cover as a 'nice to have', rather than 'need to have', stopgap.

Insuring against liabilities arising on death

While you can't be immortal, you can mitigate the financial impact on your family and any others who rely on you financially. If you are already financially independent, whether you are still working or not, there are also several situations in which life insurance might be required as part of your overall wealth plan.

Family income benefit (FIB) is a special type of life policy that provides regular payments (free of income tax) in the event of the policyholder's death until the end of the policy term. In effect it is like life insurance in instalments. An FIB policy is likely to be cheaper than a term insurance or whole-of-life policy with the same term and total benefit level. This is because the insurer's risk gradually reduces as the policy progresses. For example, with a 20-year level term policy of £500,000, if the insured died after 19 years and 330 days, the insurer would still have to pay out £500,000. With an FIB policy with £25,000 of annual benefit (a potential total payout of £500,000), if the insured died after 19 years and 330 days, the insurer would only pay out about £2,000, being 1/240th of the total initial benefit. Another benefit of FIB cover is that it avoids the need to have to invest funds to generate an income and therefore keeps things simple at what may be a very difficult time. Some policies allow future benefits to be paid as a discounted lump sum if necessary.

FIB is a very useful and under-used type of life insurance policy that has many uses. The obvious application is for those people still earning income and who want to replace it in the event of their death and where they do not want, or have insufficient resources, to self-insure. However, even if you are financially independent FIB might still be useful as part of an overall estate plan, particularly if you have agreed to fund the education of family or friends or have other regular financial commitments, such as child maintenance payments, that you would like to continue in the event of your death. In this scenario an FIB policy provides a simple and targeted solution. (Please note that to avoid inheritance tax it is usually advisable to assign life policies into a flexible trust. In Chapter 18 I explain the main types of trusts and their application.)

Another type of life assurance policy is a term protection policy. This type of policy has a set term of between 1 month and as long as 40 years during which a lump sum (whether that is level, decreasing or increasing) would be paid out upon your death providing that the premiums are paid on time. The policy never accrues a value unless a claim is paid and premiums can be guaranteed to remain the same throughout the term. Alternatively, for a lower initial level of premium, future premiums can be subject to adjustment if the insurance company's rates change.

A whole-of-life policy is designed to provide life cover, usually, until age 99. Premiums can be guaranteed or reviewable. If reviewable, premiums can be set at a lower initial level (usually the first ten years then at five-yearly intervals) but expect steep increases in the future. The key benefit of this type of policy is that the cover continues as long as you pay the premiums.

Loan protection

If you have any personal or business borrowing, check the position in the event of your death. Some loans have a clause that requires the loan to be repaid if the principal borrower or director dies. It is usually a better use of the family's or business' money to pay insurance premiums than to be scrambling around for cash to pay the bank at such times. Also check that you are getting good value for money as insurance offered by banks and other lenders is rarely the best value, particularly for large policies. The cost of life insurance has fallen a lot in the past ten years as life expectancy has increased. A term protection-only policy is usually the right type of policy in this situation.

Business protection

If you are a partner or one of several shareholders in an unquoted business then you need to ensure that your business or co-business owners have the means to fund any buyout of your share in the event of your death. There are two components to this planning: the agreement to buy and sell and the insurance or financial means to fund the transaction. A double option agreement (which allows either party to enforce it) is usual in the case of individuals, giving both sides the option to buy/sell and a life assurance policy to fund some or all of the buyout without impairing the retention of business or agricultural property relief against IHT on the business assets – see Figure 13.1.

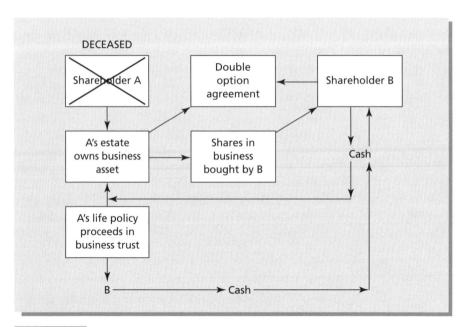

Figure 13.1 Business protection and double option agreement

The life policy can either be owned by the other business owners or by you and written in a special business trust for their benefit. You also need to make sure that you have similar agreements and policies for your other co-owners. Where the company is to be the buyer of your shares in the event of your death then the life policy will be taken out by the company and the company's articles of association need to be checked to ensure that the company is permitted to buy its own shares. Term protection or whole-of-life are suitable to provide this cover but they have different tax treatments on premiums and benefits. This is a complex area and specialist advice is required to ensure that things are structured correctly and the most beneficial tax treatment is secured.

Insuring against living too long

A traditional pension annuity is an insurance policy that allows you to exchange pension capital for a specified and usually guaranteed income throughout life. The life company usually prices an annuity based on four factors: general yields from long-term, fixed interest securities; life expectancy; administration costs; and profit margin. Those annuitants who die earlier than the average subsidise those who live longer than average. Therefore those who do best from annuities are those who live the longest. The problem is that none of us knows exactly when we are going to die and so annuities are a bit of a lucky dip. Henry Allingham is an extreme example of when buying an annuity with a pension fund can turn out to be a good choice. A veteran of the First World War, Henry died in 2010 at the age of 113, having received income from the pension annuity he purchased in 1962, aged 65, for 48 years! It was the insurance company that took the risk Henry would live too long, which turned out to be a good deal for Henry and not such a good one for the annuity provider. Figure 13.2 shows average life expectancy for various age groups.

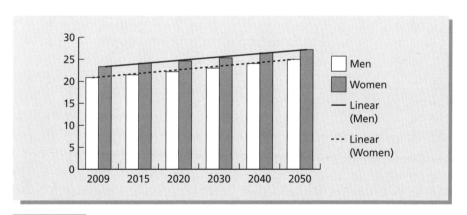

Figure 13.2 Projected current and future life expectancy for men and women at age 65

Source: PPI (2010) 'Retirement income and assets: outlook for the future'

While they do provide certainty, traditional annuities do lack flexibility and may be poor value for money if you die early or annuity
rates improve in the future. As illustrated in Figure 13.3 annuity rates
have actually been falling over the past few decades, mainly due to
a fall in the yields available from long-term gilts and improving life
expectancy. Whether this trend will continue is debatable, particularly if long-term interest rates rise in the future. As a general principle,
it doesn't make sense to take longevity risk (i.e. the risk of living too
long) and you should look to start purchasing an annuity or a series
of annuities over time between the ages of 70 and 80 at the latest. We
discuss the options for taking pension plan benefits in Chapter 15,
where you will find a fuller explanation of the key factors that will
influence your decision on whether or not, or the extent to which,
you should buy a pension annuity with your pension pot.

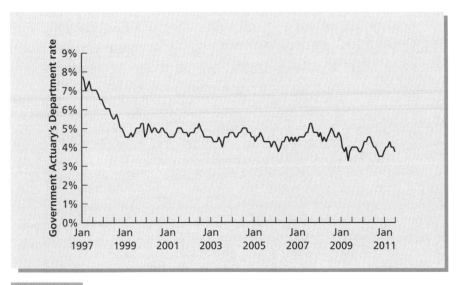

Figure 13.3   Historic annuity rates

Source: Winterthur Life

Inheritance tax (IHT)

If you have an inheritance tax liability (IHT), which you can't or don't
want to carry out any planning to reduce or avoid or perhaps you've
done as much planning as is practical or with which you are comfort-

able, but you are concerned about the loss of your family's wealth to the Exchequer, you may want to consider the role of life insurance. Sometimes it is a better use of the family money to buy life insurance equal to some or all of the IHT liability. While paying insurance is in effect the same thing as paying some of the IHT in advance, it does have the benefit, for those in reasonable health, of being simple and allows you to retain maximum flexibility and control over your wealth.

Table 13.1 illustrates the total cost of guaranteed whole-of-life and term insurance for different amounts of cover at various ages. A joint whole-of-life policy is usually the most competitive policy for couples but single people might find a term policy better value. In any case the cost of the insurance is likely to be much less than the tax liability, in some cases a lot less. Insurance is not a panacea to IHT planning but as one of a range of possible solutions it is worthy of consideration.

Table 13.1 Illustrative cost of £1 million long-term life cover – monthly premiums

Age at outset	Whole-of-life policy to age 99	Level term to age 85
55	788	307
60	1,150	472
65	1,662	704
70	2,311	937
75	3,650	1,300

Source: Avelo Exchange Comparison Services, 22 June 2011

What if you've made an outright gift for which you need to survive seven years before it falls out of your estate and you are concerned about the IHT liability that might arise in the meantime should you not survive the seven years? In these scenarios a short-term life policy is useful, with the cover equal to the tax liability. The policy can either be level or decreasing, known as a gift *inter vivos* ('in life'), depending on whether your nil rate band is available. The policy is written subject to a trust to ensure that the benefit would remain outside your estate and be available to your beneficiaries. There are only a few insurers active in this market and the costs don't seem to be significantly different for those in good health, although if you have a health condition it is probably worth making multiple, simultaneous applications (any medical examinations required can usually be carried out by the same doctor at the same time) to see which provider offers the best terms.

Buying any insurance involves a known cost in return for transferring a risk to an insurance company. In the context of wealth planning the key issue is whether the cost of insurance is a better use of family wealth compared to accepting the possibility of a high-impact but very low-probability risk.

14

State and private pensions

Most UK residents will qualify for a State pension. There are two government-administered State pensions – the basic and additional State pensions.

Basic State pension

The basic State pension (BSP) is a taxable, flat-rate pension payable from State pension age (SPA) to anyone who has built up a sufficient number of qualifying years through payment of National Insurance contributions (or received National Insurance credits – NICs). The maximum (sometimes referred to as 'full') BSP for a single person in 2011/2012 = £102.15 per week.

Since 6 April 2010 a person must have 30 qualifying years for full entitlement to BSP. Entitlement is reduced by 1/30th for each qualifying year below 30. Qualifying years relate to National Insurance contributions (or credits) having been paid.

Married/civil partnership couples

Where a spouse/civil partner does not have sufficient qualifying years for a full BSP in their own right they can apply, on reaching SPA, for a BSP based on their spouse's National Insurance record. The spouse with insufficient National Insurance will obtain 60% of the contributing spouse's BSP (if the contributing spouse has a reduced BSP then it is 60% of the reduced rate). From 6 April 2010 it is no longer a requirement that the contributing spouse has claimed their BSP, they must just be eligible to do so for the spouse with insufficient qualifying years to claim theirs (e.g. a wife reaching SPA at 62 can make a claim based on her husband's National Insurance record providing he has also reached SPA regardless of whether he is claiming or has deferred claiming BSP). Where a married woman has some qualifying years in her own right she can use her husband's National Insurance record to increase her BSP. Her BSP is increased by the lesser of:

■ the shortfall between her reduced rate BSP and the full rate BSP; and
■ the amount of BSP her spouse's record will provide.

This also applies to married men and civil partners but only where their wife/civil partner was born after 6 April 1950.

State pension age (SPA)

BSP is payable from State pension age (SPA). SPA is currently 65 for men and is being raised to 65 for women. This is being phased in over a ten-year period between 2010 and 2020. SPA is being raised to 68 for men and women from 6 April 2024 and this is also being phased in over a 22-year period, although the government has confirmed that it is considering bringing forward these increases as a result of rapid increases in life expectancy.

It is interesting to note that in 1981 individuals received the State pension for 25% of their adult life but by the year 2000 this had increased to 30% and by 2010 it had risen to 33%. To keep the proportion of adult life in receipt of the State pension constant at the 2010 level (33%) the SPA would need to be 66.5 by 2030; at the 2000 level (30%) the SPA would need to rise to 68 by 2030; and to get back to the 1981 level (25%) the SPA would need to rise to 72 by 2030.[1]

---

[1] Pensions Policy Institute (2010) 'Submission to the Work and Pensions Select Committee on the government's pension reforms', p. 4.

Annual increases

For those living in the European Economic Area, the BSP is increased every year by whichever is the highest of:

- the growth in average earnings
- the growth in prices
- or 2.5 per cent.

Additional State pension

The additional State pension is an earnings-related pension, payable on top of the BSP, at SPA. Until April 2002, the additional State pension for employees was called the State Earnings-Related Pension Scheme (SERPS). The amount of SERPS pension you received was based on a combination of your NICs, and how much you earned. In April 2002, SERPS was reformed and renamed the State Second Pension (S2P). It now gives a more generous additional State pension to low and moderate earners, certain carers and people with a long-term illness or disability. The maximum additional State pension between April 2011 and April 2012 is £159.52 each week. If you have joined an employer's pension scheme you may have been 'opted out' of the additional State pension. You can find out more from your scheme administrator or by getting a State pension forecast.

Additional State pension can arise from various different State pension schemes, each with its own different and complicated set of calculations as to benefits payable:

- the graduated retirement pension (GRP) – for earnings between 6 April 1961 and 5 April 1975
- SERPS – for earnings between 6 April 1978 and 5 April 2002[2]
- S2P – for earnings since 6 April 2002.

---

[2] Following a change of government in 1975 no additional State pension was provided until SERPS started 6 April 1978.

Other considerations

Inheriting SERPS/S2P

The surviving spouse or civil partner of a contributor to SERPS/S2P can, on the contributor's death, inherit a percentage of the contributor's SERPS/S2P entitlement. For SERPS the maximum percentage payable is dependent on the date the contributor reaches SPA: for a contributor reaching SPA after 6 October 2010 the maximum SERPS their surviving spouse/civil partner can inherit is 50%. For S2P the maximum amount a surviving spouse/civil partner can inherit is 50%.

Deferring State pension

An individual can choose to defer taking their State pension. Any deferral of at least 5 weeks or more will result in an increase of 1% of their weekly State pension (basic and additional) for every 5-week period. This equates to a 10.4% increase for a full year. If the period of deferral is 12 months or more the amount deferred (plus interest of at least 2%) may be taken as a taxable lump sum.

Annual increases

Once in payment the additional State pension is increased in line with the retail prices index. This may change in future as the coalition have plans to:

■ restore the link between BSP increases and earnings (providing a triple guarantee)

■ change the index used from the retail prices index to the consumer prices index.

The Directgov website provides further information about basic and additional State pensions, and provides a quick estimate State pension profiler tool that calculates the BSP earned to date (see **www.direct.gov. uk/en/Pensionsandretirementplanning/StatePension/DG_184319**).

The basic and additional State pensions are dependent on an individual's NICs and earnings over their working life. Additional State pension calculations are extremely complex and may be made up of a combination of GRP, SERPS and/or S2P. A comprehensive forecast based on an individual's National Insurance record can be obtained from the Pension Service part of the Department for Work and Pensions (see **www.direct.gov.uk/en/Pensionsandretirementplanning/ StatePension/StatePensionforecast/DG_10014008**).

Private pensions

Registered pension schemes are subject to limits on funding and benefits, with tax charges levied on any excesses. Below is an outline of the main features of the different types of schemes, followed by the funding limits and planning considerations.

Defined benefits

Where retirement benefits are provided by an occupational pension plan, whether a private or public-sector type, and calculated on the basis of service, salary and an accrual rate, it is the pension scheme and, by association, the sponsoring employer that bears most of the risk and costs associated with providing the pension benefits. In this sense the overall benefits are known but the future costs of providing them are not. For this reason most defined benefit schemes have closed to new members and many have closed to existing members as employers seek to minimise future funding liabilities.

However, if your benefits have yet to be paid out, either because you are still working and accruing service or have left service before the normal retirement age, you need to check the financial position of the scheme and the commitment of the sponsoring employer to continue to fund the scheme. Every three years the trustees are required to provide an assessment of the scheme's financial position and whether there are sufficient assets to secure all members' pension benefits through an insurance company if the scheme was wound up at that time.

While this assessment can be seen as the worse case scenario, it can often suggest that a scheme is underfunded, when on a going concern basis, it is not. This is because securing pensions with insurance companies is very expensive. In addition, if the assessment has been carried out when investment markets have fallen sharply, this will overstate the underfunding, when in reality members take benefits at different times, thus providing the trustees with some flexibility to ride out short-term investment volatility.

If the pension scheme fails and is unable to pay out existing or future pension benefits then a government-sponsored scheme known as the Pension Protection Fund (PPF) will step in and provide benefits up to a maximum amount. If you have reached the scheme's retirement age or are in receipt of an ill health pension or where a survivor's pension is in payment, then the protected amount will be 100% of the pension. Otherwise the protected amount will be 90% of the pension benefit. The maximum protected amount payable is currently about £30,000 per annum at age 65, but lower for younger ages and higher for older ages.

Clearly, if you have a defined pension that is significantly in excess of £30,000 and/or the pension benefit represents a significant amount of the income funding your lifetime spending, then you need to be more concerned about the financial health of the scheme and possibly investigate whether it makes sense to transfer the cash value of your benefits to either your own self-invested personal pension or your current employer's pension plan.

Other reasons why you might wish to transfer benefits, regardless of whether or not the scheme is in good financial health, include the following:

- You do not need the guarantees that the scheme provides and/or the benefits are insignificant in relation to your overall wealth and you are comfortable with taking on the investment and longevity risk (living too long).
- You envisage living abroad when you take benefits and wish to mitigate the currency risks by investing and eventually taking benefits in the currency of your new country of residence.
- You do not need some of the benefits that the scheme provides such as spouse's and dependents' pensions and would prefer to have a higher pension.
- You would like flexibility as to the level of benefits that you take from year to year, with the ability to vary these to suit your spending need.

▪ You have little confidence in the scheme trustees and/or the employer.

▪ You believe that you (or an investment manager) can obtain a better return on the pension fund than the scheme trustee.

▪ You wish to invest in a commercial property possibly to be used by your business.

A defined benefit pension is potentially a very valuable benefit and can provide a good foundation to your wealth plan. However, if benefits have yet to come into payment, it will certainly be advisable to regularly review both how the scheme fits into your overall planning as well as the financial strength of the scheme. Because assessing the merits of transferring a defined pension benefit can be complex you may need to consult an independent financial adviser who is qualified and authorised to give such advice. Expect to pay at least £1,500 for this type of advice, although the larger the benefits then the larger will be the fee to reflect the additional risks to the adviser.

Defined contribution pension plans

In contrast to a defined benefit plan, with a defined contribution (DC) plan the contribution levels are known (if continuing), whereas the eventual benefits are not. The benefits that the plan can provide will depend directly on the size of the fund (influenced by both contributions made and investment returns achieved) as well as long-term interest rates. Interest rates affect annuity rates, particularly at younger ages, which in turn will dictate the level of guaranteed income that can be secured with the fund or, alternatively, the maximum level of income which can be withdrawn directly from the fund. The member of a DC pension plan, therefore, takes on all the investment and longevity risks.

A registered pension scheme may invest up to 5% of its funds in the ordinary share capital of a sponsoring employer. Up to four sponsoring employers can be invested in as long as the total holdings are less than 20% of the fund value in total. The value is only tested at the time the investment is made and not subsequently. There is no restriction on how much of the sponsoring company's shares may be owned by a pension plan and this could, in theory, be 100%.

There are two types of DC pension: occupational and personal.

Occupational schemes

An occupational scheme is designed to provide benefits for the employees of a sponsoring employer and is subject to a detailed set of scheme rules and trust deed. The benefits that the scheme can provide will be based on the value of funds earmarked for individual members, but will be subject to overall limits set by HMRC.

Another type of occupational DC pension is the Small Self-Administered Scheme (SSAS), which was originally designed for controlling directors so that they could combine the benefits of pension tax relief but with some flexibility to use pension funds for business purposes. A SSAS may lend up to 50% of the fund to the sponsoring employer for commercial purposes, subject to taking adequate security, the loan being repaid in instalments not exceeding five years and the interest being at least 1% over the bank base rate. A loan may not be given for the purposes of keeping an ailing business afloat.

Personal

A personal plan is an individual plan in the member's own name and contributions can be made by the member, the member's employer or a combination of the two. There is no need for a sponsoring employer and all compliance with HMRC rules is handled by the pension scheme provider, not the employer. As a result, an increasing number of employers have put in place group personal pension plans (GPPPs) that combine the benefits of individual pension accounts with centralised payment and administration.

Usually the plan is derived from a master scheme trust, from which it derives its rules and compliance from the tax rules for registered pensions. However, a small number of personal pensions can be established under an individual trust arrangement that has its own set of individual scheme rules, although in practice these are based on 'model' trust wordings. I'll explain more about how and why you might want to use a master trust-type scheme shortly.

Personal plans can be provided by a wide range of suppliers including investment groups, insurance companies and professional trust companies. Increasingly plans are being offered on what is known as a self-invested basis, otherwise known as a self-invested personal pension (SIPP). This allows members a wide choice of investments in which they can invest their fund including commercial property. Alternatively a member may appoint a professional investment manager to manage the investment of some or all of their pension fund.

The contribution limits

The maximum annual contribution permitted to any pension plan is set at £50,000 and is known as the annual allowance. Pension accrued under a defined benefit plan is multiplied by 16 to determine the value for annual allowance purposes with allowance given for inflationary increases. Any personal contributions must not exceed 100% of earnings although up to £3,600 per year can be contributed without any earnings. Employer contributions may be made without reference to the member's earnings although they are, in aggregate with personal contributions, subject to the annual allowance (including any carry forward relief available).

Tax relief is given at your highest rate by extending the basic rate income tax band (although this does not change the tax position of gains arising on investment bonds). A pension contribution can thus be used to:

- bring a 40% or 50% taxpayer below the threshold at which that rate is paid
- enable capital gains otherwise taxable at 28% to be taxed at 18%
- retain the personal allowance by bringing income below the £100,000 threshold.

See Figures 14.1 and 14.2.

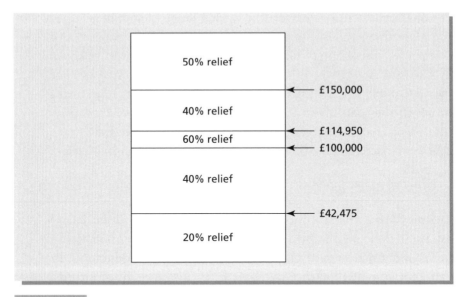

Figure 14.1 Tax relief from pension contributions against taxable income

Figure 14.2 How tax relief is given on pension contributions

Putting aside for one moment any investment returns arising, making pension contributions can be highly attractive for certain taxpayers due to the availability of a 25% pension commencement lump sum (PCLS), that is currently tax-free. Table 14.1 shows the uplift in value for different taxpayers, disregarding any investment returns. The best effect is where tax relief is obtained at the rate of 40% or more but benefits are taxed at 40% or less. Someone obtaining effective tax relief of 60% (those with taxable income over £100,000) but who only pay 20% on those pension benefits would obtain a staggering 212% uplift by making a pension contribution.

Table 14.1 Uplift in value of pension contributions assuming 25% tax-free lump sum

Tax relief on contribution	20%	40%	50%	60%
20%	6.25	−12.5	−21.87	−31.25
40%	41.67	16.67	4.17	−8.34
50%	70	40	25	10
60%*	212	75	56.25	37.5

This is the effective income tax rate for those with taxable income of between £100,000 and £114,950 due to the loss of personal allowance

Contributions in excess of the annual allowance may incur a tax charge if there is not any unused relief to carry forward from the previous three tax years. The tax charge has the effect of clawing back any tax relief provided. Carry forward is available to the extent that, in any of the previous three years, you had a registered pension plan and did not make a contribution of £50,000, regardless of whether or not you were permitted to make contributions in those years (perhaps because you had insufficient earnings or were subject to the high-earner pension restrictions introduced in April 2009). The surplus (starting with the oldest year) is then rolled forward to the current year to enable relief to be provided on the excess contribution over £50,000.

Figure 14.3 illustrates the position for Charlotte, who is a company director and has had a SIPP since 2005. She has a total of £90,000 unused relief available to carry forward to 2011/2012, allowing a maximum contribution of £140,000 to be made in that tax year.

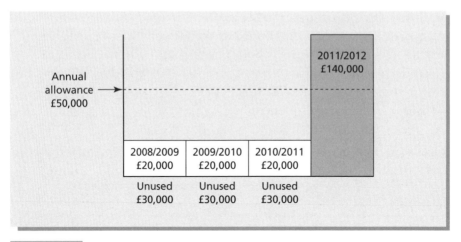

Figure 14.3 Example of carry forward of unused pension allowance – 2011/2012

Source: AXA Wealth

If you had made a contribution of £20,000 in 2008/2009 and £80,000 in 2009/2010, then the carry forward of £30,000 from 2008/2009 would be offset against the excess of £30,000 in 2009/2010. However, if the contributions had been the other way round then the excess in 2008/2009 would not be offset against the carry forward available in 2009/2010, thus permitting £30,000 of carry forward. Great care is required to ensure that you do not inadvertently incur an annual allowance tax charge and this is an area where a good adviser can be very helpful.

As time goes on the carry forward calculations could get a bit complicated. Let's assume that Charlotte or her employer made a contribution of £100,000 in the 2011/2012 tax year, making use of carry forward of £50,000 (£30,000 from 2008/2009 and £20,000 from 2009/2010). In the 2012/2013 tax year she can still make use of unused carry forward relief of £40,000 from the 2009/2010 and 2010/2011 tax years to enable her employer or herself (if she has sufficient earnings) to make a contribution of £90,000 (£50,000 + £40,000). See Figure 14.4.

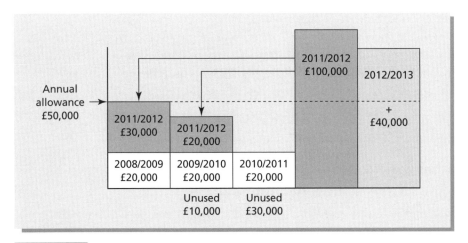

Figure 14.4   Example of carry forward of unused pension allowance – 2012/2013

Source: AXA Wealth

This is a simplified example of how the carry forward works. In practice different circumstances will cause different outcomes and considerations, particularly if you have more than one pension plan and/or you have a plan or your historic contributions may include one or more years in which you or your employer contributed more than £50,000.

The lifetime limit

The amount of benefit that you may accrue within a registered pension plan is limited to an upper limit known as the lifetime allowance. There are four types of lifetime allowance:

1 standard – £1.5 million (from 6 April 2012)

2 fixed protection – up to £1.8 million (from 6 April 2012)

3 enhanced – no limit (if applied for between 6 April 2006 and 5 April 2009)

4 primary – limit is the amount that the fund exceeded £1.5 million on 6 April 2006, increased by 20%.

For defined benefit pension plans, benefits are multiplied by 20 to determine their value for lifetime allowance purposes. If your pension fund exceeds the available lifetime allowance when you take benefits then a tax charge will apply of either 25% if you take the excess as an income or 55% if you take the excess as a lump sum.

Clearly it doesn't make sense to exceed the lifetime allowance and therefore you need to monitor the effect of:

■ any new proposed contributions

■ the investment strategy and returns arising

■ if and when to take benefits from the plan in the form of a tax-free lump sum and taxable income.

I'll explain in more detail how best to manage your pension plan in the next chapter, but for now I just want to consider the lifetime allowance in the context of whether or not you make any new contributions. As illustrated in Table 14.2, if you have no existing pension provision then it is unlikely that you will exceed the lifetime allowance unless you contribute at least £25,000 per annum for 30 years or are older and contribute the maximum and achieve quite high investment returns.

Table 14.2 Summary of growth required to reach standard lifetime allowance

Age	Annual contribution £10,000	£25,000	£50,000	Term
30	7.07%	2.82%	**−0.87%**	35
35	9.05%	4.16%	0%	30
40	12.03%	6.21%	1.38%	25
45	16.89%	9.61%	3.72%	20
50	25.98%	16.02%	8.27%	15
55	47.70%	31.38%	19.34%	10
60	145.96%	98.43%	67.17%	5

Source: AXA Wealth

Table 14.3 shows the annual investment return required to reach the lifetime allowance at different fund values and terms assuming ongoing contributions are made equal to the annual allowance of £50,000. Fund values in excess of about £900,000 with a term of more than 5 years need either low or negative returns to avoid breaching the lifetime allowance.

Table 14.3 Ready reckoner – annual growth required to fund £1.5 million lifetime allowance assuming £50,000 annual contributions

Term to retirement / Existing fund	5 years	10 years	15 years	20 years
£100,000	44.71%	14.28%	6.19%	2.66%
£200,000	33.62%	11.04%	4.69%	1.81%
£300,000	26.37%	8.65%	3.50%	1.12%
£400,000	21.06%	6.77%	2.51%	0.52%
£500,000	16.88%	5.22%	1.68%	0%
£600,000	13.47%	3.90%	0.95%	−0.46%
£700,000	10.60%	2.75%	0.30%	−0.87%
£800,000	8.12%	1.74%	−0.28%	−1.25%
£900,000	5.95%	0.83%	−0.80%	−1.59%
£1,000,000	4.03%	0%	−1.28%	−1.91%
£1,100,000	2.30%	−0.74%	−1.73%	−2.21%
£1,200,000	0.74%	−1.43%	−2.14%	−2.48%
£1,300,000	−0.69%	−2.07%	−2.52%	−2.74%
£1,400,000	−2.01%	−2.66%	−2.88%	−2.99%

Source: AXA Wealth

Qualified non-UK pension scheme (QNUPS)

This is the term given to most overseas pension plans that meet certain rules set down by HMRC. QNUPS plans fall into two types:

1 those that are classed as qualifying recognised overseas pension schemes (QROPS) because they have received a transfer in of benefits from a UK pension scheme

2 those that are not a QROPS because they do not qualify to receive a transfer in of benefits from a UK pension scheme.

The key benefits of a QNUPS, which is not also a QROPS, are as follows:

■ there is no limit on the amount that may be contributed but no tax relief is given

■ non-UK-sited investments usually grow tax-free

■ no limits on the shape of benefits provided and potential to avoid tax on amounts taken as a lump sum

■ potential to borrow from the fund between 25 and 50% depending on the jurisdiction

■ ability to invest in wide range of investments including residential property

■ no UK inheritance tax on the value of the fund as long as it is being used as a proper retirement plan.

With the exception of defined benefit plans, pension plans are merely tax wrappers within which one can hold some wealth to achieve a tax effect. The tax reliefs on offer – income tax, tax-free growth and freedom from inheritance tax – are very attractive. In the next chapter I'll explain how best to manage pension assets in the context of your overall wealth plan.

15

Managing your pension portfolio

For many people the value of their pension represents a significant element of their wealth and one that needs to be factored into a comprehensive wealth plan. In Chapter 10 we looked at the issues relating to taking regular withdrawals from an investment portfolio and the potential problems associated with funding a constant expenditure with volatile investment assets. Similar considerations apply to managing the investment strategy of your pension plan(s) and deciding how and when to take benefits, but with the added complication of the tax treatment being affected by how benefits are taken, particularly with larger funds.

The main factors that you need to consider in the management of your pension assets are as follows:

■ cashflow needs

■ life expectancy and dependants' situation

■ income tax, capital gains tax and residency status

■ pension lifetime allowance

■ investment risk and taxation of investments

■ estate planning considerations.

Cashflow needs

As we saw in Chapter 3 having an idea of your cashflow needs is likely to help you to make better financial decisions and should form the cornerstone of your wealth plan. With pensions this is even more important so that you can determine how and when to take benefits, what risks you need to take and how best to minimise or avoid tax. It is essential to bear in mind that your pension fund should not be looked at in isolation. You will need to consider the level of cashflow net of tax, that your non-pension investment portfolio can provide. If your investment portfolio was established in the expectation of no withdrawals being required, it may need to be reviewed if it is tax-inefficient or unfeasible for your pension portfolio to meet all your lifestyle costs.

The earliest age at which you can take benefits from your pension is usually 55, unless you are in a special occupation that permits earlier access (e.g. sports person, model, etc.) or you qualify for a severe and permanent ill-health pension. There is no longer a time limit for taking pension benefits, whether that is as an income or lump sum.

Life expectancy and dependants

How long you expect to live has important implications for how you manage your wealth generally but it is particularly important in the context of pension assets because it dictates the time horizon that your fund needs to last. As I explained in Chapter 3 life expectancy has been rising in the UK over the past 50 years. Unless you have a chronic/terminal health condition, it is impossible to know how long you are likely to live, but the evidence suggests that it will be a lot longer than you think. As a general rule it doesn't make sense to take longevity risk, particularly if you expect above-average life expectancy, so you might find purchasing a guaranteed pension annuity a more attractive option for some or your entire fund. In this context the annuity is insurance against living too long.

Income tax, etc.

Pension benefits are usually available in the form of a tax-free lump sum, known as a pension commencement lump sum (in most cases this is 25% of the fund value) and a taxable income. If you have secure pension income of at least £20,000 per annum you may also take the entire fund (after deducting the 25% tax-free amount) as a taxable lump sum. The tax rate applied to this lump sum is determined by adding it to your other taxable income in the tax year when you take the benefit.

Pension income (or a taxable lump sum) forms the bottom element of taxable income together with State pensions and income from employment and self-employment as illustrated in Figure 15.1. As such, it uses up some of your lower- and/or higher-rate income tax band and can affect whether or not you retain your personal income tax allowance. With income tax rates as high as 50% and capital gains tax also affected by whether you are a basic- or higher-rate taxpayer, it makes sense to carefully consider the income tax effect of different ways of taking pension benefits.

It may be that that you can take pension benefits gradually over a number of years and use tax-free lump sums to provide cash inflow to meet income needs each year, together with taxable income either directly from the fund or from the purchase of an annuity. Although your pension can only be paid to you and taxed as your income, you could take the maximum pension commencement lump sum from your whole pension, whether you take an income or not, and give it to your spouse or civil partner to buy a 'purchased life annuity' or income-generating investments, if your spouse/civil partner would then be subject to a lower rate of tax on their own income than you would be.

If you have investments outside of tax wrappers or pensions that generate capital gains more than your annual exemption, the rate of taxable capital gains will be determined by the total amount of taxable income you receive from all sources, including your pension plan. If any part of the taxable gain, when aggregated with your taxable income, falls into the basic rate income tax band, then it will be taxed at 18%. Otherwise the capital gains tax rate will be 28%. It can be very useful, therefore, to have the flexibility to control how much taxable income you receive from your pension portfolio, where you anticipate ongoing capital gains arising from an investment portfolio or variable taxable income.

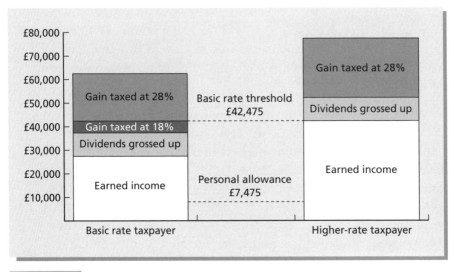

Figure 15.1 Order in which income and gains are taxed

Pension lifetime allowance

The lifetime allowance represents the maximum amount of pension fund (or cash equivalent for defined benefit schemes) that you are permitted to have. The limit will reduce from £1.8 million to £1.5 million on 6 April 2012. Any excess over the lifetime allowance is subject to a tax surcharge of 25% plus income tax at your marginal rate if the excess is taken as an income or 55% if the excess is taken as a lump sum. Although the lifetime limit will reduce from £1.8 million to £1.5 million on 6 April 2012, the old limit of £1.8 million continues to apply if you have applied for fixed protection by 6 April 2012 and cease to make further contributions from that date.

Fixed protection makes sense if you anticipate the growth of your fund causing you to exceed the new £1.5 million limit. However, if your fund is significantly below the new £1.5 million lifetime allowance and you and/or your employer would still have scope to make further contributions and obtain tax relief of 50% with regard to any personal contributions, you might prefer to adopt a very cautious investment approach and not apply for fixed protection to enable you to continue to make tax-relievable contributions.

Investment risk and tax efficiency

Investment returns arising within a pension plan grow free of tax. With the exception of withholding tax on dividends from equities, there is no tax on interest, dividends, property, rental income or capital gains arising within the fund. It is therefore more tax-efficient to hold interest, rental-producing commercial property or capital gains-generating investments than those producing dividends.

Table 15.1 Ready reckoner – annual returns required to achieve £1.5 million lifetime allowance with no new contributions

Term to retirement / Existing fund value	5 years	10 years	15 years	20 years
£100,000	71.83%	31.08%	19.78%	14.49%
£200,000	49.60%	22.31%	14.37%	10.60%
£300,000	37.95%	17.45%	11.32%	8.38%
£400,000	30.24%	14.12%	9.21%	6.83%
£500,000	24.56%	11.61%	7.60%	5.65%
£600,000	20.11%	9.59%	6.30%	4.69%
£700,000	16.46%	7.92%	5.21%	3.89%
£800,000	13.39%	6.49%	4.28%	3.20%
£900,000	10.76%	5.24%	3.47%	2.59%
£1,000,000	8.45%	4.14%	2.74%	2.05%
£1,100,000	6.40%	3.15%	2.09%	1.57%
£1,200,000	4,57%	2.26%	1.50%	1.13%
£1,300,000	2.91%	1.45%	0.96%	0.72%
£1,400,000	1.39%	0.70%	0.47%	0.35%

Source: AXA Wealth

If you are near to the lifetime limit of £1.5 million (or £1.8 million if fixed protection applies) then you should follow a cautious investment strategy because there is no reason to take 100% of the risk of capital loss and only 45% of any returns, due to the tax charge levied if you exceed the lifetime allowance. Table 15.1 shows the annual returns required at different fund values to reach the £1.5 million standard lifetime allowance. The larger fund values and longer terms require the lowest growth to reach the limit. If you benefit from enhanced or primary protection because you had significant pension benefits before 6 April 2006, then these considerations do not apply and you are free to pursue whatever investment strategy you wish.

Estate planning

The value of pension funds is usually exempt from inheritance tax at all ages. Any lump sum you choose to take from your pension plan (whether tax-free or taxable if you qualify for flexible drawdown), will immediately form part of your estate for inheritance tax to the extent that you do not spend it. How death benefits are distributed from your pension plan will depend on the way the plan has been set up and whether it has an integrated or master trust. Most plans are under a master trust and the member gives the trustees an expression of wishes or nomination form specifying who they would like to benefit in the event of their death. There could be advantages to setting up a special pension 'by-pass' trust and nominating any death benefits to be paid to that trust. See Chapter 18 for more details.

A flat rate tax charge of 55% is payable on lump sum death benefits paid from a scheme (or part of a scheme) from which benefits have been taken (known as benefit crystallisation) or for any plan, regardless of whether or not benefits have been taken, where the member is aged 75 or over.

Taking benefits

Extracting benefits from an approved pension scheme used to be straightforward – they were paid as an annuity, some of which could be sacrificed in exchange for a tax-free lump sum. Over the years the number of options has increased considerably, culminating in the introduction in April 2011 of capped and flexible income drawdown, which provide even greater options to avoid annuity purchase altogether.

The following is a brief summary of the current options available to pension investors for the vesting of benefits. They are not mutually exclusive and, in many cases, a combination of them together with, possibly, ongoing earnings and/or drawings from an investment portfolio or other assets will prove to be the preferred route to provide for ongoing expenditure requirements when full-time paid work has ceased to become a necessity.

Annuities
Conventional annuity

An annuity is not an investment but an insurance policy against living too long. Although this is the most straightforward option it is still worthwhile to use the open market option, which allows the annuity to be purchased from any provider, not just the one with whom the existing fund is held (assuming that the existing provider offers annuities, which it will not unless it is an insurance company). Annuity rates depend on several factors, of which the most important are the level of long-term interest rates and expected mortality rates. Important factors to consider then are the following.

■ Should you take the maximum pension commencement lump sum (i.e. tax-free cash)?

■ Should you purchase a single life annuity or an annuity based on the joint lives of you and your spouse?

■ In the event of your death what proportion (usually 50%, 66% or 100%) of your pension should continue to your spouse or civil partner?

■ Should your pension increase each year and, if so, by how much, given that the higher the level of annual increases, the lower the starting amount?

■ Should you build in a guarantee period of five or ten years in case you die soon after commencement?

■ Could you qualify for an enhanced or impaired life annuity because of your medical history or lifestyle (e.g. if you smoke)?

All of these options affect the income you will receive. You need to know how much each one costs and find the right balance of benefits for your circumstances, as the extent to which you have other assets and sources of income will affect the suitability of each option – the pension income should not be considered in isolation from your other assets. I recommend that a conventional annuity be the default choice, against which all the other options are compared to on the basis that it is the cheapest, simplest, lowest-risk and lowest-cost option for the majority of people. The Financial Services Authority has endorsed this view.

A regulator's view

An increasing number of consumers, especially those moving from defined benefit to defined contribution pension schemes, may demand products that allow decumulation of capital. However, this is an area where consumer financial capability is particularly low.

For many, an annuity will be the most appropriate option. However, people approaching retirement may be more susceptible to sales of income drawdown because, as discussed earlier, annuity rates are lower and could generate an income below consumers' expectations. These factors create the conditions for potential misselling of products that generate higher fees or commissions than annuities, even when annuities would be more appropriate

A related risk is that consumers who buy drawdown products do not understand the need for regular review or take the after-sales advice offered to them to help decide when to purchase an annuity. While the market for income drawdown is small, there has been a significant increase in the volume of sales in recent years.

Financial Services Authority (2010) 'Financial risk, outlook report', March

---

Projected benefits from guaranteed annuities are shown in Figure 15.2.

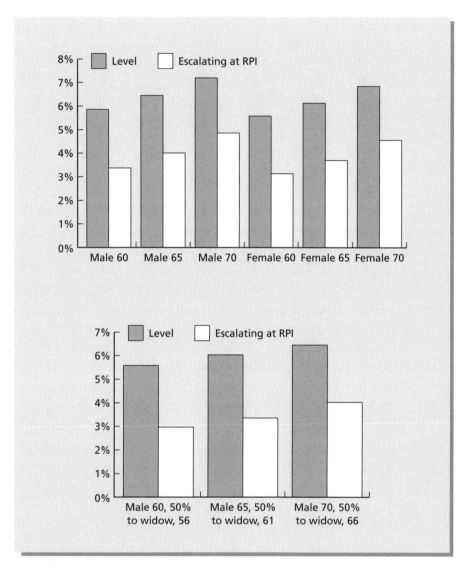

Figure 15.2 Projected benefits from guaranteed annuities

Source: www.moneymadeclear.org.uk (24 June 2011)

With profits annuity

A with profits annuity provides an income that is linked to the investment returns of an insurance company's with profits fund. As for all investment-linked annuities, the income payable can go down as well as up in the future. With profit annuities do however provide smoothed investment returns, so that in poor years, your income will not necessarily go down as much as the underlying investments have gone down, while in good years, not all of the investment return is necessarily paid out (as some is retained to cover the bad years). With profit fund returns should therefore be less volatile than other investment funds.

Typically, income is made up of two parts.

1 **A minimum starting income.** This is set at a low level but, unless investment conditions are very bad, you will usually get at least this much income provided you select a 0% anticipated bonus rate. Some with profits annuities guarantee it.

2 **Bonuses.** The insurance company usually announces bonus rates once a year. Bonuses can be both 'reversionary' (usually announced once a year and then guaranteed to pay out for the duration of your annuity) and 'special' (which only pay out for a year or so until the next bonus announcement). The amount of bonuses depends on many factors, the most important of which is the performance of the underlying assets within the with profits fund itself. However, the insurer's expectations for future mortality and its financial strength are also an influence.

When you start a with profits annuity, you normally select an anticipated bonus rate. The minimum and maximum rates of anticipated bonus rate you can choose vary by provider, but typically, the range is from 0% to 5% and normally once selected it cannot be changed. A very cautious person wishing to use a with profits annuity would choose a 0% anticipated bonus rate. Selecting a higher anticipated rate gives a higher initial income but lower future increases and the income could fall if actual bonuses do not match the anticipated ones.

Some providers allow you to convert to a conventional annuity (which must be purchased with the same provider) at given points in the future. This means that you can change your annuity to one that provides set income levels and no investment risk. This can be useful if your circumstances change or standard annuity rates change.

The main drawback of with profit annuities are that the underlying asset mix is tailored to the liability stream of the insurer, not the investor. There is consequently no inherent relationship between the investment risk that you take and your risk tolerance or capacity and the composition of the underlying fund can change quite dramatically over a relatively short period of time, often without it being obvious until some months later. There is also the fact that some insurers have used their with profit funds to meet the costs of poor past business decisions, such as buying into estate agencies in an attempt to buy market share and meeting the compensation costs for inappropriate advice.

Unit-linked annuity

With a unit-linked annuity, your income in retirement will be linked directly to the value of an underlying fund of investments. Generally, you can choose the types of funds, for example:

■ one or more managed funds whose managers select from a broad range of different assets and may vary the exposure to each over time

■ one or more actively managed sector funds whose managers selects investments from within particular countries or sectors

■ index-tracking funds that track the performance of a particular stock market index.

The riskier the underlying fund you choose, the more your retirement income may vary – both up and down. Some unit-linked annuities work in a similar way to with profits annuities, in that your starting income is based on an assumed growth rate and if the fund grows at that assumed rate, your income stays the same. If growth exceeds the assumed rate, your income increases. If growth is less than the assumed rate, your income falls.

A few unit-linked annuities offer access to a 'protected fund' that limits the fall in your income, although most unit-linked annuities do not guarantee any minimum income. The drawback is that you are restricted to the range of funds offered by the insurer whose annuity product you purchase. It may therefore be difficult or impossible to find a mix of funds that meets your requirements at a reasonable cost, if at all.

Third way products

A few providers now provide what are called 'third way' annuities that combine limited guarantees with some investment upside. While there may be some situations where these are useful, such as where someone needs more income than a guaranteed annuity but can't accept the full risk of income drawdown, their use by affluent and wealthy individuals is likely to be limited.

Self-invested annuities

If you transfer your pension to a Qualified Recognised Overseas Pension Scheme (QROPS) you can use your fund to provide a self-invested annuity. There are two potential benefits of a self-invested annuity. Firstly, you have more flexibility over the amount of income that you may take, usually between 50 and 120% of the average of the best three annuities on the open market, including impaired lives. However, you will be taking the longevity risk yourself rather than passing this to an insurance company. Secondly, you can leave any residual fund available on death to an offshore trust and, as such, avoid the 55% flat rate death charge that would apply if in drawdown. See Table 15.2.

Figure 15.2 Death benefits comparison of SIPP drawdown and open annuity [1]

	Aged 70	Aged 75	Aged 85
SIPP drawdrown fund value	£522,452	£625,844	£727,947
EU open annuity fund value	£500,836	£535,015	£578,836
Difference in fund value	–£51,616	–£90,829	–£149,111
SIPP lump sum death benefit paid to beneficiaries assuming new 55% tax rate	£248,603	£281,629	£327,576
EU open annuity mortality profit paid to offshore trust upon death	£500,836	£535,015	£578,836
Difference	**+£252,233**	**+£253,386**	**+£251,260**

Source: London & Colonial – data provided June 2011

---

[1] Illustration based on a male aged 65 with a pension fund of £500,000 with investment returns of 7% per annum and from which he elects to take annual income of £25,000

Phased retirement or staggered vesting

Phased retirement is the process of taking pension benefits (whether by way of annuity purchase or taking income directly from the fund) over a period of time rather than in one go. Although it used to be necessary for personal pensions to be arranged not as a single plan, but as a cluster of many separate plans or segments for phased retirement to be an option, the introduction of the pensions simplification regime in April 2006 eliminated this requirement and even non-segmented plans can take advantage of the facility. Each time you use part of the fund to purchase an annuity or provide income withdrawals, you can first take part of it as a pension commencement lump sum of up to 25% of the total amount being vested. Repeating the process regularly means that you can effectively use the pension commencement lump sum as well as the annuity or income withdrawal to provide your cashflow for each year, as Figure 15.3 shows.

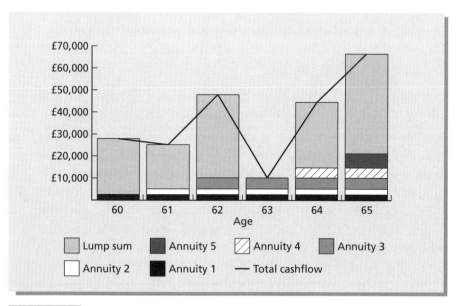

Figure 15.3 Phased pension benefit crystallisation

The drawback of the approach is that if you stagger the vesting of your pension fund in this way, you will not be able to take all your pension commencement lump sum from your total pension fund at once as a single lump sum. Phased retirement can be a very useful financial planning tool, for example, if you want to ease back gradually on work and start to replace your earnings with pension income. It also provides more flexible help for your survivors if you die before converting the whole of your fund to annuities. It is possible to vary the type of annuity you purchase on each occasion and it need not be on the same basis as the first or subsequent years. You can also purchase each annuity from a different provider. Any unvested fund that has not yet been converted to annuities can provide a pension for your surviving dependants or a lump sum, depending on the terms of the pension scheme, although these may be subject to tax if the value of your total pension benefits exceeds the lifetime limit.

Phased retirement is generally suitable only if you have a fairly large pension fund or have other assets or income on which to live. This is because the bulk of your pension savings remain invested, which may be riskier and more expensive than buying an annuity straight away.

Capped drawdown

Originally introduced in 1995 under the name of 'pension fund withdrawal', capped drawdown allows you to take a pension commencement lump sum of up to 25% and an *income directly from your fund* whilst deferring the purchase of an annuity. Your pension fund remains invested and you may draw an income from it each year if you wish, although there is now no requirement for a minimum income to be drawn. The maximum annual income limit is calculated by the Government Actuary's Department (GAD) and is determined by your age and sex and is 100% of the yearly income that could be paid if the pension fund were used to buy a level (i.e. non-escalating) single life annuity for someone of your age at the time of vesting. The amount must be formally reviewed every three years below age 75 and yearly thereafter. You may have to change the level of the amounts being drawn down to fall within the new maximum limit at each review, particularly if you are drawing near the maximum.

Importantly, the GAD factors vary according to long-term interest rates, so if interest rates fall, GAD factors can fall, too. They are also reviewed periodically to take account of changes in life expectancy of the population as a whole. In practice, with life expectancy generally increasing, this translates to a downward pressure on the factors. You have considerable flexibility in setting the amount you draw and can vary it (from nil up to the maximum) from year to year to meet changing personal or financial circumstances throughout your life.

Because you do not buy an annuity at the outset, you can keep your options open as regards ancillary benefits such as survivors' pensions and escalation and do not end up paying for benefits that might not be needed (e.g. were one or more of your dependants to pre-decease you). The pension fund remains under your control, so can be invested according to your objectives and risk capacity. On death, the whole of your remaining pension fund, less a 55% tax charge, is available to provide lump-sum benefits to your family or beneficiaries. This means that if you are under age 75, activating capped drawdown will reduce the potential fund value that could be passed to your heirs. For those who die aged 75 or over the fund is subject to the 55% tax charge regardless of whether or not drawdown has been activated. It may be possible for a dependant's pension to be payable subject to the provider offering this option. A dependant's pension will not attract a 55% tax charge until the fund is paid out as a lump sum.

If you are risk-averse and need a high level of income in retirement you're unlikely to gain any benefit from an unsecured pension and may end up with an inferior pension to that which you could have had simply by purchasing an annuity at the outset. This is partly because the cross-subsidy from those who die early, which helps to maintain annuity rates, does not apply to unsecured pension (this is known as the mortality drag), as well as the additional costs involved in the ongoing portfolio management and advice. See Figure 15.4.

The cost of mortality drag is less than 0.5% per year for someone effecting drawdown at age 60, but this rises to nearly 3% pa at age 75 and 5% pa by age 85. Therefore, unless there are other special factors, such as having no need to use the pension pot to fund retirement income or health issues, you should buy an annuity or start to buy a series of

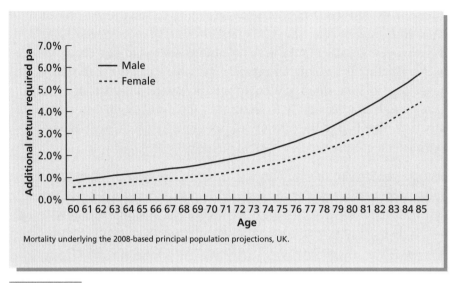

Mortality underlying the 2008-based principal population projections, UK.

Figure 15.4 **Mortality drag**

Source: Office for National Statistics

annuities over time, by the time you reach age 70. Unsecured pension is therefore most appropriate for those circumstances when financial planning concerns (such as cashflow planning) are dominant.

Deferring annuity purchase in the expectation of annuity rates rising is unlikely to be an effective strategy as even if long-term interest rates do rise sufficiently to overcome the effect of increased longevity, the income foregone by deferral may never be recouped over the remainder of your lifetime.

Flexible drawdown

If you have secure pension income of at least £20,000 pa in the tax year in which you take benefits, you are permitted to take any amount of your pension fund as a taxable lump sum, in addition to the normal, tax-free, lump sum of 25% of the fund. The taxable amount is taxed through the PAYE system and, as such, will be taxed at your highest marginal rate of income tax. The definition of what counts as secure pension income is quite strict and broadly includes State pensions, scheme pensions (i.e. where a prescribed pension is paid directly by an occupational pension scheme and larger private schemes where the scheme has at least 20 pensioner members entitled to a scheme pension) and guaranteed pension annuities. The advantage of being able to get access to all of your pension fund needs to be weighed against the disadvantages of paying income tax on the amount and bringing the capital into your estate for inheritance tax.

Phased retirement and capped drawdown pension combined

Combining both phased retirement and a capped or flexible draw-down pension means you would start to draw an income or lump sum from just part of your pension fund on one date, leaving the rest of the fund intact. If, in the future, you wish to increase your income you could either increase the rate of withdrawal (provided that you did not exceed the maximum limit if in capped drawdown) or start to draw an income from a further part of your pension fund.

Self-Invested Personal Pensions (SIPPs)

A Self-Invested Personal Pension (SIPP) is essentially a pension wrapper that is capable of holding investments and providing you with the same tax advantages as other personal pension plans. You can choose from a number of different investments, unlike other traditional pension schemes, giving you control over where your money is invested. One of the major advantages of a SIPP is that you can transfer in other pensions and this allows you to consolidate and bring together your retirement savings. This makes it simpler for you to manage your investment portfolio and makes regular investment reviews easier.

In a full SIPP there is a wide range of investment options:

- stocks and shares
- government securities
- mutual investment funds
- investment trusts
- insurance company funds
- traded endowment policies

■ deposit accounts with bank and building societies

■ National Savings products

■ commercial property (such as offices, shops or factory premises).

This level of choice can be expensive to offer and many people find that they do not need it, so lower-cost SIPPs have been developed that focus on investment funds only. These lower-cost SIPPs usually offer significantly more fund options than would a traditional pension scheme. If you are working with a wealth manager they should integrate the management of your SIPP, including taking benefits over time, into the overall management of your wealth.

The family SIPP

A family SIPP is a pooled arrangement where all members may also be trustees (if over the age of 18). The key aspect of this type of scheme is that all the members pool their capital for the purposes of investment, whether in funds, property or both, and this is known as the 'common' fund. No member has a right to any investment returns and the members can decide how returns are distributed as they see fit, either at the outset or each year, subject to the scheme rules. For example, where a member has a fund approaching the lifetime limit, this ability for the trustees to allocate investment growth to different members might help mitigate against the effects of the lifetime allowance charge and provide other valuable tax-planning opportunities.

A family SIPP can also offer a scheme pension, which is not something that standard SIPPs offer. A scheme pension is where the trustees agree to pay an income directly from the fund. For the purposes of testing against the member's lifetime allowance, the value of the scheme pension is multiplied by a factor of 20 when it commences. Thus someone without fixed protection could receive a scheme pension directly from the family SIPP of £75,000 per annum fully inflation protected, without exceeding the standard lifetime limit. A scheme pension of up to £90,000 per annum is possible if fixed protection applies. See figure 15.5.

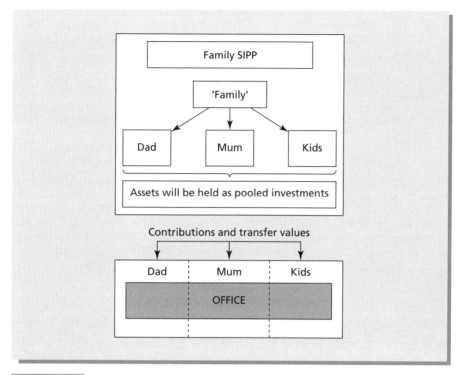

Figure 15.5 The family SIPP

Qualifying Recognised Overseas Pension Schemes (QROPS)

It is only possible to transfer benefits from a UK-registered pension scheme to either another UK-registered pension scheme or an overseas pension that meets strict rules set down by the UK tax authorities. Since 2006 overseas schemes that meet these requirements have been called Qualifying Recognised Overseas Pension Schemes (QROPS). If you expect to retire abroad permanently (this means being non-UK-resident for a minimum of five complete tax years) or have already done so, you are likely to want to transfer your UK pension benefits to a QROPS for a number of reasons:

- to avoid UK income tax on the income
- to avoid the GAD income withdrawal limits that apply to capped drawdown
- to avoid the income tax charge that would apply on any lump sum withdrawn under 'flexible drawdown'
- to remove the currency risk of receiving a pension denominated in sterling
- to avoid the 55% tax charge payable on lump sum death benefits for those aged 75 or younger individuals who have taken benefits from their fund
- to improve investment flexibility.

Even if you don't intend to retire abroad, a QROPS could be useful for two reasons. Firstly, the pension fund is tested against the lifetime allowance at the time it is transferred and thereafter any growth beyond the lifetime allowance would not be subject to the lifetime allowance tax charge on future growth as it would not be tested again. Secondly, a QROPS will allow the purchase of a European self-invested annuity that offers improved income limits and the possibility to pass any residual fund value to your beneficaries free of tax.

A QROPS provider must continue to report to the UK tax authorities on any benefits taken from members' plans while they are UK tax resident and for five tax years after they cease to be UK tax resident. Thereafter, the QROPS provider is not required to make further disclosures to the UK tax authorities.

16

Later life planning

As identified in Chapter 3, we are all living much longer and the outlook is for life expectancy to continue to increase, but perhaps not at the same rate is it has over the past 30 years or so. Increased life expectancy, however, also brings with it a multitude of issues that may have a bearing on your own wealth planning and possibly that of your parents or relatives.

Dementia is one of the main causes of mental incapacity in older people in the UK, affecting about 750,000 people and this number is set to rise to over 1 million people by 2025. The chances of suffering dementia increase significantly with age and roughly double with every five-year age group.

Power of attorney

A lasting power of attorney (LPA) is a legal document that provides one or more people (known as attorneys) whom you appoint, to deal with your affairs as if they were you, subject to certain conditions and obligations. LPAs replaced enduring powers of attorney (EPA) in England and Wales in 2008, although EPAs executed prior to the change remain valid. Although existing EPAs are still valid, no new agreements may be created from 1 October 2007. An LPA is arguably more important in your later life stages, given the higher likelihood of losing mental capacity compared to middle age. Ensuring that someone has the legal means to make important legal, financial and medical decisions on your (or your parents') behalf when you (or your parents) are not capable of making those decisions is a prudent and responsible piece of forward planning.

A person acting as an attorney must follow certain principles that govern what they can and cannot do. These principles include:

- only acting within the powers set out in the LPA
- acting in the best interests of the donor
- involving the donor in decision making as far as possible
- not taking advantage of the donor's situation to benefit the attorney personally
- keeping property and money separate from the attorney's.

An LPA must be registered with the Office of the Public Guardian (OPG) in order to be valid. However, because it can take up to four months to register an LPA I recommend that you register it at the outset to avoid delays if it needs to be used. LPAs can be wide-ranging, including allowing your attorney to sell property, operate your bank accounts or even provide guidance as to what type of health treatment you would like in certain scenarios. Alternatively you could make your LPA very limited in scope to deal with only a narrow range of scenarios.

The old style EPA only needs to be registered with the OPG in the event that it is to be used when the person subject to the EPA (known as the donor) has lost mental capacity. If the donor hasn't lost mental capacity the EPA can be used without being registered although there can be practical difficulties with banks and investment providers refusing to deal with an attorney where the EPA is unregistered.

There are two types of LPA: a property and affairs LPA, which covers financial and legal issues, and a personal welfare LPA, covering things like where you will live and medical preferences. Since 2005 it has also been possible to create what is known as an advance decision to state preferences for medical treatment that one would like or not like if one were no longer able to decide for oneself.

If you have very strong views on medical treatment then you should set these out in either a personal welfare LPA or an advance decision but ensure that your general practitioner and your next of kin know about it. In most cases a personal welfare LPA will override an advance decision as long as the LPA is prepared after the advance decision and it specifically confers authority on the attorney.

If someone loses mental capacity but they have not established an EPA or LPA then it is possible for a friend or relative to make a deputyship application to the Court of Protection. The Court will then consider conferring specific powers on the prospective deputy making the application, to deal with the person's legal and financial affairs, together with various legal obligations. The Court also has power to appoint someone else as the deputy if they think the applicant isn't suitable (e.g. they have a criminal record).

Making wills in old age

There are a number of potential problems associated with older people making wills, particularly when they deprive relatives of inheritance. The case of Golda Bechal highlight these.[1] Mrs Bechal left her £10 million estate to a couple who ran her favourite Chinese restaurant, to the detriment of her immediate family. The family contested the will on the basis that Mrs Bechal executed it without being fully aware of what she was doing. The case was eventually settled in favour of the beneficiaries of Mrs Bechal's will but not after several years of legal wrangling.

Another case involved Dr Christine Gill, whose parents, John and Joyce Gill, had left their entire estate of over £2 million to the RSPCA charity.[2] The court was told the Gills were a 'very close family' and there had been no major rifts to explain cutting their only child out of the will. Indeed, the daughter did thousands of hours of unpaid work helping to run the family's 287-acre farm and selflessly supported her troubled mother Joyce, who suffered from various phobias.

---

[1] 'Thanks for the tip: Restaurant keeps £9 million from favourite customer's £10 million contested will', *London Evening Standard,* 28 June 2008.

[2] Brooke, C. (2009) 'Daughter wins back £2million estate left to RSPCA after overturning parents' will', *Mail*Online 10 October.

Dr Gill argued in court that her mother had been coerced into making the will by her 'domineering' father John, who died in 1999. Judge James Allen QC said Mr Gill was a bully and a 'stubborn, self-opinionated, domineering man, who was prone to losing his temper'. His wife, a shy woman, deferred to what he wanted, said the judge. In 1993 Mrs Gill signed a will leaving everything to the RSPCA, despite being said to have an 'avowed dislike' of the organisation. Judge Allen found that Joyce Gill had been coerced into making a will that was against her wishes and awarded the estate to the daughter.

To avoid disputes about your (or any elderly relative's) will after death, you need to prove that you (or your relative) had 'testamentary capacity' at the time you made the will. In other words you had the mental capacity to make decisions. Although the test for testamentary capacity is not quite the same as the medical test for mental capacity, it is still a good idea to obtain a statement from your family doctor that confirms you have mental capacity. In addition, to avoid legal claims from those with legitimate claims as your 'dependants', you should make reasonable provision for them in your will. Otherwise such individuals might be able to contest your will.[3]

However, all is not lost if someone loses mental capacity to make a will as it is possible to create a statutory will providing that the person wishing to make the will is either an attorney under a registered EPA or LPA or has been granted a deputyship by the Court of Protection and subsequently applies to the OPG with a formal proposal for the terms of a statutory will. However, sophisticated estate planning is unlikely to figure highly on the list of permitted actions!

Long-term care fees

Much attention is focused on the issue of long-term residential care costs and the impact it can have on a family's wealth. The consensus of all the available research seems to be that one in three people will need some form of long-term care. In many situations, funding care

---

[3] The Inheritance (Family and Dependants) Act 1975 provides certain protections for family members and dependants who have not been adequately provided for financially as a result of the deceased's will.

fees while remaining in your own home can actually be more expensive than residential or nursing home care costs, because of the need to meet the cost of care and of running and maintaining the home. It has been estimated[4] that the average cost of care at home varies from £12,600 per annum for two hours a day to £40,000 to £150,000 for live in care. The cost of residential or nursing home care depends on the location as illustrated by Table 16.1.

Table 16.1 Average weekly care home fees around the UK 2009/2010

Area	Care homes	Care homes with nursing
London	£561	£801
East Anglia	£482	£635
Southern Home Counties	£537	£767
Northern Home Counties	£582	£855
South West	£496	£730
West Midlands	£444	£618
East Midlands	£448	£582
North West	£419	£618
Yorkshire and Humber	£423	£597
North	£451	£555
Wales	£419	£589
Scotland	£482	£608
Northern Ireland	£407	£556

Source: Partnership Insurance estimate, 2011

Care costs are fully funded by the NHS if the 'primary' need is for healthcare. This is assessed by the NHS when the patient is discharged from hospital or moves into a care home and since 1 October 2007 has been covered by the National Framework for NHS Continuing Healthcare and NHS-funded Nursing Care. However, like hospital

---

[4] Partnership Insurance estimate 2011.

stays, such funding affects an individual's entitlement to a State pension and certain other benefits. In addition, the individual has no say in the choice of care provider or establishment.

Part-funded care: non-means tested

If a registered nurse assesses that an individual needs nursing care as part of their care needs then the NHS will, regardless of that person's wealth or income, contribute a flat weekly rate (currently this is £106.30 in England and £119.66 in Wales). If the assessment was carried out before 1 October 2007 and the person qualified for the higher rate of nursing care funding then this will continue (this is £146.30 in England and Wales).

The situation in Scotland is different in that those aged 65 and over who self-fund their care benefit from an NHS contribution towards nursing and personal care (this currently amounts to £222 per week). Those aged under 65 benefit from a contribution towards personal care only (this is currently £69 per week).

Means-tested care funding

Means-tested care fees funding is assessed and provided by the social services departments of local authorities. Each local authority can choose its own eligibility criteria, although national guidelines set out the core rules and legal obligations. As a general rule any person who is assessed with having more than a modest amount of income or capital is not eligible for means-tested care fees funding. The current capital upper limit of £23,250 (April 2010) means that most affluent people will need to fund all of their care fees, at least until their capital falls below the upper limit.

Certain assets are excluded from the means-tested care fees funding assessment, including:

■ an individual's home that continues to be occupied by a spouse, civil partner or someone living with the claimant as a spouse or civil partner

■ an individual's home that continues to be occupied by a relative aged over 60 or who is incapacitated

- the proceeds of the sale of the home to the extent that the capital is used to buy a replacement property for the resident spouse, civil partner or qualifying resident
- previous outright gifts to individuals or trustees as long as these were not, and can't be shown to have been, made with an intention to deliberately avoid paying care fees
- the surrender value of life insurance policies including investment bonds but not capital redemption bonds.

If the local authority can prove that the individual (or their attorney) deliberately deprived themselves of assets to avoid paying care fees, then the local authority can seek payment from the recipient of the capital, including placing a charge on any assets. Although any transfer of assets made by the individual within the six months before they required care will always be treated as a deliberate deprivation of assets, in theory the local authority can go back many years before that if it thinks it has sufficient evidence avoiding care fees was the main motivation for giving away assets or capital.

Protecting assets from assessment

The whole issue of deliberate deprivation of assets is a bit of a 'grey' area as the test will depend on the facts of each case as well as a degree of subjectivity. Any preventative planning needs to be done in the context of one's overall wealth plan and should avoid the accusation that '[while] avoiding the charge need not be the main motive... it must be a significant one'.[5] The guidelines state that it is reasonable to ignore disposals made when the individual 'was fit and healthy and could not have foreseen the need for a move to residential accommodation'. The length of time between any planning action and requiring care funding would seem to be an important element of any defence against a charge of deliberate deprivation of assets.

The following planning areas are worth considering as part of your wider wealth plan as they may minimise how much you and/or your spouse or civil partner have to pay towards care fees:

[5] Department of Health (2010) 'Charging for residential accommodation guide (CRAG)', para 6.062, The Stationery Office.

- ■ making gifts to a discretionary trust from which you can't benefit and was done for the purpose of minimising inheritance tax
- ■ in your will, directing an amount equal to the available nil rate band to a trust from which your surviving spouse (and wider family) can receive benefit, ideally by way of loans (as well as outright income and capital), for the purpose of providing flexibility over who can benefit and to minimise inheritance tax
- ■ making a nomination for any pension lump sum death benefit (whether the plan is in income drawdown or not) to be paid to a pension by-pass discretionary trust that will allow your surviving spouse (and wider family) to receive benefit, ideally by way of loans (as well as outright income and capital), for the purpose of providing flexibility over who can benefit and to minimise inheritance tax
- ■ effecting a discounted gift trust (which is explained in more detail in Chapters 17 and 18)
- ■ considering using your home and a trust structure to carry out inheritance tax planning, taking care that the main objective is inheritance tax planning and it is effective[6]
- ■ holding capital within an onshore or offshore life insurance investment bond.

Life assurance bonds

Although some local authorities do try to include investment bonds in care fees funding assessments, the legislation and guidance is quite clear that such capital must be disregarded.[7] However, any 'income' taken from an investment will be assessed as income for fees funding purposes, but if the 'income' is stopped when care fees start such income will then cease to exist and, as such, will be disregarded under means testing. A capital redemption bond is not one that is treated as providing life insurance and therefore is not disregarded for care fees funding assessment.

---

6 The Law Society advises its members against planning using the family home but you might disagree.

7 National Assistance (Assessment of Resources) Regulations 1992, Schedule 4, para 13; Department of Health, (2010) 'Charging for residential accommodation guide (CRAG)', para 6.002B, The Stationery Office.

The reality of care fees funding

Most people want to know that they will have a choice about the type and quality of care, if required, that they will receive in later life. Doing financial planning that has the effect of avoiding having to fund care fees means you will, to a large extent, give away your choice to the local authority. This may not be a key objective. However, you might be of the opinion that any planning having, as a long-term additional benefit, the potential effect of giving you and your family the choice of whether or not to use family wealth to fund care fees, either in whole or to top up local authority provision, is better than not having the choice!

The reality for most affluent and wealthy people is they will have to use their own income and capital to fund most, if not all, of the cost of any long-term care fees that might arise in later life. The two key questions that arise, therefore, are: 'What implication does this have for your own financial security?'; and 'How will it affect your ability to give away assets and/or income in your lifetime or leave legacies on your death?'

It is possible to take out care fees insurance either before you know whether you need it or by way of an immediate needs annuity when you know that you have to fund care fees. Whether buying care fees insurance is a good use of family wealth or not depends on whether you need it (in the case of pre-funded care insurance). If so, and you buy an immediate needs care annuity, you need to assess how long care fees need to be paid. Pre-funded policies are useful if you wish to transfer to an insurance company some or all of the risk of funding care fees over the long term, but are happy to meet the cost in the short term (usually between one and five years). Immediate care annuities are useful if you would prefer to make a known payment up front in return for passing to an insurance company the risk of meeting the agreed level of fees for the rest of your life. There is only a handful of insurers active in this market and the maximum amount of fees benefit is usually limited to £5,000 per month. While care fees benefit can also be protected against general inflation, care fees inflation has, historically, risen at a higher rate. Therefore, claims over the long term might see the cost of care exceed the insurance benefit.

17

Wealth succession

Wealth succession is all about ensuring that the right people and/or causes receive the right amount of your surplus wealth, at the right time, in the most tax-efficient manner. It is not about giving away all your money to avoid inheritance tax (IHT), although that may well be a legitimate concern of yours. If you've done your strategic wealth planning properly then you should have a good idea of whether you have any surplus capital or income available in your lifetime. However, before you start thinking of giving any of your wealth away or nominating beneficiaries in your will, I suggest that you carefully consider what really matters to you and the impact that any gift might have on the recipient.

You might have concerns that your gift could have a detrimental effect on the recipient or cause tension within the family. Sometimes giving young people large amounts of money can have a negative impact on their motivation and life choices and lead to unhappiness. Treating beneficiaries differently can also cause friction between family members and you'll need to think through the implications carefully. Leaving any gifting until your death might not be the best approach if the beneficiaries are having a tough time now and a financial gift could have a positive impact on their life. The key is to strike the right balance between helping and hindering beneficiaries.

Some people are worried about their beneficiaries getting divorced and the gifted wealth disappearing in any subsequent financial settlement. In some cases your intended beneficiary might not want your

gift and/or it might worsen their own estate and IHT planning problems. Significant wealth can also have a negative impact, particularly on
young people, where it may lead to loss of motivation and purpose. You
might find it helpful to draw up a family mindmap or organisational
chart like the one shown in Figure 17.1, noting all relevant facts and
issues so that you can discuss this with your estate planning adviser and
agree a plan that avoids, as far as possible, any potential problems.

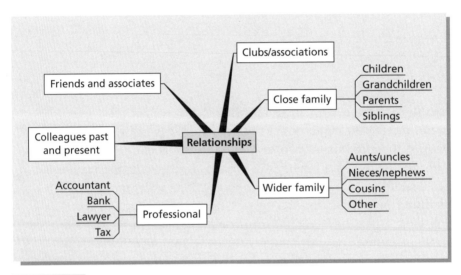

Figure 17.1   The family map

You might want to give directly to family members or a family trust
during your lifetime and leave any charitable gifts to be made on your
death or vice versa. It is highly likely that one or more trusts would
be required to help achieve your objectives. For many people, providing their children and grandchildren with a good education is an
important priority, which is seen as a good 'investment'. In some cases
parents and grandparents view funding school fees as a more practical and positive method of transferring wealth to the next generation
than giving them money either during their lifetime or on death.

Funding a private education, however, is not an insignificant commitment and could well equate to over £300,000 (about £250,000 in
present-value terms) based on a cost of £5,000 per term. University
fees and costs will add another £45,000 to that total cost, although

this is likely to increase further when tuition fees increase. In addition, school fees inflation (see Figure 17.2) continues to be well above price inflation, with latest figures from the Independent Schools Council (ISC) showing this to be 4.5% in 2010.

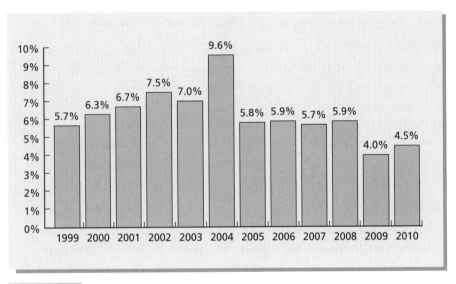

Figure 17.2   UK school fees inflation 1999–2010

Source: Independent Schools Council

Inheritance tax (IHT)

IHT is a tax levied on your estate when you die. The tax charge is currently a flat 40% and applies to your worldwide assets if you are UK domiciled (regardless of residence) or most of your UK assets if you are non-UK domiciled (although there are some exemptions). The first £325,000 of your estate is effectively tax-free and this is known as the nil rate band, more of which later. Any assets left to your surviving spouse or civil partner are also exempt from IHT as long as they are UK domiciled. If you are UK domiciled (or deemed to be) but your spouse or civil partner is non-UK domiciled then the maximum amount you can leave them free of IHT is £55,000.

Certain assets are exempt from IHT and these include holdings in unquoted trading businesses (including assets used by such a business), agricultural land and buildings and woodland. Gifts to political parties and registered charities are exempt from IHT whether made in your lifetime or upon your death. In addition, from April 2012 it is proposed that where at least 10% of your taxable estate is left to a registered charity, then the tax on the rest of your estate is reduced by 10% to 36%. This isn't sufficient to make your beneficiaries better off but it's useful if you intend to leave some of your wealth to charity.

As a general rule, you can give away any amount of your estate during your lifetime to individuals or bare/absolute trusts and as long as you derive no use or benefit from the gifted amount and survive for at least seven years afterwards, the gift will fall out of your estate for IHT purposes. This type of gift is known as a potentially exempt transfer (PET). However, there are ways of making gifts that are immediately exempt from IHT and allow you to retain some benefit without offending these requirements.

Gifts to most types of trusts (other than bare/absolute trusts) are chargeable lifetime transfers (CLTs) and, as such, attract an immediate tax charge of 20% of the amount of the gift over the available nil rate band and the annual exemption(s). However, if the gift to the trust, together with any other gifts made to the same or other trusts in the past seven years, is equal to or less than the nil rate band (currently £325,000) then no immediate charge to IHT is due. As long as you derive no use or benefit from the gifted amount and survive for at least seven years afterwards, the gift will fall out of your estate for IHT purposes and no further IHT will be payable. For this reason it makes sense to gift as much as you can up to the maximum of the NRB to a trust every seven years if you can afford to do so.

Estate planning basics

Having a valid will is essential to help others deal with your affairs following your death. If you don't have a will in place when you die, then you will die **intestate**. This means that your assets will be distributed in accordance with the rules of intestacy, which are set out in Figure 17.3. Depending on the amount of your wealth, the types of assets you own

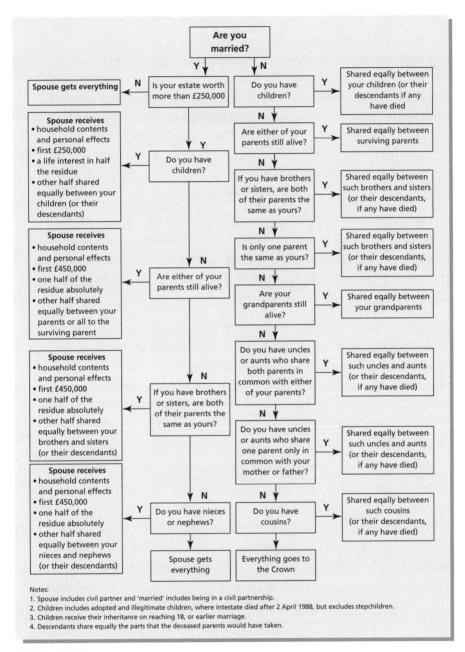

Figure 17.3 The law of intestacy – England and Wales

Source: This expanded version was created by the author, based on the simplified version from 'IHTM12111–Intestacy (E&W): summary of the main rules of intestacy', available online at: www.hmrc.gov.uk/manuals/ihtmanual/ihtm12111.htm

and the makeup of your family, dying intestate is unlikely to be recommended. For example, a spouse or civil partner is unlikely to inherit all your assets under the intestacy rules. Although it is possible to do a deed of variation to override the intestacy rules and vary the basis on which an estate is to be distributed (it is possible to do this with a will as well), this relies on the various beneficiaries who are entitled to the inheritance all agreeing to the terms of any variation of intestacy. This is fine if everyone agrees but not if they don't! Also if there are any minor beneficiaries involved, the variation has to be approved by the court, which is obviously expensive and uncertain.

Ideally you need to have a will in any country in which you own real property as some countries like France have forced heirship rules that are different to the rules in the UK. If you need a will in more than one country then you should take legal advice to ensure that these are co-ordinated.

I do not recommend using a will-writing company to draw up your will unless your affairs are very simple and modest. Many of the will-writing companies use non-legally qualified representatives to take instructions and see to the signing of documents. This can lead to mistakes and misunderstandings that can turn out to be costly and problematic further down the line. In addition, some will-writing companies have no or very modest professional negligence insurance cover.

There are a number of ways that you can increase the tax efficiency and flexibility of your will to deal with things like business assets, second marriages, unequal gifts of property or other assets. A good lawyer is worth paying for and, as long as they have a clear grasp of what you own and the overall context of your wealth strategy and personal objectives, they can help to craft a more sophisticated will that reflects your wishes and is tax-efficient. The more wealth you have and the more complex your financial affairs, then the more important and valuable this will be.

Life and pension policies

If you have life policies or pension plans, then you should ensure that these are written under an appropriate trust so that they do not form part of your estate for IHT and to enable the proceeds to be paid out quickly, side-stepping the process of probate on the rest of your estate. However, you need to be careful when putting existing policies into a trust in case they are deemed to have a value and, as such, could trigger an immediate tax charge. Most term policies with no cash in value will not cause a tax problem on transfer as long as you are in good health, but some investment-based policies, particularly whole-of-life types, could have a significant value, so good legal advice is essential.

Although a trust will never fail because there is no trustee available to act, it is advisable to appoint at least two other trustees other than yourself, so that there are no undue delays in distributing life policy proceeds to beneficiaries, if required. Your trustees should be people you trust both to make good financial decisions and who would be comfortable dealing with the trust's business.

Death-in-service benefits from occupational pension schemes and personal pension plans written under a 'master' trust-type arrangement usually pay out at the discretion of the scheme's trustees. However, you may complete a written nomination stating to whom you would like the trustees to consider paying out any death benefits. It is essential that you complete and keep up to date this nomination as it is the first thing that the trustees will refer to in the event of your death, although they will not be bound by it. Instead of nominating your spouse (or civil partner) or other beneficiaries as your preferred recipients, you might instead create and nominate a special trust known as a 'pilot' or 'by-pass' trust to receive any death-in-service or pension plan death payment (see Figure 17.4). The benefit of doing this is that it enables the lump sum to be paid into the trust and avoids the capital falling into the estate of your chosen beneficiaries and thus avoids IHT being charged on that capital if any of your beneficiaries subsequently die. In addition, it will help avoid other 'hostile' creditors, including local authorities (care fees), ex spouses or civil partners, or bankruptcy proceedings that may be experienced by your beneficiaries.

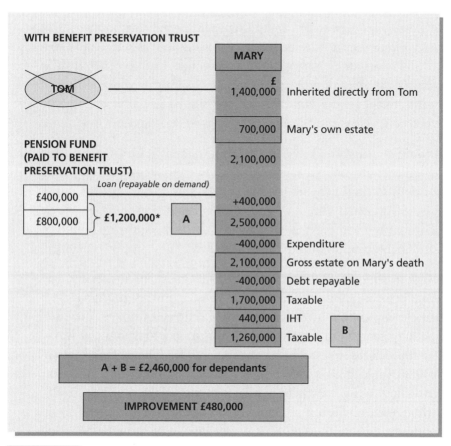

Figure 17.4   The pension by-pass trust

The following is a quick checklist of the main planning points worth considering in your estate plan that will help minimise IHT and avoid other 'hostile creditors'.

Checklist |

■ Use your current annual gift exemption of £3,000 (the previous year can also be used if you have not already done so).

■ Make annual gifts of £250 capital to any number of beneficiaries (no one person can receive more than £250 unless this is part of the £3,000 annual exemption and you cannot add these exemptions together to give £3,250 to one person).

■ Make gifts in consideration of marriage (£5,000 for your own children, £2,500 for grandchildren, £1,000 to anyone else) if relevant.

■ Make regular gifts out of surplus income (see below) to individuals or, if the amounts are meaningful, a discretionary trust, as the amount falls out of your estate immediately.

■ Lend capital to individuals or a trust to 'freeze' the value for IHT purposes.

■ Gift up to the nil rate exemption band to a trust to freeze the value of assets and remove them from your estate after seven years (currently the limit is £325,000 every 7 years).

■ Invest in assets that qualify for business property relief or agricultural property relief (effective after two years of ownership) to avoid IHT on the value on death.

■ Make gifts to charities or, if the amounts are significant and you have particular objectives, to your own charitable foundation to remove them from your estate immediately for IHT purposes.

■ Effect a long-term insurance policy on your life in trust to pay out some or the entire IHT bill on your death (or the second of you to die if you are married or in a civil partnership).

Normal expenditure out of surplus income exemption |

This is one of the most underused IHT exemptions but also one of the most effective and simplest to use. If you meet the conditions then the gifted amount falls out of your estate immediately and does not use up any of your nil rate band. The conditions that must be satisfied are as follows:

■ the gifted amount must form part of your usual expenditure

■ it must be made out of income

■ it must leave you with sufficient income to maintain your normal standard of living.

Using life insurance

If you have made a gift that is classed as a PET and might become taxable if you die within seven years of the gift, to the extent that it exceeds the available nil rate band on death, life insurance can provide the funds to enable the recipient of the gift (known as the donee) to meet the IHT which will become due. The nil rate band can also be used up for these purposes if you have made a gift to a trust (other than a bare trust) in the seven years prior to the PET. It is worth noting that responsibility to pay the tax due is in the following order:

1 donor (or their personal representatives)

2 donee

3 anyone in whom the property is now vested

4 any beneficiary of a trust who receives the asset in question.

If you still have a residual IHT liability and either can't or don't want to carry out other planning, and are in reasonable health, then you could take out long-term life assurance for some or all of the tax liability to reduce the loss to your beneficiaries. The policy would need to be written under trust to avoid it forming part of your estate. Please refer to Chapter 13 for a fuller explanation of the role of life insurance in IHT planning.

Getting a bit more creative

There are numerous planning solutions that are usually (but not always) more complicated and costly than the standard planning referred to earlier. The benefits include quicker or higher IHT savings; being able to retain some use, enjoyment or benefit from the asset or capital; and/or greater flexibility in how and when wealth can be distributed to beneficiaries. The following is a non-exhaustive list of some of the more widely used planning concepts, a number of which are explained in more detail in Chapter 18.

Some widely used planning concepts

- A discounted gift trust immediately removes a proportion of gifted capital from your estate while still allowing you to benefit from a preselected 'income' during your lifetime. As a general rule the higher the amount of income and the younger your age then the greater the immediate discount.
- Use trusts to obtain IHT reductions on property, including your main home, second home and investment properties.

- Restructure businesses to maximise IHT exemptions, the main one of which is business property relief (BPR), which provides complete exemption from IHT once owned for two years.
- Use multiple trusts to avoid or minimise ongoing IHT charges.
- Loan capital on interest-free terms to a trust of which you are not a beneficiary in order to freeze the value of your capital for IHT purposes but allow you access to the capital through repayments of the loan on terms agreeable to you.
- Do gifting in the right order to minimise IHT. The general order should be: 1) set up any lifetime pilot trusts (to receive pension death benefits, etc.); 2) make loans to individuals or trusts; 3) gift exempt assets; 4) make chargeable lifetime transfers; 5) make potentially exempt transfers.
- Gift assets to a special type of 'reversionary' trust that allows you to remove assets from your estate while still benefiting from some or all of the gifted capital by way of a future 'reversion' of the gifted asset (see Chapter 18).
- For non-domiciled or mixed-domiciled marriages/civil partnerships deal with any domicile mismatch issues.
- If you are non-UK-domiciled and have not been a UK resident for more than 17 out of the last 20 years, or you have a short life expectancy, consider using an excluded property trust to avoid UK IHT.
- Pass a minority interest in a property to a trust via your will that benefits unconnected beneficiaries, i.e. not your spouse or civil partner, so as to create a discount of the value of the surviving spouse or civil partner's retained share for IHT purposes.
- If you have a spouse or civil partner create a nil rate band trust on your death and have the trustees of your residual estate enter into a debt arrangement with the trustees of your nil rate band trust. With the passage of time during which your spouse or civil partner survives you, the debt has the effect of 'sucking' value out of their estate and placing it in the nil rate band trust.
- Borrow assets/capital from a trust interest-free and then gift those assets/capital to another trust so as to create a debt on your estate that reduces the value of your estate for IHT purposes, as long as you survive for seven years. Alternatively invest the borrowed funds in assets such as business or agricultural property, which then become exempt from IHT after two years.
- Leave any asset that qualifies for BPR/APR in a discretionary trust and have your surviving spouse/civil partner exchange an equivalent amount of their own assets for the BPR/APR assets so that they own IHT-exempt assets (after two years' ownership) and the trust owns the assets that would have been subject to IHT.
- Invest in a Qualifying Non-UK Pension Scheme (QNUPS) to build up capital that would also not be subject to IHT, as long as the main objective is retirement savings and you can justify the need to save for retirement.

The key point to bear in mind about some creative planning, particularly that which involves the family home or other property, is that there is always a risk the tax authorities may change the rules to render the planning ineffective retrospectively. Over the past ten years alone we have seen a barrage of anti-avoidance rules that have removed any tax benefit from thousands of 'schemes'. In addition, new IHT planning 'schemes' are now included within the Disclosure of Tax Avoidance Scheme (DoTAS) rules that already apply to income and capital gains tax planning.

Ensuring that your financial affairs are well-organised means that you will not leave a mess for your family to sort out if they have to deal with your financial affairs in the event of your death. Wealth succession planning can be as simple or complicated as you wish but it must be viewed in the context of your own needs, values, resources and tax position. In any event a decent private client lawyer is essential to help you form a sensible wealth succession strategy that is in context with your own financial needs and overall financial plan.

18

Using trusts and alternative structures

A trust is a legal agreement where a person, known as the settlor, transfers the ownership of their assets to another party – a trustee. The trustee holds the assets for the benefit of a person, group of people, charity or organisation – the beneficiaries – without giving them full access to the assets for the time being. Because children (those aged under 18) cannot own assets in their own name, these will always be held in trust until at least age 18.

As well as holding assets for children, trusts are used for a number of other reasons including:

- reducing inheritance tax (IHT)
- providing formal oversight and controls about how assets will be used
- providing flexibility to defer decisions about how assets will be distributed or otherwise to benefit different beneficiaries
- ensuring that assets are legally separated from one's personal assets, and thus potentially protected against unforeseen situations like divorce or bankruptcy
- providing a means for managing assets for those unable to do so themselves.

A trust can be created either in your lifetime or through your will. Sometimes a trust can arise through your action, without any formal documentation. Changes in the tax treatment of trusts over recent years have seen a reduction in the types of new trust that may be worth establishing, although many of the other types remain in existence.

There are three parties involved in setting up a trust:

1 the **settlor** sets up the initial asset (e.g. an insurance or pension contract) and then transfers the ownership of the assets to one or more trustees

2 the **trustee** is the legal owner of the assets who holds and manages them for the benefit of the beneficiaries according to the terms of the trust deed or trust law

3 the **beneficiaries** are the individuals or groups of people selected by the settlor to receive the benefits of the trust.

A trust is typically a single-settlor trust or a joint-settlor trust with two settlors. The settlor can appoint individuals as trustees, a corporate trustee or a trust corporation (a company constituted to carry out trustee duties with several authorised directors). If the trust holds land then you will need to appoint at least two individual or corporate trustees or a single trust corporation. Individual trustees could be another family member, a close friend or someone else you trust to deal with financial and legal issues. The basic rule is that a trustee must be at least 18 years old and of sound mind. The named trustees must also accept the appointment for it to be valid. A settlor can, and almost always does, appoint themselves as a trustee and this gives them some control over the trust property during their lifetime.

The trust deed will set out the basis on which trustees can be changed and it is usual to give the power to change a trustee to the settlor in their lifetime. If the trust deed is silent on who has power to appoint and remove trustees then trust law provides for current trustees to appoint their own replacements. The trustees must also take minutes of a meeting regarding the change of trustee. The legal rules relating to appointing and retiring trustees are strict and must be followed carefully.

The two main types of trusts

The two main types of trusts that are most likely to be created today are a bare/absolute trust or a discretionary trust.

Bare/absolute trusts

This type of trust is the simplest and is used to hold assets on behalf of someone else where it is intended that the beneficiary has the definite right to benefit from or take ownership of an asset. The trust is called a bare trust where the beneficiary is aged under 18 and is called an absolute trust where they are 18 and over. The asset will form part of the beneficiary's estate for IHT purposes and they have a legal right of ownership at age 18.

Gifts to a bare or absolute trust are treated as a potentially exempt transfer (PET) for IHT purposes, in the same way as gifts of assets to individuals. This means that no IHT is due at the time the gift is made to the trust and, as long as the person making the gift survives for seven compete years, the gift will fall out of account for IHT purposes. There is also no periodic (ten-yearly) charge on the trust's assets (see below). However, the assets subject to a bare or absolute trust will count as the beneficiary's for IHT purposes and will also be exposed to other potential 'hostile' creditors such as divorce and bankruptcy proceedings that might be brought against them in the future.

Income and gains arising from assets held in a bare trust are taxed as if they were the beneficiary's, subject to them having full use of their own personal income and capital gains tax allowance. The tax rate paid will, therefore, depend on the beneficiary's other taxable income and capital gains. However, if the capital within the trust was provided by a parent (or joint parents), then while the child is aged under 18, any income arising from that capital over £100 per annum (£200 if joint parents) would be taxed at the parent's (or parents' if jointly gifted) highest marginal income tax rate.

Where you are comfortable to make an outright gift to someone, but they are under 18, then you will have to own it (or have someone else own it) in a bare trust. This can be as simple as opening a savings or investment account in your name with the child's initials to signify you are not the beneficial owner. In this case you will be governed by the Trustee Act 2000, which includes rules on investments and how the trust should be managed. Alternatively you could have a formal trust deed drawn up to override the Trustee Act's default provision. As a general rule, for small amounts and simple assets such as a savings account or investment funds a simple designation (initials) should be adequate. However, for more significant amounts or, in the case of land or other more complicated assets, a formal deed is likely to be desirable.

Clearly the larger the amount, the greater the potential problem. If you have already made a gift to a discretionary trust up to the nil rate band, then a bare trust is the only way that you can make a gift without an immediate charge to IHT. One of the potential problems with a bare trust is that the beneficiary has an absolute right to the trust's assets at age 18; many people are uncomfortable at the thought of an 18-year-old having access to capital without any restrictions.

One potential solution to this problem for larger amounts (£100,000 or more) is to invest in a special type of offshore insurance bond, which has specific policy conditions that govern when the policy may be encashed and the values available. So while the beneficiary would have the right to the capital at 18, in fact all they would have a right to is an offshore insurance bond/policy that has prescribed policy conditions. The conditions of the policy are set at the outset but can, for example, stipulate that the policy has no cash in value until, say, the beneficiary's 25th or 30th birthday. This enables you to combine the benefits of a PET while restricting access to the capital until the beneficiary is older. It is also possible to use a bare or absolute trust within more complicated IHT planning arrangements such as gift and loan and discounted gift plans.

Discretionary trusts

This type of trust, also sometimes known as a flexible trust, allows the trustees to choose who can benefit from the trust, from a wide class of potential beneficiaries, including those yet to be born, such as future grandchildren, etc. As well as giving the trustees maximum flexibility over who can benefit, in what proportions and when, this type of trust offers the possibility of avoiding IHT both against the estate of the person making the gift (known as the **donor**) and the estate of beneficiaries (known as **donees**).

All discretionary trusts created after 5 April 2010 may continue in existence for up to 125 years. In addition to providing flexibility over who might receive outright distributions of trust capital and/or income, trustees of a discretionary trust might also prefer to lend capital to beneficiaries, provided that the trust powers permit this. Lending capital to beneficiaries can sometimes be a better way of protecting the family wealth from 'hostile' creditors such as bankruptcy or divorce proceedings being brought against a beneficiary because, being a loan, the capital is not assessed as part of the beneficiary's personal assets. Loans can also preserve beneficiaries' entitlements to means-tested State benefits, assuming that any loan were called in by the trustees. Any loan owed by beneficiaries to a trust are also deductible from each beneficiary's estate for IHT purposes, thus potentially saving up to 40% in IHT.

Tax charges on transfer to a discretionary trust

As explained in Chapter 17, the transfer of most assets to a discretionary trust will be treated as a chargeable lifetime transfer (CLT) for IHT purposes. As long as there have been no previous gifts to a discretionary trust in the previous seven years, the gift to this trust is within the nil rate band (currently £325,000) and any unused current and previous annual gift exemption (£3,000 per year), then no immediate charge to IHT will arise. However, if the settlor dies within seven years of the date of the transfer to the trust then the gift will become chargeable and utilise some or the entire nil rate band applicable at the date of death, effectively pushing other assets into charge.

If the gift, when made to the trust, exceeds the available nil rate band then the excess will be subject to an immediate charge to IHT of currently 20% (i.e. half of the normal rate) if paid by the donee or 25% if paid by the donor. The available nil rate band will be the current nil rate band, less any other CLTs that have been made in the previous seven years. Whether or not the gift is subject to tax at outset, after seven years, assuming no other gifts have been made, the gift will fall out of account for IHT purposes and the nil rate band will become available again to enable further lifetime gifts or a tax-free amount of the estate to pass free of IHT on death.

Certain assets, however, are *exempt* from IHT, such as qualifying business assets, qualifying agricultural property and lump sum death benefits from registered UK or qualified non-UK pension schemes. If this is the case then no immediate charge to IHT can apply on the initial transfer value transferred to a trust. In the case of exempt assets gifted during a lifetime, as long as the settlor survives for seven further years, the asset will fall out of their estate completely for IHT purposes, assuming that they can't benefit from the trust. It is possible, however, for a settlor's spouse or civil partner to be a beneficiary of that same trust but this will cause the income and capital gains arising within the trust to be taxed on the settlor during their lifetime. Exempt assets can also be passed, free of IHT, to a trust via your will, whether that trust is an existing one or created within your will.

The discretionary trust periodic charge

If the value of the trust exceeds the available nil rate band at the time (currently a maximum of £325,000), on each 10-year anniversary of the trust or when capital is distributed out of the trust, it may incur a tax charge of up to 6% of the value above the available nil rate band at the time. For example, if the trust fund were £100,000 above the nil rate band, then £6,000 could be payable every 10 years by the trustees. However, this is still a fraction of the next-generation tax benefits it can deliver.

Each discretionary trust benefits from its own periodic charge allowance, as long as each trust was established on a different day and there were no prior gifts that used up some or all of the nil rate band. This can be very useful where trusts have been established, for example, to hold large life insurance policies or assets have been transferred to trusts that do not attract an immediate charge to IHT but which are subsequently sold and become chargeable assets. Any asset owned by the trust that is treated as exempt, such as a trading business, will also avoid the periodic charge.

Discretionary trusts created by a will, no matter what date they come into effect, are treated as being created on the same day (the date of death) and thus are subject to *one* periodic charge nil rate band for all trusts created this way. The exception to this rule is where the trust created via the will is specifically designated to receive only lump sum death benefits from a pension trust. In this situation the will trust is deemed to have been created on the date that the deceased joined the pension scheme.

For higher-value estates with substantial non-exempt assets, and where no spouse or civil partner is available to receive assets, it is usually advisable to create trusts during your lifetime, on different days, for a nominal sum and direct assets to each trust via the will as required. There are, however, two important points to bear in mind when creating multiple trusts and these relate to lifetime gifts and the order in which trusts are created.

Prior lifetime gifts

If you make a gift to a non-bare trust in your lifetime, which counts as a CLT, but you subsequently die within seven years of that gift, then the nil rate band will have been used up to the extent of that gift. When each of the trusts reaches its ten-year anniversary, it will only benefit from the available nil rate band, not the full amount.

Consider Shelia, a widow, who creates 10 trusts for £10 each on different days, thus the initial gift for each trust is within her annual gift exemption. A month later Shelia makes a gift of £325,000 to a further discretionary trust, being the maximum amount she can gift without incurring an immediate tax charge. In her will Shelia leaves her net residual estate, worth £3.25 million (after IHT), to the 10 pilot trusts.

Sadly Shelia dies three years later. Seven years after her death the pilot trusts reach their ten-year anniversaries for periodic tax charge purposes. When working out whether any tax is due on the trusts' assets the trustees are permitted to deduct the available nil rate band from the trust's value. But because Shelia did not survive the £325,000 gift to the discretionary trust by seven years, each trust will not have any tax-free amount (£325,000 – £325,000) to deduct from the trust fund for periodic charge purposes unless the nil rate band has been increased by then. However, if Shelia had survived at least seven years after the gift to the trust, then the entire nil rate band would be available. If the value of each pilot trust at the ten-year anniversary were below the value of the nil rate band applicable, then no tax would be due.

Order of trusts

If Shelia had made the £325,000 lifetime gift to the trust first and then created the 10 pilot trusts, then regardless of whether or not she survived the 7-year gift period, each pilot trust would only have available, at the 10-year anniversary, a nil rate band to the extent that it exceeded the value of the original nil rate band. Therefore, if the nil rate band amount remains at £325,000 then none of the pilot trusts would have a tax-free amount at the 10-year anniversary. Even if the nil rate band is increased by that time, the first £325,000 will have been used by the lifetime gift made within the seven-year prior to the establishment of the pilot trusts.

It is, therefore, very important to ensure that any pilot trusts are created at least seven years after any lifetime gifts to a trust but *before* any subsequent lifetime gifts to a trust, even if this is just a few days.

Taxation of trust investments

Most trusts (i.e. not bare/absolute or old-style, life interest trusts) are subject to what is known as the rate applicable to trusts (RAT) and, as such, pay income tax of 50% on income arising (42.5% on dividend income) in excess of the trust personal allowance and 28% on capital gains tax (CGT) above the CGT annual exemption.

The taxation of discretionary trusts is a complicated subject and beyond the scope of this book, but as a general rule dividend income is best avoided where this is being accumulated by the trustees. Alternatively, income can be 'streamed' directly to basic rate taxpaying beneficiaries, so that it avoids higher-rate tax, without the underlying capital forming part of the beneficiary's own estate for IHT purposes.

The trustees could also invest in capital growth assets, which are taxed at a much lower rate than income. Another solution could be to hold investments within an insurance bond 'wrapper', as this is treated as being non-income-producing and not subject to income tax unless or until the bond is completely encashed or more than 5% of the original investment per policy year is withdrawn (the amount is cumulative so after 10 years, say, up to 50% of the original investment could be withdrawn without an immediate charge to income tax). An insurance bond makes most sense where most, or a significant amount, of the total return arises from interest and/or dividends and the trustees wish to accumulate all returns.

An insurance bond (or parts of it) can also be assigned to a benefici-ary, who would then be taxed on the gain within the bond when it is finally encashed by them. If the beneficiary is a non- or basic rate tax-payer then they will pay less than had the trustees encashed the bond.

Practical uses of trusts

There are several ways in which you might use a trust as part of your wealth plan.

Flexibility for lifetime gifts

Where you want to make gifts now but don't want to make a deci-sion on who gets what and when until some time in the future, a discretionary trust is ideal. The trustees usually have wide powers to invest, distribute, lend assets or borrow funds, depending on the needs of the beneficiaries. Although the trustees (who will usually include yourself in your lifetime) have the discretion to decide how benefits are provided, you can provide them with a side letter setting out some guidelines that you would like them to take into account. Although such guidance doesn't bind the trustees, it can provide a useful ref-erence point where trustees are faced with competing demands or difficult decisions. Making lifetime gifts to a discretionary trust is also useful if giving assets directly to your chosen beneficiaries would exac-erbate their own IHT position or where there is a concern about the beneficiary getting divorced or becoming bankrupt.

No immediate IHT charge will apply on gifts to a trust that:

- are within the available nil rate band (currently £325,000) every 7 years
- are within the annual gift exemption of currently £3,000 (plus £3,000 for the previous year if not used)
- meet the test for gifts out of surplus income
- are exempt assets such as unquoted business shares or agricultural property
- are derived from the death benefits from a UK or qualifying non-UK pension scheme.

Using trusts to diminish the value of jointly owned assets

If a property is owned by two people who are not married to each other or in a civil partnership, then each person's share is, for IHT purposes, subject to a discount in value. The discount is typically between 10 and 15%. If you are married or in a civil partnership you can take advantage of the joint property discount by ensuring that you have appropriate provisions in your and your spouse's/partner's will to deal with the ownership of your or their share of the home depending on who dies first. Under this arrangement a small part of the share of the house belonging to the first spouse/civil partner to die is placed in trust for your children or grandchildren. The rest of the deceased's share of the property is held in a life interest trust for the surviving spouse/civil partner. This has the effect of reducing the value, for IHT purposes, of the share that is owned (both personally and via the trust) by the surviving spouse/civil partner.

Example

Charles and Penny own a £1,000,000 house in equal shares as tenants in common. Sadly Charles dies and his executors decide to transfer £55,000 of his £500,000 share to a trust for the benefit of his adult children. This uses up £55,000 of Charles' nil rate band, with the balance (£270,000) available for Penny to carry forward to offset against her estate when she eventually dies. The balance of Charles' share is passed to a life interest trust for Penny's benefit. Penny now owns £945,000 of the property by virtue of her own £500,000 share that she owned already and the £445,000 that is held in trust for her. Penny continues to be able to enjoy the use of all of the property and does not need to pay rent to the children for their share.

The immediate effect is that the value of Penny's share of the property will be reduced for IHT purposes on her subsequent death, to reflect the open market value of her share and the fact that a small element is owned by the children's trust. Using a discount factor of 12.5% on Penny's £945,000 share of the property, this represents an immediate IHT saving of £47,250. However, the potential savings are even higher depending on how long Penny lives and after, say, 12 years, this might increase to £116,500 based on the growth in the children's trust (£55,000 × 40%) and the growth in Penny's discounted fund (945,000 × 40%) in addition to the immediate savings.

The joint property discount is shown in Figure 18.1.

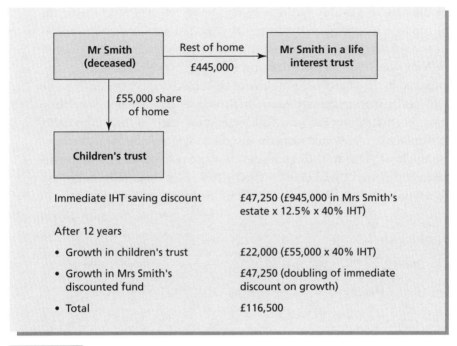

Source: Speechly Bircham

Figure 18.1   The joint property discount

Spousal by-pass

It is common for exempt assets, such as business or agricultural property, to be passed to a surviving spouse or civil partner who then disposes of it for cash. Alternatively the executors will dispose of the exempt assets and pass cash to the surviving spouse or civil partner. In both cases the surviving spouse or civil partner ends up with cash that will potentially be chargeable to IHT on their subsequent death. A better approach would be to create one or more discretionary trust(s) either in your lifetime, or via your will, of which your surviving spouse or civil partner would be a potential beneficiary, and pass any exempt business or agricultural property to the trust(s) to avoid the exempt asset falling into your spouse's or civil partner's estate and thus avoid 40% IHT on his or her subsequent death.

In the case of a family business that is to be retained after the death of the first spouse or civil partner, the surviving spouse or civil partner could purchase the business from the trustees using their personal cash or assets. This means that the surviving spouse/civil partner has swapped assets that would otherwise be subject to IHT on their eventual death with business assets which will be IHT exempt once they have been held for two years. The by-pass trust would then hold family assets that would only be subject to IHT at a maximum of 6% on the trust value to the extent that it exceeds the then applicable nil rate band (currently £325,000). Figure 18.2 illustrates graphically how this type of trust would operate in simplified form.

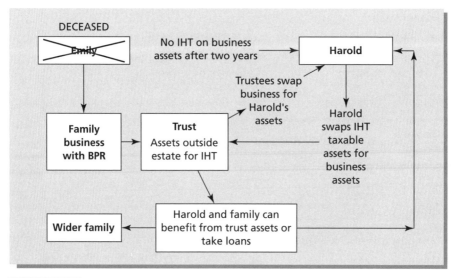

Figure 18.2   The spousal by-pass trust

Life insurance policies

Personally owned life policies should always be written under a suitable trust deed, to avoid the proceeds falling into your estate for IHT purposes and to speed up the distribution of assets. Assuming the life policy has no value or is a new policy at the time the trust is declared, there should be no immediate charge to IHT. Subsequent payment of premiums will be exempt from IHT as long as they are paid from 'surplus' income (and meet the conditions for expenditure out of surplus income) or are within the annual gift allowance of £3,000.

Where the life cover amount required is more than £325,000 (or whatever the IHT nil rate exemption band is), and the intention is not to distribute policy proceeds immediately, it might make sense to arrange multiple policies each limited to £325,000 and placed in a separate trust created on different days (see Figure 18.3). This will help avoid the periodic tax charge that would otherwise arise on the ten-year anniversary of the trust, in the event that the policy pays out. Make sure that you do this before you make any gifts to a discretionary trust that would count as a CLT. A number of life insurance companies will issue segmented or multiple policies to facilitate this and to avoid the need to make multiple life policy applications. If you are affecting a policy to fund a possible IHT liability then there will be no need to arrange multiple policies and trusts as the proceeds will be paid out well before the ten-year anniversary to meet the IHT liability.

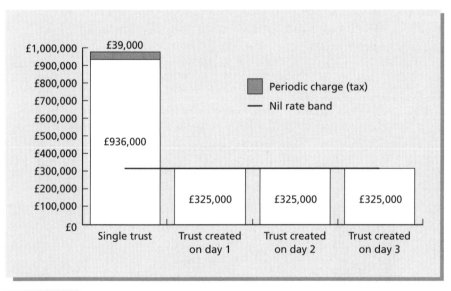

Figure 18.3   Life policy in trust and the periodic charge

The pension by-pass trust

As previously detailed in Chapter 17 a lump sum death benefit payment from a registered pension (and certain overseas pensions) is exempt from IHT. Depending on the type of trust under which the pension has been established, it can make sense to nominate a separate lifetime or will trust for any death lump sum payments, so that this can pass free of IHT and avoid falling into the estate of your surviving spouse or other family members. The trust should permit the trustees to make loans available to beneficiaries to further improve the IHT efficiency.

The loan trust

As I briefly mentioned in Chapter 17 you could set up a trust (discretionary is usually best) for a nominal amount (say £10) and then loan capital, usually interest-free, to the trustees to invest as appropriate. Any future growth generated by the invested trust capital will arise outside of your estate and also outside of any of the beneficiaries if it is a discretionary trust. This allows you to freeze the value of the loaned capital, which remains in your estate, while retaining access to it by way of repayments on terms that you agree with the trustees. The ten-year periodic tax charge is calculated on the value in excess of the available IHT nil rate band but after deducting any outstanding loan due to you. See Figure 18.4.

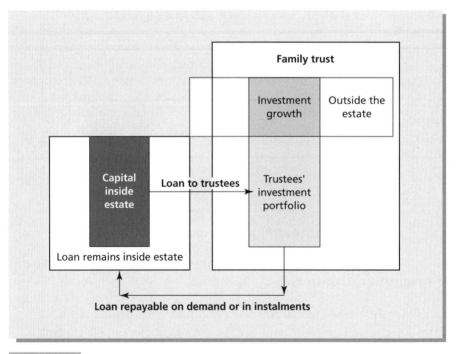

Figure 18.4   **The loan trust**

Discounted gift trust

A discounted gift trust allows you to give away capital that then qualifies for an immediate IHT saving, which increases if you survive seven years. However, you have to agree a fixed amount of 'income' that the trust will pay you throughout your lifetime and it is not possible to vary or stop this amount. As such, it is important that you spend such 'income' otherwise the arrangement won't be as IHT-efficient as possible. The amount of immediate IHT saving, which is prescribed by HMRC and subject to medical underwriting by an insurance company, is obtained by applying a discount to the amount that is gifted to the trust. The discount will vary depending on your age and the amount of income taken, with the highest discount given to younger ages taking a high income. Table 18.1 sets out a range of discounts based on various levels of income and ages.

Table 18.1 Discounted gift factors

Age	% discount single male	% discount single female	% discount joint lives
60	55.63	61.02	68.12
65	50.21	56.53	64.40
70	44.16	51.19	59.67
75	37.78	45.05	53.82
80	31.52	38.30	47.02

Note: The above discounts are based on a discount factor of 5.5% and assume acceptance on normal terms. In the case of joint lives these factors assume both lives are the same age. Income is assumed to be 5% of the original investment.
Source: Canada Life International

Reversionary trust

Although the general rule is that you can't give an asset away and then benefit from it (the gift with reservation rule), there is a little known exception[1] that applies to what is known as a 'reversionary trust'. This is achieved by creating a discretionary form of a reversionary trust from

---

[1] 'In the case where... the retention by the settlor (donor) of a reversionary interest under the trust is not considered to constitute a reservation...' (see paragraph 7 of the Inland Revenue's letter to the Law Society dated 18 May 1987 at p. 346, in, *Tolley's Yellow Tax Handbook, 2010–11, Part 3*).

the gift of the current value, death benefit or extension benefits of a single-premium, investment-based 'life' policy (although the underlying investment could be an investment fund if desired), but you benefit from the trust by way of regular maturities (reversions) of the policy.

The initial gift to the reversionary trust is treated as a CLT and as long as it is within the nil rate band (currently £325,000) there will be no immediate charge to IHT. The growth on the trust fund accrues outside of your estate from day two and, as long as you live for seven years, the original gift will fall out of your estate for IHT purposes. The amount and frequency of 'reversions' must be selected at the outset and will fall back into your estate for IHT purposes if not spent. However, and this is the clever part, if you don't want to receive a reversion of the trust capital, you can disclaim this by advising the trustees before the reversion date and they will effectively defer it to a later date. The act of 'disclaiming' the reversion is not treated as a further gift and, as such, does not fall into your estate. Figure 18.5 illustrates how this arrangement works.

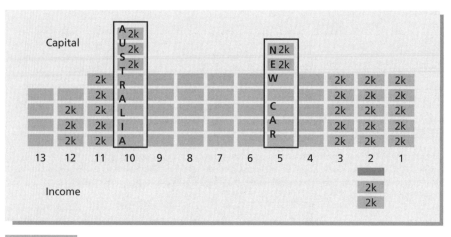

Figure 18.5 Reversionary trust and single-premium life policy

Source: Reproduced by kind permission of Canada Life International

Combining a loan and reversionary trust

If you have substantial assets but only want to make a small commitment to estate planning initially, gradually protect your estate from IHT and preserve maximum flexibility for the rest of your life, you could consider combining a gift and loan trust and a reversionary trust. This involves first creating a trust (usually discretionary) with a modest gift, say £10, and then loaning capital to it. You can draw down the loan at any time and, as such, retain full access to that capital, although any growth arising occurs outside of your estate immediately.

Shortly after creating the gift and loan trust, you then gift £325,000 (or whatever your available nil rate band is) to a reversionary interest trust and set this up to provide yearly optional 'income' by way of regular maturities. Any growth arises outside your estate immediately and, as long as you live for seven years, then the gift will also fall out of your estate for IHT purposes. You then repeat this process every seven years, creating additional reversionary trusts equal to the nil rate band, while being able to benefit from the regular but optional 'income' reversions. Figure 18.6 illustrates how this would work with £1.5 million of capital where £1.2 million is lent to the first trust and £300,000 (i.e. below the current nil rate band) is gifted to the reversionary trust. If you are married or in a civil partnership then you

	Inside estate (Assumming loan repayments are spent)	Outside estate
At outset	£ 1.5 million cash	Investment growth in reversionary trust plus investment growth on loan trust
7 years	£ 1.2 million cash	£300,000 CLT to reversionary trust and investment growth plus growth on loan trust
14 years	£ 900,000 cash	£600,000 CLT to reversionary trust and investment growth plus growth on loan trust
21 years	£ 600,000 cash Loan fully repaid	£900,000 CLT to reversionary trust and investment growth plus growth on loan trust
28 years	£ 300,000 cash	£1.2 million CLT to reversionary trust and investment growth plus growth on loan trust

Figure 18.6 Components of combined trust loan and gifts to reversionary trust

Source: Reproduced by kind permission of Canada Life International

could gift up to £650,000 to the reversionary trust if neither of you have made gifts to a discretionary trust in the previous seven years.

As illustrated in Figure 18.7 everything should be outside the estate after 35 years while providing the individual with access to the £1.5 million during that period through a mixture of loan repayments and regular reversions of capital. Based on an assumed 6% pa investment return net of tax and charges, the amount held outside the estate would amount to nearly £8 million! In addition, because in this scenario there would be five separate settlements the periodic (ten-yearly) charge is also minimised.

Other structures

Family limited partnerships (FLPs) have been around in various forms for many years but have become more popular since the changes to trust rules in 2006. FLPs provide a structure that enables a family to bring together assets under common management, oversight and control of, say, the parents, but to obtain IHT and other benefits. The use of FLPs is a complex area and most suited to large-value estates that have already made maximum use of discretionary trusts. Expert advice should be sought from a legal and tax adviser who is familiar with this area.

Foundations are an international structure that can be used to create very sophisticated intergenerational and charitable planning and are usually based in places like Latin America, Luxembourg and Liechtenstein. They are unlikely to be suitable for most families, with the exception of those with at least tens of millions of pounds' worth of assets.

A word of caution. Using trusts and other structures to hold family wealth can help to avoid IHT and a range of other hostile creditors and also provide proper oversight of those assets so that they can be preserved within the family for their use. However, it is essential to make sure that you make decisions about the use of trusts within the context of your overall wealth plan. In addition, make sure that you have any trust correctly drafted, choose your trustees very carefully and make sure that they are aware of their responsibilities and duties. Finally, take personalised professional advice on the establishment, management and investment of trust assets. At the very least you need to ensure that the trustees know what they are doing and are well-supported in the ongoing management and operation of the trust. That way your family will reap the rewards of good planning without it becoming a drama!

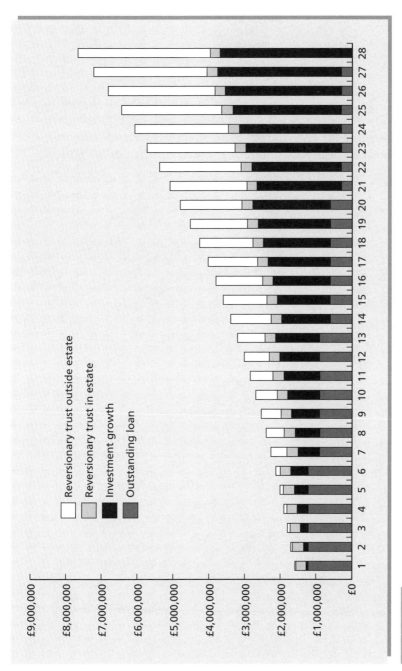

Figure 18.7 Projected value of combined £1.5 million loan and reversion trust

Source: Reproduced by kind permission of Canada Life International. Assumes 6% of annual growth before changes and taxation.

19

Philanthropy

In Chapter 1 we looked at Maslow's hierarchy of needs and the fact that, as our own and our immediate family's needs are met, it is natural to seek a higher level of fulfilment, meaning and purpose; the process of self-actualisation. Giving time or money to causes from which neither you nor your family can directly benefit is clearly an altruistic and selfless act and may help you to achieve that feeling of greater meaning and purpose in your life.

Giving time

Helping people or causes doesn't have to mean giving away your wealth. Giving your time can be equally valuable and, in many cases, more fulfilling. There are numerous organisations throughout the UK that offer ways for people to volunteer their time and expertise across a diverse range of roles, examples of which are:

- magistrate
- special police constable
- school governor
- working with prisoners or detainees
- hospital visitor
- advocate for vulnerable individuals
- visiting elderly people
- education support
- National Trust, RSPCA, RSPB, etc.

Sometimes, particularly in poorer countries, sharing your skills and knowledge can be extremely valuable. Voluntary Service Overseas (VSO) is one of the world's largest independent international development organisations, which works through volunteers to fight poverty in developing countries. 'VSO's high-impact approach involves bringing people together to share skills, build capabilities, promote international understanding and action, and change lives to make the world a fairer place for all.'[1] There is high demand for teachers, engineers and health workers, as the provision of education, infrastructure and health services is sparse in many developing countries.

An acquaintance of mine, who is very successful and wealthy, derives great meaning and pleasure from supporting the building and upkeep of schools in Africa. As well as making cash donations, he and a few friends also go to Africa to provide hands-on help with the building and painting. This has the added benefit of enabling him to see the real difference that he is making on the ground by meeting the staff and pupils of the schools he has helped, thus motivating him to continue his support.

Giving money

While philanthropy is something that is well understood and practised in the United States, it less so among wealthy people in the UK. A study[2] found that only 18% of wealthy individuals in the UK said that charitable giving is one of their top three spending priorities, compared with 41% of their US counterparts.

This reticence to give certainly doesn't seem to be related to wealth. Over the years I've met modestly affluent people who give 10% of their earnings to charity, even though they have not achieved financial independence themselves. In other cases I've met multimillionaires with far more wealth than they or their family could ever spend, but they only make very modest charitable gifts. Research[3] shows that the poorest 10% of donors give 3.6% of their total spending to charity, whereas the richest 10% give only 1.1%.

[1] www.vso.org.uk/about/

[2] Ledbury Research and Barclays Wealth (2010) 'Global giving: The culture of philanthropy'.

[3] Cowley, E., Smith, S., McKenzie, T. and Pharaoh, C. (2011) The New State of Donation: Three decades of household giving to charity, 1978–2008. Cass Business School and University of Bristol.

A common barrier to higher giving is that wealthy people often feel they can't afford to give much to charity until they feel financially more stable. A study[4] found that 71% of wealthy people give only when they feel financially secure. It is natural for people to feel less secure, given the tumultuous events since the global credit crisis hit, but that is unlikely to be the only or even the main reason for reticence to gift more meaningful amounts to charity.

It is probable that some people see giving to charity as complicated, or worry that it will unleash a rush of begging letters! Others see charities as inefficient and think that very little of their gift will be used to make a real difference, once administration charges have taken their share. In my experience, the biggest reason that charitable giving isn't a bigger priority among affluent and wealthy individuals is because they haven't given it any real thought or consideration. While they might respond to disaster requests or to Children in Need, it is the exception, not the norm, for people to seriously consider how charity fits into their wealth planning.

Let's go back to that question in Chapter 1: 'What's important about money to you?'. If you can identify a cause with which you really connect and develop a passion for, then you are much more likely to be motivated to make more meaningful gifts in your lifetime and/or through your will. This is where a good wealth manager can add value, by helping you to work out what causes are important to you and selecting charities – possibly by engaging a charitable giving adviser – and determining how to give easily and tax-efficiently and, more importantly, to monitor the impact of your giving.

Financial giving can be done in your lifetime on a planned or *ad hoc* basis and/or left for the executors of your will to deal with after your death. Clearly, if you give in your lifetime, you can derive some personal satisfaction from the outcome. I use a philanthropy questionnaire with clients to help them identify what, if any, philanthropic aims they have and this is reproduced at Figure 19.1 below should you wish to use it. You can also download a blank copy from **www.wealthpartner.co.uk**

[4] Bank of America Merrill Lynch (2010) 'Study of HNW Philanthropy: Issues driving charitable activities among affluent households'.

Philanthropy survey: an act of kindness, a generous gift
Name: **Date:**
1. Charities or causes into which I feel a need to invest my time and energy:
2. Charities or causes to which I currently contribute:
3. Causes that I would like to support on a perpetual or annual basis:
4. Charities that I would like to provide for in my will:
5. Endowment funds I would like to establish:

Figure 19.1   Philanthropy survey

Reasons for giving

There are six key reasons why you might want to make charitable giving a serious part of your own wealth plan, as set out in Figure 19.2 and discussed further below.

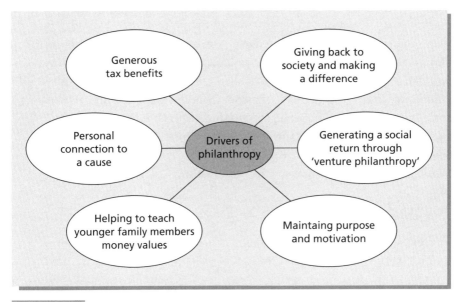

Figure 19.2 The main drivers of philanthropy

Giving back to society and making a difference

Bill and Melinda Gates and Warren Buffett have given billions of dollars to the Bill and Melinda Gates Foundation, which is the largest transparent, managed independent foundation in the world, with an endowment of $36.3 billion. The Foundation aims to advance education and technology use in the United States and to eradicate malaria, polio, HIV/Aids and poverty in the developing world and has distributed $25.36 billion to date[5]. Gates and Buffett announced that over 50 prominent businesspeople have made a public pledge to make more substantial charitable donations. Warren Buffett said:

---

[5] Gates Foundation factsheet, as at 30 June 2011.

We want the general level of giving to step up. We want the Pledge to help society become even more generous. We hope the norm will change towards even greater and smarter philanthropy.[6]

While you may not be able to make donations on the same scale as the Gateses and Buffett, you could almost certainly make donations that would have a high impact and make a big difference. The problem with making small donations to lots of charities without any real strategy is that it dilutes the impact of the donations and erodes the satisfaction derived from giving. The power of philanthropy comes from the focus and drive of the philanthropist. It also allows affluent and wealthy families to stay connected with the wider world, each other and to give something back, making a difference that will last beyond their lifetimes. The purpose of philanthropy is, therefore, to make an impact, change things about which you are not happy and, to a large extent, pass on these positive values to your wider family – more of which later.

Generating a social return through 'venture philantrophy'

Increasingly, charitable giving is being channelled into enterprises that seek social as well as financial returns. For example, CAF Venturesome was one of the first funds set up to support UK social investment. The fund provides loan capital to charities, social enterprises and community groups so they can deliver services that have a high social impact. The charities and social enterprises repay the loan capital with interest and the fund then reinvests in other projects to multiply the social impact of the original donation. Clearly not all loans will be repaid, but, if you invest in a reputable social investment fund, the manager will carry out thorough due diligence so that loans are only made to well-managed organisations with sound business plans.

Maintaining purpose and motivation

Many successful people maintain a strong sense of purpose and motivation by generating wealth to fund charitable causes about which they care deeply. The singer Elton John is well known for the fund-

---

[6] Bill and Melinda Gates Foundation website – Just Giving pledge **www.gatesfoundation. org**/annual-letter/2011/Pages/giving-pledge.asp

raising that he does for his AIDS charity. The singer and actor Roger Daltrey has been a keen supporter of the Teenage Cancer Trust, which he helped to establish in 2000, and he speaks with passion and conviction about how this helps him to stay positive and enthusiastic about his life purpose, as well as keeping in touch with those much less fortunate than himself.

Successful businesspeople are increasingly making sizeable gifts to their own charitable foundations or established charities, at the expense of leaving a larger legacy to their own family and friends. Sometimes this provides a business owner with the motivation to continue in business and defer, indefinitely, any notion of 'retiring'. Tom Hunter, the Scottish entrepreneur, is a good example of a self-made person who keeps working to fulfil his higher calling in life. After selling his business, Sports Division, to JJB Sports for £290 million in July 1998, Sir Tom moved to Monaco for tax reasons. At the same time, he established a charitable foundation – The Hunter Foundation – with £10 million, initially as a tax mitigation tool.

Hunter explained that he had realised making money was 'only half the equation' and announced, after setting aside enough money to keep him and his family comfortable throughout their lifetimes, he would return to live in the UK and continue to invest in and nurture new businesses via his own private equity company – West Coast Capital. He intends to channel gains and profits arising from his private equity investment into charitable causes in what he calls 'venture philanthropy'. To date, the foundation has invested £50 million.[7] Hunter said in an interview:

> There is more great wealth in fewer hands than ever before in history. My own personal belief is that with great wealth comes great responsibility … all the material goals have all been settled some time ago, so now the philanthropy is the real motivator to continue to make money. The aim is to redouble our efforts in wealth creation in order that we can, over time, invest £1 billion in venture philanthropy through our foundation.[8]

[7] www.thehunterfoundation.co.uk/, as at 30 June 2011.

[8] Sir Tom Hunter, announcing his philanthropic intentions in an interview with Robert Peston, *BBC News* July 2007.

Helping to teach younger family members money values

Teaching young people the value of money and a sense of responsibility in terms of how to manage wealth sensibly can often be made easier by engaging family members in the process of giving. While this could be as elaborate as a family 'board' to guide giving by a dedicated family charitable trust, it can also be a simple matter of making sure that giving is a regular part of family dialogue.

In my family, for example, once a year, each of us has to choose one large and one small charity to which we would like to make a charitable donation and explain why. In the case of my daughters, they each have to donate £1 of their own savings for every £10 given by my wife and I. This achieves a number of objectives:

- my daughters know that planned charitable giving is a key priority for my wife and me
- by each supporting a large and a small charity, we strike a balance between those organisations that may have a high impact in terms of results but are not as well funded as the more visable and more established charities, which are well-funded, proven and have economies of scale
- making our own donation subject to our daughters also making their own contributions causes them to make a small sacrifice of their own money and to appreciate what they have compared to others
- the act of actively choosing our charities gives each of us a sense of ownership and engagement in the giving process
- talking and thinking about charitable giving causes us as a family to think more about others and less about ourselves, which also helps to give us all a greater sense of meaning and purpose in life
- it gives us all more motivation to do our best in our lives and share the financial fruits of our efforts.

Just like it's never the 'right' time to start a family, it's never the right time to start charitable giving! If you wait until you feel wealthy enough, the opportunity to make a real difference to others is likely to have been missed.

Personal connection to a cause

The reason that cancer and heart disease charities are well funded is because almost everyone knows someone who has been affected by those conditions. I have a particular interest in education and parenting, as they are both issues that I feel go to the heart of many of society's problems and my own experiences of both were less than ideal! The more you connect with and feel passionate about a cause or issue, then the more likely it is that you will be motivated to support it. In addition, you will probably derive more pleasure and satisfaction from charitable giving to that cause, particularly if you are clear what your gift is being used for and can see tangible results being achieved.

I suggest that you widen your net a bit more than the usual charities and think carefully about whether there are less mainstream, but equally worthy, causes with which you connect and are important to you personally, as a gift to one or more of these might have a much higher impact and social return. I have known clients who feel strongly about the value of a good education and they have provided funds for free or subsidised education for disadvantaged pupils at some of the best independent schools. Although not a charitable gift, I've also known people agree to fund some or all of the educational needs of their relatives' or friends' children, sometimes requiring a matching contribution, pound for pound, to ensure a sense of ownership and responsibility on the part of the child's parent.

Generous tax benefits

The government is keen to support charitable giving and wants to encourage a more giving society. One of the ways that giving is encouraged is by giving a number of very generous tax benefits. These include income tax relief, freedom from capital gains tax on assets gifted and exemption from inheritance tax on lifetime gifts or those made on death, as summarised in Figure 19.3 below.

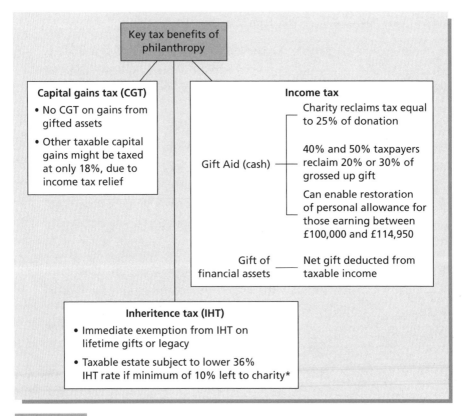

Figure 19.3 UK tax benefits for charitable gifts made by individuals

* This applies to deaths occuring from 6 April 2012

Gift Aid

For cash gifts it is better for all concerned to make a gift that falls within the Gift Aid scheme. Gift Aid allows a charity to reclaim basic rate tax on donations from UK taxpayers and enables higher rate and additional rate taxpayers to claim 20% or 30% tax relief, respectively, on the amount of the gift grossed up for basic rate tax. If the amount of UK tax (income tax and/or capital gains) paid by the donor is less than the amount of basic rate tax that the charity can reclaim, then the shortfall has to be repaid by the donor to HMRC, although in practice this is rarely done.

Example

Claudia is a higher-rate taxpayer and gives £8,000 to a recognised charity. Under the Gift Aid scheme, this will be treated as a gift of £10,000 (£8,000 grossed up by 25%), from which the basic rate tax of £2,000 has been deducted at source. The charity can reclaim the basic rate tax of £2,000 directly from HMRC, so it will receive a total of £10,000.

As Claudia is a higher-rate taxpayer with taxable income of £45,000, she may claim higher-rate tax relief on the gift. This is calculated as follows:

Grossed gift	£10,000
Tax relief at 40%	£4,000
Less: tax deducted when gift made	(£2,000)
Reduction in Claudia's tax liability	£2,000

If Claudia were an additional (50%) rate taxpayer, the corresponding reduction in liability would be £3,000 (i.e. 30% of £10,000).

Other income tax benefits

The reduction in higher/additional rate tax is given by an increase in the basic rate income tax band equal to the grossed up gift. In the example, Claudia's basic rate band would be increased from £35,000 to £45,000 for the tax year 2011/12. This means that any dividend income otherwise taxable at 32.5% (less the 10% credit) could fall within the extended basic rate band with no extra tax payable.

If Claudia had taxable income of £114,950 and, as such, had lost her personal income tax allowance,[9] then a gift of £11,960 would gross up to £14,950 and extend her basic rate income tax band by the same amount. This would bring Claudia's taxable income down to £100,000 and enable her to retain her personal income tax allowance, thus providing effective personal tax relief of 50% on the net cash donation and 75% including the tax reclaimed directly by the charity[10].

---

[9] The personal income tax allowance is reduced by £1 for every £2 that taxable income exceeds £100,000 until the allowance is nil and as a result, the effective marginal rate of income tax on taxable income between £100,000 and £114,950 can be as high as 60%, depending on the source of income ((£14,950 x 40%) + (£7,475 x 40%) = £8,970) so (£8,970/£14,950) x 100 = 60%).

[10] The effect of the gift is that Claudia would receive £2,990 as a tax reduction on the grossed up gift of £14,950 and avoid £2,990 of higher-rate tax due to the reinstatement of her personal allowance of £7,475. This equates to marginal tax relief of 50% on the net cash donation (£5,980/£11,960). When combined with the tax reclaimed at source by the charity of £2,990, this equates to total tax relief equivalent to 75% (£8,970/£11,960).

It is also possible to make a gift and carry this back to the previous tax year, subject to you having paid sufficient income tax in that tax year to meet the tax claim by the charity. The deadline for carrying back a gift is on or before the time you make the donation but no later than 31 October (if you file a paper tax return) or 31 January (if you file an online tax return) in the year that the gift is made.

Gift Aid and chargeable events on insurance bonds

It is important to note that the basic rate tax band is not extended for the purpose of computing relief on top-sliced[11] gains under a life assurance policy. For example, if Claudia had taxable income of £34,000 after allowances for the tax year 2011/12 and the top-sliced gain under a single-premium bond were, say, £2,000, then higher-rate tax would usually be calculated on £1,000 (i.e. £35,000 − £34,000).

Were Claudia to make a gross Gift Aid payment of £1,000, then, although the basic rate threshold would be increased to £36,000, for top-slicing relief it would be held at £35,000, so the higher-rate tax would still be based on a chargeable gain slice of £1,000.

Capital gains tax and Gift Aid

As explained in Chapter 15 (see Figure 15.1) taxable capital gains (after deducting exemptions, reliefs and the annual capital gains tax exemption) are taxed at 28% unless the taxable gain falls within your unused basic rate income tax band of, currently, £35,000. The taxable capital gain will, therefore, be taxable at 18% to the extent that it falls within the basic rate band.

For example, Stephen has total taxable income after personal allowance of £35,000 and taxable capital gains of £25,000.

Gains that fall within basic rate tax band	Nil
Gains that exceed the basic rate tax band	£25,000

All of the gain will be taxed at 28%, resulting in a liability of £7,000. If, however, Stephen made a charitable donation under Gift Aid of £20,000, his basic rate income tax band would be increased by the amount of the grossed up gift (£25,000), to be £60,000. After deducting his taxable income of £35,000, this means that he has £25,000 of

---

[11] For an explanation of top-slicing relief, see Table 11.1 in Chapter 11.

unused basic rate income tax band and, as such, the entire taxable capital gain will be taxed at 18% – i.e., £4,500 rather than £7,000 had he not made the contribution.

Non-cash gifts to charities

Although the Gift Aid scheme does not extend to non-cash gifts, it is also possible to obtain tax relief at your marginal rate(s) of income tax, as well as exemption from capital gains tax (CGT) and inheritance tax (IHT), by donating 'qualifying assets' to a registered charity or foundation, including one created by yourself.

Such 'qualifying assets' include:

- quoted shares (on a recognised exchange)
- units or shares in a unit trust or OEIC
- shares or units in an offshore fund
- A freehold interest in land in the UK or a leasehold interest in such land for a term of years absolute.

Relief is given by way of deduction against income otherwise subject to tax. The amount that can be deducted is broadly the market value of the asset gifted plus the incidental costs of disposal, e.g. commission, costs of transfer. So, if a donor with a taxable income of say £125,000 gave qualifying shares worth £50,000 to a charity, then the donor's taxable income would be reduced to £75,000, resulting in an income tax saving of £20,000 (40% of £50,000).

In addition:

- there would be no capital gains tax to pay on the gift, even if the shares had appreciated in value since their acquisition; and
- there would be no inheritance tax on the gift.

It is also possible to sell an asset to a charity at below its market value and, in this situation, the proceeds are deducted from the gift value for the purposes of determining both exemption from capital gains and reducing taxable income.

Charitable legacy IHT reduction

It is proposed that, from 6 April 2012, where at least 10% of your taxable estate is left to a registered charity, the remainder of your taxable estate will be taxed at 36% rather than the standard 40% IHT rate. If you were not going to leave money to charity on your death then the new rules will not motivate you to do so. However, if you were planning to leave at least 10% of your taxable estate to charity, then your beneficiaries will be better off by 6.70%, as shown in Table 19.1.

Table 19.1 Effects on net estate of new charitable legacy rule

	No charitable legacy	With charitable legacy (before 6 April 2012)	With charitable legacy (on or after 6 April 2012)
Taxable estate	£1,000,000	£1,000,000	£1,000,000
Charitable legacy	NIL	(£100,000)	(£100,000)
Net taxable estate	£1,000,000	£900,000	£900,000
IHT charge	(£400,000)	(£360,000)	(£324,000)
Net estate for beneficiaries	£600,000	£540,000	£576,000

> Increase of 6.7%

Ways to give

There are four main ways to give to charities, as set out in Figure 19.4. The receiving entity must, however, have a charity reference number issued by Her Majesty's Revenue and Customs (HMRC).

Direct to charity

This means that you gift cash or a financial asset directly to your chosen charity. This is simple and is best if your overall level of giving is modest, ad hoc and you are good at keeping on top of paperwork for when you come to complete your tax return.

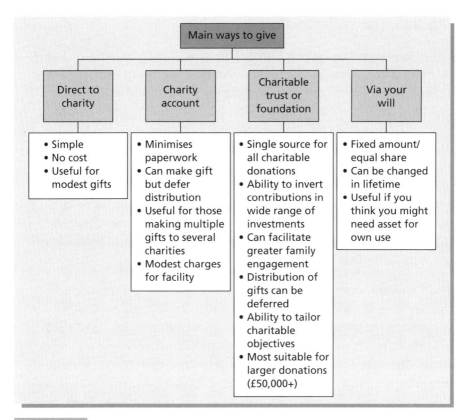

Figure 19.4 Main ways to give

Charity account

If you want simplicity, particularly if you make gifts to lots of charities each year, and/or you want to obtain the tax benefits now but defer a decision on which charities to support, then a charity account can be very useful. These accounts are similar to a normal bank current account, in that you pay cash donations into the account, which usually earns a modest amount of interest. Withdrawals are only permitted in order to make donations to your chosen registered charities and these can be done electronically or by issuing cheques. Charity accounts are provided by a number of organisations, including the Charities Aid Foundation (CAF) and Charities Trust, although they do make a small charge on each contribution and a small annual charge.

Charitable trust or foundation

This is a personalised type of trust that attracts charitable status and provides a high degree of flexibility over how funds can be deployed, although neither you nor your family may benefit from the trust personally. Like a charity account, a charitable trust allows you to make substantial donations but defer deciding which charities are to benefit. Alternatively, you could build up capital, of which you could delegate the management to a professional investment manager, which will fund ongoing charitable giving long after you've ceased to make contributions. In addition, there is greater flexibility to invest in businesses, whether social or normal commercial enterprises, that you think will have a high social impact and/or generate significant profits or capital gains that can be distributed to charities.

The Charity Commission[12] however, is getting hot on making sure that charities *do* distribute funds rather than leave them to stockpile. So, you could have problems if you set up a charitable trust and then contribute funds to it for a period of years without ever paying anything. The best approach is probably to ensure that you do start to make distributions within a few years of setting the trust up and to keep making distributions, even if these are less than the ongoing contributions and any investment growth.

Because the costs of setting up and managing a charitable trust are higher than for a charity account, they are most suited to those making a more substantial gift – usually £50,000 or more. In practice, however, contributions to this type of structure are usually in excess of £250,000. Although a charitable trust or foundation is usually set up by a lawyer, organisations like CAF can provide you with your own charitable trust that is pre-approved with HMRC and for which they handle all ongoing administration and compliance for a very competitive price. In addition, they have a range of external investment options at preferential rates. However, if you have very specific needs and objectives or you like the idea of having a bespoke charitable trust, then go ahead and have your legal adviser create the entity for you.

---

[12] The Charity Commission regulates charities in England and Wales

Via your will

Leaving a legacy to one or more charities via your will is easy. It can be changed at any time while you are alive and avoids you having to give away cash or assets that you might need to call on for your personal use in your lifetime. You could stipulate a fixed amount or specific asset or give all or part of your residue estate. There can be issues with each, particularly where confusion can arise if you have a list of gifts in your will, some of which are tax-free and some are not. You need to make clear your intentions – i.e, whether they each receive the same amount net or the charity receives more because it's tax-free.

In the next and final chapter we'll go back to where we started in Chapter 1, when I asked 'What's important about money to you?' I'll share with you a few final thoughts on living a life of purpose to help with the motivation needed to ensure that your wealth helps to achieve all that is important to you.

20

A life with a purpose

I am successful today because someone believed in me and I didn't have the heart to let them down.

Abraham Lincoln

One of the most important attributes of those who enjoy a long and fulfilling life is having a strong sense of purpose. As I said in Chapter 1, the more you know what is important to you and why, the easier it will be to determine an appropriate wealth strategy and associated solutions. If you've read the entire book and got this far, then well done, but, before you go, I just want to give you some of my personal perspectives and pose some thought-provoking questions.

Are you inspired by your life?

Do you appreciate the people you've met and experiences you've had so far? You might find it useful to keep a journal of what you've learned and keep updating it. We are a product of our thoughts and feelings and we usually get what we expect or tolerate in our lives. The two biggest excuses in life are 'I'm too young' and 'I'm too old'. Why believe that you have arrived; why not keep growing? There are people becoming first time authors in their sixties, starting businesses in their seventies, taking exams in their eighties and running marathons in their nineties!

The standards that we set for ourselves will usually be in a comfort zone that is well below our potential. Personally, I am grateful for what I have experienced and achieved so far, but I'm also very excited about what the future holds. How excited are you about your future and those of the people you love and care about?

The power of knowing your 'why'

Passion comes from enthusiasm and enthusiasm comes from belief. Knowing what's really important to you and what your higher calling is are key elements of belief in yourself. While you might think that leaving a financial legacy is important, what about leaving a legacy of character? By character I mean that unique combination of human attributes of integrity, principles and authenticity.

Was there someone who acted as your mentor, who helped you to become the person you are today? If you aren't already, could you be a mentor to others to provide inspiration, support and encouragement? My view is that our example is the only thing that influences others. Think about your actions, deeds and messages. What impact do these have on your family, friends and colleagues and are they the impacts that you want?

Happiness is not the same as pleasure

Pleasure can only be sustained by the activity that produces it, whereas happiness is a state of mind that comes from a series of actions, thoughts, feelings and attitudes. If you find it hard to be happy and contented, try acting happy for the first two hours of every day and eventually it will become a habit.

The news is mainly negative and not intended to make us happy. For most of us, 90% of life is great and 10% is not so great so why not focus on the 90% that *is* great and forget the other 10%? Control what you can control and don't worry about what you can't (investment returns, taxes and politicians!) and instead focus on what you have, not on what you don't have or may have lost. Silence is the key to contemplation and wisdom, so try to avoid being stimulated and electronically connected *all* the time (personally, I avoid Twitter and social networks and I try to keep email to a minimum).

At the end of each week in my firm, we ask each member of the team to score their happiness on a scale of one to ten. Our current average is eight but we are aiming for ten! What's your happiness score and why is that so? Each week at the dinner table, I ask my family what's the best thing that happened to them that week. The idea is to focus on the good rather than the negative things and we find it helps us to stay positive and appreciative of the good things in life.

Who do you have around you?

We are judged and affected by the company we keep. If you have negative and unpleasant people around you then that can rub off and make you the same as them. My experience (and I've interviewed nearly 1000 people over the past 20 years) is that people are either drains or radiators. Drains sap you of energy and enthusiasm, so avoid people who are drains and those who have no love of life! Who do you have around you and are they the right people?

A thought to leave you with

Your life isn't defined by money or your net worth but the things that you do, see and experience on a daily basis and make you happy and fulfilled. It's not my job to tell you what's important to you or how to live your life. I do hope, however, that you are clear on your life's purpose so you know the 'why' and 'what' (the mission, vision, values and goals) of your wealth plan. If you understand those, then the 'how' of your wealth plan (the strategies, tactics and tools set out in this book) will fall neatly into place. In that context, I hope that your future will be even bigger and more exciting than your past.

Useful websites and further reading

Websites

Wealthpartner: Dedicated website for readers of The Financial Times Guide to Wealth Management. You can download a range of templates, tools and questionnaires to assist you with creating your own plan. www.wealthpartner.co.uk You will need to enter the password lifeofpurpose to gain access to the website.

Institute of financial Planning: Official website for professional body that awards and monitors the international Certified Financial Planner CM (CFP) accreditation. Online searchable registry of CFPs in the UK is avaliable at http://www.financialplanning.org.uk/consumers/cfp_search.cfm

Findanadviser: Consumer website of the The Personal Finance Society – the professional body which awards and monitors the Chartered Financial Planner designtion. Online searchable database of Chartered Financial Planners http://www.findanadviser.org/

The Money Advice Service: A government-backed, comprehensive, independent and free source of information and guidance on a wide range of personal finance issues. Includes access to an online personal finance 'health check' analyser; interactive money planners; in-depth money guides and a product comparison tool for insurance, annuities, pensions and other financial products. Free general advice is also available via telephone or face to face. http://moneyadviceservice.org.uk/default.aspx

Which? Savings rates booster comparison tables.
http://www.which.co.uk/money/savings-and-investments/guides/saving-rates-booster

BBC Radio 4 Moneybox: Website of the long-running Radio 4 personal finance programme with a range of articles, videos and links to other websites on personal finance issues.
http://news.bbc.co.uk/1/hi/programmes/moneybox/default.stm

The Pensions Advisory Service: Useful source of independent information and guidance on pension-related issues.
www.pensionsadvisoryservice.org.uk

HM Revenue & Customs, Pensioners portal: Useful information and guidance on a range of tax-related issues affecting those receiving pension benefits.
http://hmrc.gov.uk/pensioners/index.htm

Directgov: A wide range of information on money, tax, pensions, education funding and State benefits.
www.direct.gov.uk/en/index.htm

Disability Law Service: Free information and guidance for people with disabilities.
www.dls.org.uk

Schmidt Tax Report: Subscription-based online and printed tax planning newsletter aimed at successful individuals and business owners.
http://schmidtreport.co.uk/index.htm

Registered Pension Schemes Manual (RPSM): HM Revenue & Customs' (HMRC) comprehensive, in-depth technical guide to registered pension schemes.
www.hmrc.gov.uk/manuals/rpsmmanual/index.htm

Books

Financial DNA: Discovering your unique financial personality for a quality life by Hugh Massie (ISBN-10: 0471784206)

The Energy of Money: A spiritual guide to financial and personal fulfilment by Maria Nemeth (ISBN-13: 978-0345434975)

Money and the Meaning of Life by Jacob Needleman (ISBN-13: 978-0385262422)

The Seven Stages of Money Maturity by George Kinder (ISBN-13: 978-0385324045)

Man's Search for Meaning by Viktor E. Frankl (ISBN-13: 978-1844132393)

The Millionaire Next Door by Thomas J. Stanley and William D. Danko (ISBN-13: 978-0671015206)

3 Dimensional Wealth by Monroe M. Diefendorf, Jr., and Robert Sterling Madden (ISBN-13: 978-0976901402)

Wealthy and Wise: Secrets about money by Heidi L. Steiger (ISBN-13: 978-0471221418)

Smart Couples Finish Rich: 9 steps to creating a rich future for you and your partner by David Bach (ISBN-13: 978-0767904834)

Values-based Financial Planning: The art of creating and inspiring financial strategy by Bill Bachrach (ISBN-13: 978-1887006033)

Enough!: True measures of money, business, and life by John C. Bogle (ISBN-13: 978-0470398517)

The Number: A completely different way to think about the rest of your life by Lee Eisenburg (ISBN-13: 978-0743270311)

Sorted! DIY financial planning: How to get the life you want by Jane Wheeler (ISBN-13: 978-1845493264)

Sudden Money: Managing a financial windfall by Susan Bradley (ISBN-13: 978-0471380863)

A Random Walk Down Wall Street by Burton G. Malkiel (ISBN-13: 978-0-393325350)

Against the Gods: The remarkable story of risk by Peter Bernstein (ISBN-13: 978-0471295631)

The Little Book of Common Sense Investing, John C. Bogle (ISBN-13: 978-0-470102107)

The Investment Answer by Daniel C. Goldie and Gordon S. Murray (ISBN-13: 978-0982894705)

Smarter Investing: Simpler decisions for better results by Tim Hale (ISBN-13: 978-0273708001)

Winning the Loser's Game: Timeless strategies for successful investing by Charles D. Ellis (ISBN-13: 978-0071545495)

No Monkey Business: What investors need to know and why by Stuart Fowler (ISBN-13: 978-0273656586)

Index

Comprehensive. Authoritative. Trusted

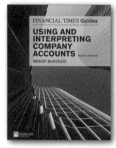

FINANCIAL TIMES Guides

USING AND INTERPRETING COMPANY ACCOUNTS FOURTH EDITION

WENDY McKENZIE

9780273723967

FINANCIAL TIMES Guides

USING THE FINANCIAL PAGES SIXTH EDITION

ROMESH VAITILINGAM

9780273727873

FINANCIAL TIMES Guides

INVESTING

THE DEFINITIVE COMPANION TO INVESTMENT AND THE FINANCIAL MARKETS
SECOND EDITION

GLEN ARNOLD

9780273723745

FINANCIAL TIMES Guides

BUSINESS NETWORKING

HOW TO USE THE POWER OF ONLINE AND OFFLINE NETWORKING FOR BUSINESS SUCCESS

HEATHER TOWNSEND

9780273745822

FINANCIAL TIMES Guides

ANALYSIS FOR MANAGERS

EFFECTIVE PLANNING TOOLS AND TECHNIQUES

BABETTE BENSOUSSAN AND CRAIG FLEISHER

9780273722014

FINANCIAL TIMES Guides

MAKING THE RIGHT INVESTMENT DECISIONS SECOND EDITION

HOW TO ANALYSE COMPANIES AND VALUE SHARES

MICHAEL CAHILL

9780273729846

FINANCIAL TIMES Guides

SELECTING SHARES THAT PERFORM FOURTH EDITION

10 WAYS TO BEAT THE STOCK MARKET

RICHARD KOCH AND LEO GOUGH

9780273712671

FINANCIAL TIMES Guides

VALUE INVESTING SECOND EDITION

HOW TO BECOME A DISCIPLINED INVESTOR

GLEN ARNOLD

9780273724520

FINANCIAL TIMES Guides

CORPORATE VALUATION SECOND EDITION

DAVID FRYKMAN AND JAKOB TOLLERYD

9780273729105

FINANCIAL TIMES Guides

EXCHANGE TRADED FUNDS AND INDEX FUNDS

HOW TO USE TRACKER FUNDS IN YOUR INVESTMENT PORTFOLIO

DAVID STEVENSON

9780273727835

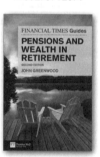

FINANCIAL TIMES Guides

PENSIONS AND WEALTH IN RETIREMENT
SECOND EDITION

JOHN GREENWOOD

9780273763031

FINANCIAL TIMES Guides

INHERITANCE TAX, PROBATE AND ESTATE PLANNING

AMANDA FISHER

9780273729969

FINANCIAL TIMES Guides

OPTIONS

THE PLAIN AND SIMPLE GUIDE TO SUCCESSFUL STRATEGIES
SECOND EDITION

LENNY JORDAN

9780273736868

FINANCIAL TIMES Guides

BUSINESS START UP 2012

THE MOST COMPREHENSIVE ANNUALLY UPDATED GUIDE FOR ENTREPRENEURS

SARA WILLIAMS

9780273761990

OVER 200 TOP TAX-SAVING TIPS

FINANCIAL TIMES Guides

PERSONAL TAX 2011–12

SARA WILLIAMS AND JOHN BLOXHAM

9780273756668

ALWAYS LEARNING   PEARSON

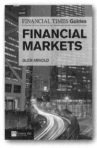

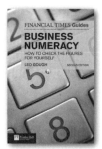